CRY OF MURDER ON BROADWAY

CRY OF MURDER ON BROADWAY

A Woman's Ruin and Revenge in Old New York

JULIE MILLER

THREE HILLS
AN IMPRINT OF
CORNELL UNIVERSITY PRESS
ITHACA AND LONDON

First published 2020 by Cornell University Press

Printed in the United States of America

Library of Congress Cataloging-in-Publication Data

Names: Miller, Julie, 1959– author.
Title: Cry of murder on Broadway : a woman's ruin and revenge in old New York / Julie Miller.
Description: Ithaca [New York] : Three Hills, an imprint of Cornell University Press, 2020. | Includes bibliographical references and index.
Identifiers: LCCN 2020012520 (print) | LCCN 2020012521 (ebook) | ISBN 9781501751486 (hardcover) | ISBN 9781501751509 (pdf) | ISBN 9781501751493 (epub)
Subjects: LCSH: Norman, Amelia, approximately 1818– | Child, Lydia Maria, 1802–1880—Friends and associates. | Seduction—New York (State)—New York—History—19th century. | Attempted murder— New York (State)—New York—History—19th century. | Female offenders—New York (State)—New York—History—19th century. | Women—Legal status, laws, etc.—New York (State)—History—19th century. | New York (N.Y.)—Moral conditions—19th century. | New York (N.Y.)—Social conditions—19th century.
Classification: LCC HV6587.N4 M55 2020 (print) | LCC HV6587.N4 (ebook) | DDC 364.152/3092—dc23
LC record available at https://lccn.loc.gov/2020012520
LC ebook record available at https://lccn.loc.gov/2020012521

In memory of Minnie Singer Miller and Mollie Meyerowitz Silver, my grandmothers, who began their American lives as immigrant girls in New York

CONTENTS

Illustrations

PROLOGUE

Defending Amelia Norman

The wonder being, all the while, as we look at the world, how
absolutely, how inordinately, the Isabel Archers, and even much
smaller female fry, insist on mattering.

HENRY JAMES, *PORTRAIT OF A LADY*, PREFACE TO THE
NEW YORK EDITION, 1908

On November 1, 1843, a young woman dressed in black and carrying a
large fur muff followed a man up the steps of the magnificent new Astor
House Hotel on Broadway in New York. After what appeared to witnesses to be a brief conversation, she pulled out a folding knife—and
stabbed him.

The reporters who later saw her recognized the horror of what she had
done, but they were also quick to conclude that because she was the heroine of a story, she must be beautiful. Over the next two days the *New York
Express* reported that "the wretched female who thus sought to imbrue
her hands in blood is an elegant appearing woman, tall and of beautiful
figure and form," wearing a "splendid black dress." When she appeared
in court the following January, James Gordon Bennett, editor of the *New
York Herald*, made a deeper observation, noting that she was "a girl evidently of no ordinary character. Her hair and complexion are fair, but her
eyebrows and eyes are very dark, giving an expression of sternness to a
face which otherwise would justly be considered strikingly handsome." A

Herald reporter saw the expression of character that his editor described, but described her physical appearance somewhat differently. According to him, Norman had "very dark brown hair, expansive forehead, heavy eye brows and lashes, with a melancholy but very determined expression of countenance." In the woodcut portrait the *Herald* published during Norman's trial, her hands, face, and body are so obscured by her tiered dress, large fur muff, hat, and veil that it is almost impossible to tell what she looked like, allowing the paper's readers to imagine whatever they liked best or expected to find.

The woman was twenty-five-year-old New Jersey–born Amelia Norman, a servant, seamstress, and sometime prostitute. The man she tried and failed to kill was thirty-one-year-old Henry Ballard, a prosperous merchant originally from Boston. Norman had become Ballard's mistress in the spring of 1841 during the depression that followed the economic collapse known as the Panic of 1837. After little over a year, during which Ballard moved her from one boardinghouse to another, he left the country, abandoning her and their child. When he returned, Norman pleaded with him to help support them, but Ballard refused. Instead he told her to "go and get her living as other prostitutes did." It was this rebuff that evidently created the state of mind that pushed Norman to pursue Ballard up the stone steps of the Astor House on the night of November 1, 1843, and put a knife in him. Or, as Bennett put it, "the vengeance of a woman upon her despoiler cannot be checked, when jealousy and desertion goad her to its accomplishment."

The trial of Amelia Norman attracted the excited attention of the penny press, particularly Bennett's *Herald*, which thrived on sensation. Newspaper editors around the country, recognizing the interest the story was generating, republished it for the benefit of their own readers. People daily filled all three hundred seats in the courtroom, crowding the room "to excess," while as many as a thousand more who couldn't get in packed the lobby and spilled out the door, down the steps, and into the street. Years after the trial an observer remembered that "so great was the public interest in her that on the night the verdict was rendered, the courthouse was besieged by thousands of our citizens, and when the result was announced, the welkin rang with the plaudits of an excited populace!"

What was it about this would-be murderess that attracted the attention not only of the press and the public, but also of a coterie of
influential supporters? These supporters included the members of the
American Female Moral Reform Society, who had been working since
the 1830s to criminalize "seduction," the concept then current in common law that allowed a woman's father or master to sue her seducer
on the basis of loss of services to himself. After her trial, and probably partly as a result of it, one of Norman's lawyers, David Graham
Jr., attacked the seduction tort from a different angle, seeking to make
it possible for a woman to sue on her own behalf. In the age of the
movements for abolition and women's rights, reformers, including legal
reformers like Graham, were seeking to jettison the idea that anyone
could own the labor of another.

Two very different voices that spoke out in support of Norman belonged to Mike Walsh and George Wilkes, who were in jail when she
was and met her there. Walsh, then around twenty-eight years old,
was a leader of a radical splinter of New York's Democratic Party
and the editor of a weekly labor paper, the *Subterranean*, in which
he published two editorials on Norman's plight. He was in jail after
convictions for libel, and assault and battery. His lawyer was the same
David Graham who represented Norman. His friend Wilkes, twenty-
seven, was a journalist who had coedited the *Sunday Flash*, one of
the first examples in New York of the "flash," or "sporting" press
directed at men. In 1843 Wilkes was in jail for violating the terms of
the suspended sentence he had received after being convicted for libel
and publishing an obscene paper. While in jail Wilkes wrote a prison
memoir, *Mysteries of the Tombs: A Journal of Thirty Days Imprisonment in the New York City Prison for Libel*, in which he recorded his
observations of Norman and his feelings about her predicament. Like
Walsh, Wilkes was a champion of the small artisans and workingmen
who were struggling to maintain their livelihoods and their identities
as men in the industrializing economy. Even though the focus of Walsh
and Wilkes was chiefly on the difficulties of men like themselves, and
even though they narrowly equated manhood with selfhood, both saw
enough of their own plight in Norman to sympathize with her, and did
so in their writings.

Of all Norman's supporters the closest and most steadfast was the abolitionist and popular author Lydia Maria Child. Child helped find Norman a lawyer, accompanied her in the courtroom, took her home when the trial was over, and tried to help her get back on her feet afterward. Child wove elements of Norman's story into her fiction, and she devoted a newspaper column, one in a series titled "Letters from New-York," to her. Child's writings about Norman were an avenue for her to develop her position on the cause of women's rights, just then starting to coalesce into a movement. They were also an outlet for her anger at what she called the "false structure of society" that allowed men to dominate women. In her "Letter from New-York No. V," published in the *Boston Courier* immediately after Norman's trial, Child erupted so angrily, and veered so close to condoning Norman's violence, that fearing for her literary reputation, she excised six particularly heated paragraphs when the column was reprinted two weeks later in the *National Anti-Slavery Standard*.

What these supporters had in common, disparate as they were, was that they all read into Norman's predicament a parable ready-made for their own use. Storytelling is central to understanding what made Norman matter to so many people. Her crime and trial unfolded at a period of heightened interest in narrative, whether written or spoken. In the 1830s and 1840s in the United States, crowds eagerly listened for hours to political speeches, abolitionist lectures, and revivalist sermons. The mystery novel and investigative journalism are both products of these decades. Rising literacy, mechanization of the processes of papermaking and printing, and spreading democracy all meant that more people read novels and newspapers.

In this atmosphere the boundaries between fiction and factual reporting sometimes blended. Lydia Maria Child, who inserted real people and events (including events from the life of Amelia Norman) into her stories, titled a book of them *Fact and Fiction*. Novelists, including Edgar Allan Poe and Herman Melville, borrowed elements of their stories from the news. Poe, for example, based *The Mystery of Marie Roget* on the story of Mary Rogers, a young cigar seller who disappeared from her boardinghouse and then reappeared floating in the Hudson several days later, an apparent murder victim. During the period of Amelia Norman's crime and trial, New Yorkers were fascinated by Eugène Sue's novel *The Mysteries of Paris*, newly translated from French. George Wilkes read and admired it and was influenced by it when he wrote his *Mysteries of the Tombs*. Some let their excitement about Sue's fictional heroine, Fleur de Marie, color how they understood Norman.

The penny press, which was central to these developments, was born in New York City in 1833 when Benjamin Day founded the *New York Sun*. In 1835 Scottish immigrant James Gordon Bennett quickly followed with the *New York Herald*. The newspapers that came before, many of them party organs, were directed at well-to-do men who paid an annual subscription of eight to ten dollars so they could follow the political and business news and keep up with the shipping columns and public notices. Penny papers were different. Sold cheaply on the streets by newsboys, they were written to attract a wide audience. The penny papers introduced local news and, above all, sensational stories, many of which were found in the city's courtrooms by a new species of journalist, the investigative reporter.

Bennett of the *Herald* was one of the earliest to use the techniques of the investigative reporter. In 1836, his paper just a year old, Bennett rushed to one of the city's exclusive brothels to see the just-murdered prostitute Helen Jewett. After viewing Jewett's body, Bennett constructed for his readers an eroticized vision of the murdered woman, "a beautiful female corpse—that surpassed the finest statue of antiquity." (Although he tried, he was unable to do the same for Norman, who was the aggressor, not the victim—alive, and, in Bennett's own words, "determined.") Investigating Jewett's past, Bennett presented his readers with a young woman from Maine who, in a story that was similar to Norman's, had worked as a servant, then migrated to New York, where she became a prostitute.

Bennett at first chose to believe in Richard P. Robinson, the man who was acquitted of the murder of Jewett, but who most likely did commit the crime. Bennett, who was probably swayed by the crowds of young men who supported Robinson, came around after Robinson's trial, when presented with better evidence. Bennett's *Herald* led the rest of the city's press in pursuit of Jewett's story, and his paper's circulation jumped as a result. He learned from this experience, and his paper again took an aggressive lead when he learned of Amelia Norman's attack on Henry Ballard in 1843.

When it came to pursuing Norman's story, Bennett initially sympathized with Henry Ballard, "a man of credit and standing," as he had with Robinson. He argued that Ballard, in "the pardonable excesses of youth," had taken up with Norman, "whose position in society placed her at the command of any one whose purse could satisfy her demands," until, when feeling "the nature of this connection derogatory to his position," he wisely cut her off. But Bennett was again swayed by popular feeling, and came to side with Norman, even coming to advocate for the criminalization of seduction.

Some of the audience for crime in the nineteenth century went directly to the source. People attended trials for entertainment, just as they did the theater, and they expected lawyers to have the oratorical and performative skills of actors. Lawyers at Amelia Norman's trial quoted poetry and Shakespeare because they knew that their reading, theatergoing audience would understand it. New York's antebellum courtroom was often crowded with spectators who watched what amounted to a serial drama, as one trial after another cycled through it, with lawyers, judges, and sometimes defendants appearing repeatedly in different roles. These stories formed an ongoing pageant of crime, the narrative cycle in which Amelia Norman's story was set.

On the surface it seems that Norman, preoccupied with the events of her own life, accidentally propelled herself into the center of a set of causes that had nothing to do with her. It is hard to know what she thought about the plight of workers in an industrializing society, or the criminalization of seduction, or the just-forming movement for women's rights. This is because almost none of her own speech survives. Only a few fragments were recorded in writing, and every one of them was filtered through someone else—Lydia Maria Child, the witnesses who gave testimony to the police or at her trial, and the newspaper reporters who took it all down—and then only at the one, highly charged moment when she stepped into the public spotlight. She recorded none of her own thoughts because she did not know how to write. When she was asked to sign the interview she gave after her arrest, she signed with an X, the symbol traditionally used in place of a signature by people who cannot write. Because of that, and unlike her very prolific supporters, she left no letters, diaries, speeches, or newspaper columns.

But as I became more familiar with Norman's story, I came to feel that her act of violence on the Astor House steps was more than simply a personal act of revenge. She may not have been able to read or write about the careening economy that crushed the poor, and particularly poor women, while it barely clipped the wings of prosperous merchants like Henry Ballard, or the inequalities that the burgeoning movement for women's rights was beginning to identify. Instead, these things were embodied in the circumstances of her life. Her violence was the wrong mode of expression, but it seems to me that when she attacked Henry Ballard so publicly on the Astor House steps, she, like Henry James's Isabel Archer, insisted on mattering.

Amelia Norman's story has significance as a story, but it is also more than that. I am as guilty as any of the people who wrote about her almost two hundred years ago in exploiting it for your pleasure and mine. I hope, however, in reading it you will see that it is also a piece of evidence that shows how change occurs, how history, in other words, is made. Norman's actions did not, on their own, "change history." Her dramatic moment on the stage created by the steps of the Astor House was brief. The two changes in seduction law that her actions unintentionally helped bring into being were rooted in the values and preoccupations of the mid-nineteenth century, and they fizzled and died by the early twentieth when the notion of "seduction" became obsolete.

Instead, Norman's attack on Henry Ballard and its reception by her contemporaries reveal the machinery of history, the way it progresses in twisty and unexpected ways, one step forward and two steps back, enmeshed in contemporary values and circumstances that later become obscure, propelled by chance events and unlikely actors who are unaware that forces of history are working through them. Norman could not write as Lydia Maria Child did, or speak like Mike Walsh did when he stood up in front of roaring political crowds, or effect changes in the law, as the moral reformers and David Graham did, but their words were made out of her experience. Historians want to know what forces, human and otherwise, brought us from there to here. In that story all the moving parts of the machine, even the tiny ones, even the broken ones, matter.

In 1845 a friend of Lydia Maria Child's, the pioneering feminist author Margaret Fuller, published *Woman in the Nineteenth Century*. In it she commended Child for supporting Norman. She argued that Child had used Norman's story to make people see that men as well as women ought to behave with "virtue." Child, she wrote, "was successful in arresting the attention of many who had before shrugged their shoulders, and let sin pass as necessarily a part of the company of men. They begin to ask whether virtue is not possible, perhaps necessary, to man as well as to woman. They begin to fear that the perdition of a woman must involve that of a man. This is a crisis. The results of this case will be important." As I write in 2019, the "me too" movement, which calls powerful men to account for their behavior toward women, is evolving. The balance of power between men and women has only now, after many decades of feminist effort, tipped just enough to make this movement effective. Margaret Fuller, it now appears, was right.

1

I Am Murdered

Yesterday has been a great day—an important day. The exciting
events which marked its close will render it a memorable day in
New York. Scarce had the air ceased to reverberate the shouts of
the unterrified democracy—the unflinching subterraneans and the
conflicting cries of "Van Buren or death," "Calhoun and victory,"
when the cry of murder was heard in Broadway.

"Horrible Attempt at Murder in Broadway,"
New York Herald, November 2, 1843

On the evening of October 31, 1843, Joel Behrend noticed that the young
woman who worked in his household as a servant, Amelia Norman, was
agitated. Norman had gone to work for Behrend, a German immigrant
who owned a wholesale shirt store on New York's William Street, in late
August. She ironed shirts for the store, did housework for Behrend and
his wife, and lived with them in their home at 53 West Broadway just west
of City Hall. Behrend found Norman, whom he knew as "Mrs. Ballard,"
to be pleasant and, in his judgment, "very lady like," but in the middle
of October she began to act strangely. She would cry as she worked, so
that her tears soiled the shirts she was ironing and they had to be washed
again. Then she would laugh in a way that looked to him like "a kind of
mad-laughter" and that was sometimes prolonged for as much as half an
hour. In addition to this peculiar behavior, Norman, who had previously
been so polite, would no longer reply to him when he spoke to her.

That evening, in an effort to distract her, Behrend, an amateur photographer, gave her some daguerreotype plates to clean, but instead of cleaning them "she rubbed the cotton and oil on the table instead of on the type, and would laugh and cry at the same time." He and his wife anxiously agreed that their servant was, in the word he would choose when he gave testimony at her trial, "crazy."

On the afternoon of the following day, November 1, as Behrend was on his way home from his store for dinner, he saw Norman on Greenwich Street, walking back and forth, carrying "a large bundle of cakes in her hand, eating and acting strangely." He was distressed to see his servant eating so indecorously in the street, but instead of approaching her himself he went home to get his wife to bring her home. Before she could do so, Norman walked home by herself. Once at home, Norman continued her odd behavior. She cried throughout dinner and refused to speak, and even though she cut up her food into small pieces, she ate nothing. After the meal she sat in a rocking chair and cried. When Mrs. Behrend handed her some work to do, probably sewing, she threw it on the floor.

Now the Behrends were really frightened. "She was very much excited," Behrend recalled at the trial, "more so than I ever saw her for the three months she lived with me." She remained that way all afternoon. When he left the house to return to work he told his wife not to let Norman go out again because he was afraid she might "fall down in the street." But Mrs. Behrend could not restrain her, and by the time her husband came home again for the evening, Amelia Norman was gone.

That same evening, sometime shortly before seven, Henry Ballard, a young Boston-born merchant, wearing an overcoat against the cool, windy weather, stepped out of 15 Warren Street, the home he shared with his brother Francis, and set off for the Astor House Hotel on Broadway, opposite City Hall.

His walk was short, just two blocks east on Warren Street, then three more south on Broadway. The Broadway Ballard strolled down on the evening of November 1, 1843, was no longer the street of quiet mansions it had been when President George Washington lived at its southern end.

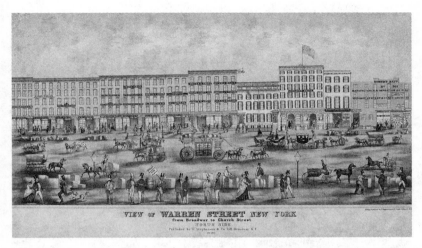

Figure 1.1. Warren Street, from Broadway to Church Street. Henry Ballard lived on this block, at number 15. Frederick Heppenheimer, 1854. Museum of the City of New York, 39.253.4.

Advancing northward along with the expanding city, Broadway had become a much commented-on symbol of everything that was urban, modern, and fast: a corridor of stores, restaurants, hotels, traffic, and crowds. Bustling along rapidly through tight spaces, people of every class and kind rubbed past one another. English novelist Charles Dickens, who visited the city in 1842, noted the density, diversity, and flash of both people and vehicles on Broadway: "No stint of omnibuses here! Half-a-dozen have gone by within as many minutes. Plenty of hackney cabs and coaches too; gigs, phaetons, large-wheeled tilburies, and private carriages." Dickens noted the "many-coloured crowd and glittering shops" and exclaimed, "Heaven save the ladies, how they dress! We have seen more colours in these ten minutes, than we should have seen elsewhere, in as many days." He also noticed the men, fashionable "Byrons of the desk and counter," young clerks and merchants like Henry Ballard.

Dickens also saw that the glitter of Broadway was deceptive. Close by the sparkling commercial boulevard was the city's darkest slum, the Five Points. He invited the readers of his travelogue, *American Notes*, to go along with him and "plunge into the Five Points" as into a murky

Figure 1.2. Broadway, looking downtown. The columned entrance of the Astor House is visible on the right, and the entrance to City Hall Park is on the left. N. Currier, 1846. New York Public Library, Print Collection.

hell. "Poverty, wretchedness, and vice are rife enough where we are going now," he warned, to explain the "two heads of the police" he took along for protection. New York journalist George G. Foster, whose exposés of city life were published in New York in the 1840s and 1850s, took his readers on a similar walk on Broadway. "Fashionable, aristocratic Broadway! Certainly we shall find nothing *here* to shock our sense and make our very nerves thrill with horror," he taunted, then stirred up vicarious thrills with his descriptions of "two ladies approaching us, magnificently attired, with their large arms and voluptuous bosoms half naked," trolling for innocent newcomers, and a group of "flashily-rigged young men who stand at the entrance of an oyster cellar" who were also "on the look-out for victims."

Visible seepage from the city's shadowy side to its bright side was one danger created by the density of urban life. There were also dangers one could not see. These included the brothels masquerading as quiet residences on the side streets along Broadway and the well-dressed prostitutes who mingled in the Broadway crowds, camouflaged by their fine clothing, visible only to those who knew how to recognize them. Another was the business carried out nearby on Wall Street, which those who feared the tricky, protean nature of financial speculation saw mimicked in miniature by the street-level cons of the hucksters in Broadway doorways. Dickens, no admirer of "your model republics," as he sarcastically classed the United States, observed that the "fine streets of spacious houses" along Broadway had been "furnished and dismantled many of them very often" by Wall Street. He was referring to the crashes or "panics" that periodically shook the nineteenth-century economy. One of these, the Panic of 1837, had created a financial depression that lingered into the first half of the 1840s. The speculator, no less than the prostitute and the petty con man, brought temptation and danger to all who strolled down Broadway.

As Ballard, walking down Broadway, reached the Astor House, he passed the leafy triangular park, today known as City Hall Park (then, before the construction of Central Park, known simply as "the park"), on the opposite side of the street.

At four o'clock that afternoon, members of the Democratic Party met in the park to nominate candidates for the local election that was to be held the following week. Tammany Hall, the political club that in a few decades would be defined by the corrupt excesses of its leader, William "Boss" Tweed, controlled the Democratic Party in 1843, but it was boisterously challenged from within by groups of urban workingmen who sought to remake what had once been the party of Thomas Jefferson in their own urban, working-class image.

The meeting, whose estimated size ranged from five to twelve thousand, depending on which newspaper one read, united many factions of the Democratic Party. The "dense mass of human beings" that assembled in the park represented "all classes and conditions, from the well fed, well dressed merchant down town, to the ragged, greasy loafer, who vegetates on the 'Five Points.'" James Gordon Bennett's *New York Herald* laughingly listed the many splinters of the fractured Democratic Party: "'regulars' and 'irregulars,' 'regular irregulars,' 'irregular regulars,' 'old democrats' and 'young democrats,' 'old hunkers' and 'young hunkers,' 'huge-paws,' 'spank-enders,' 'indomitables,' 'subterraneans,' blackguards

NEW YORK CITY HALL, PARK AND ENVIRONS.

Figure 1.3. City Hall Park with Broadway at left. City Hall is at the center of the park, facing the fountain. John Bachmann, 1849. Library of Congress, Prints and Photographs Division, pga.04311.

of every description." But it was the workingmen who set the tone of the meeting that day. In 1821 New York was one among a wave of states that in this period dropped property requirements for voting, ushering in an age of political participation for poor white men (and for a very few black men) who had earlier been partly or fully disenfranchised.

Using language that evoked the rough exuberance and passionate political engagement of these men, the *Herald* described the "hard fisted, red flannel ranks of the great democratic party" packed around the platform set up outside City Hall and the "genteel classes mustered strong about the portico, on the balcony, and at the windows of the Hall." The mayor "sat quietly in his office," protected by a "posse of police officers" in his anteroom, evidently intimidated by the scene outside. Meanwhile the "immense mass," the "magnificent mob," that had poured into the park from every Democratic ward in the city created a "delicious uproar . . . tumbling about like an ocean in a storm, yelling, shouting, hissing, hurraing, to such an extent as to defy all description, all calculation—and all intelligible results."

Ascending the platform in the midst of this uproar was Mike Walsh, an Irish-born political radical and publisher of the short-lived workingman's newspaper the *Subterranean*. That day, the faction of the Democratic Party he represented, known variously as the Spartan Association, the Spartan Band, or the Subterraneans, had nominated him for state senator. "We are all engaged in the same great and glorious cause—the elevation of the downtrodden masses," he boomed to the applauding crowd.

The following day the *Herald* printed its description of the meeting and Walsh's speech next to the report of Amelia Norman's attack on Henry Ballard. Walsh would later devote two columns in his own paper to Norman, writing sympathetically about her and scathingly about Ballard: "What kind of a heart the abject craven wretch has, is to me an impenetrable mystery." That evening, however, Henry Ballard was still unknown to Walsh, and they could have brushed by each other in the dispersing remnants of the Democratic meeting in the Broadway crowd.

When Ballard reached the intersection of Broadway and Park Place, just a block from the Astor House, Norman approached him. To a stranger she might have been mistaken for a modest version of one of the Broadway prostitutes George Foster described, but these two had a history. To George Washington Matsell, the police justice who went to the Astor House on the night of the crime to take his story, Ballard later said that she "pretended to have something to say to him" and tried to persuade him to walk with her. Ignoring her, Ballard continued on his way. Amelia, refusing to be dismissed, followed behind him. Together, they reached the steps of the Astor House.

The Astor House, the largest, newest, and most luxurious hotel in the city, was well known to Henry Ballard. Ballard lived there between 1838 and 1842, and that evening he was probably on his way there to dine, as he was still in the habit of doing. Where the stone steps of the Astor House met Broadway, the flow of urban foot traffic pooled and eddied. The steps, which descended from between the columns surrounding the hotel's Broadway entrance, were a gathering place where locals and visitors mixed. Walt Whitman reputedly "loved to bask on its steps for hours." English traveler Isabella Bird described the entrances of the Astor and other big New York hotels: "Groups of extraordinary-looking human beings are always lounging on the door-steps, smoking, whittling, and reading newspapers."

When Ballard and Norman reached the Astor House steps, he walked up, and she followed him. When he reached the top he pulled open the door to go into the hotel, but he was halted when Norman grabbed him by the coat. Leaning against one of the columns that framed the hotel's entrance was William Crummie, an Astor House driver. Crummie was close enough to see the encounter at the hotel entrance, but could not hear what Ballard said to Norman as he freed himself from her and stepped back from the door. Later Crummie told the court he could see clearly, even though it was about seven o'clock by this time, the sun had set, and the gas lamps had not yet been lit. Perhaps he was assisted by the light from the moon, which had waxed past its first quarter but was not yet full.

Crummie then saw Norman, wearing a dark dress and veil, put her hand into the muff she carried, or, he wasn't sure which, into her pocket. As she did so, a small piece of cloth fell out onto the ground. Crummie politely approached, bent down, picked up the piece of cloth, and offered it back to Norman, but she, evidently too preoccupied to worry about a fragment of cloth, would not take it from him. Ballard, meanwhile, walked down a few steps and stopped to talk to a clot of acquaintances he found there. Norman retreated and went to stand behind one of the columns. Ballard, surrounded by men he knew, in the convivial early evening bustle of the Astor House steps, evidently felt safe enough to turn his back on her.

He quickly found out that he was wrong. Remarking to his friends, "That woman is coming up again," Ballard walked back up the steps toward the door. When he reached it, Norman, like a villain in a melodrama, stepped out from behind the column and confronted him, again preventing him from walking in. At just that moment Samuel Floyd, a commission merchant, was also approaching the hotel entrance. Seeing the close conclave the couple formed on the landing outside the door, he thought he was witnessing a conversation. As he arrived he saw Ballard push Amelia away from him with his hands, "gently," Floyd thought. But then Norman unfolded a short, sharp knife, pointed it at Ballard's heart, and plunged. "I am stabbed—oh, God, I am murdered," Ballard cried out. Blood poured out of the hole the little folding knife had made in his light overcoat.

After that, events began to move quickly. As Norman tried to strike Ballard again, Crummie, the hotel driver, "ran up and catched her within my arms and held her still." As he held her, Norman again tried to reach

Ballard with her knife, but Crummie held her tightly. Floyd, the passing merchant, alerted by Ballard's cry and aware by this time of what was happening, grabbed Norman's wrist and pulled the knife away from her. In the false calm that sometimes follows sudden catastrophe, Norman, according to Crummie, "did not seem to be angry, nor attempt to escape." Floyd, however, remembered her saying " 'Do not hold me,' or 'Let me go.' " Ballard, too, Crummie thought, "did not seem alarmed." A lawyer, John Liston, who was walking out of the Astor House just in time to see Crummie holding Norman on the steps, thought she looked "very pale and languid" and "prostrate from past excitement." By this time the crowd on the steps had realized that something had happened. Liston reported that "there were loud exclamations and inquiries of what was the matter. The excitement was great," and "a crowd was rushing." Crummie too began to sense "a little excitement," and as he held Norman he could feel it in her body. The drama finally over, the two men, Crummie with his arms around Norman's waist, and Floyd holding her by the arm, walked her, still grasping her muff, into the Astor House.

Once inside the hotel lobby, Samuel Floyd left William Crummie holding Norman and walked over to the bar to send for a police officer from the local watch house. At the bar he saw Ballard, who had walked in on his own, with blood pouring onto his coat and down onto his hand, and went to help him. Norman, still in Crummie's grasp, must have seen him too. Disappointed to see him alive and on his feet, she said that she "was sorry she had not killed him." In the confusion, Crummie did not wait for Floyd to return with the officer but instead took her himself in a cab to the nearby city jail known grimly as the Tombs. When he told her where they were going she replied, with what sounds like resignation, that that was all he could do with her.

In the cab on the way to jail, William Crummie and Amelia Norman talked. Although he had seen her stab Ballard, he had only glimpsed the knife, which he at first thought might have been a ring or a breast pin. In the cab he asked her "what sized knife she used," and Norman told him, "Oh, only a small one—it is a pity it wasn't larger." And then she repeated, with more venom, the sentiment she expressed when she saw Ballard standing, bleeding but alive, near the Astor House bar. Crummie later repeated it for the benefit of the jury at her trial: she said she "regretted she had not killed the damned yankee."

2

JERSEY MAID AND DAMN YANKEE

Would that heaven might inspire some Jersey maid to spirit up her
countrymen, and save her fair fellow sufferers from ravage and
ravishment!

THOMAS PAINE, "THE CRISIS NO. 1," 1776

Amelia Norman was born around 1818 on a farm near the village of Sparta
in Sussex County in New Jersey's mountainous northwest. The household
she grew up in was troubled. In a coincidence of timing, two of Amelia's
brothers, within days of her attack on Henry Ballard, were raising hell at
home in New Jersey. On November 3, 1843, as their sister sat in jail in New
York, Oliver Norman, eighteen, and Charles Norman, thirty-three, robbed
two of their neighbors, Job Kelsey, "honeyman," and John Rochelle, another beekeeper, of a total of four bee skeps (hives of twined straw made by
beekeepers to house their swarms) and two hundred pounds of honey. The
sticky, buzzing haul was valued at a total of sixteen dollars, about what a
New York City laborer could earn carting fifty-one loads of bricks.

Less than two weeks later Oliver was at it again. This time without
Charles, but with a new companion, the appropriately named Henry Bird,
he stole two geese, twelve fowls, twelve hens, twelve pullets, and twelve
chickens from yet another neighbor, Sering Wade. Later the same night
Oliver Norman and Henry Bird broke into the still house of a fourth
neighbor, James Decker, and stole three gallons of whiskey.

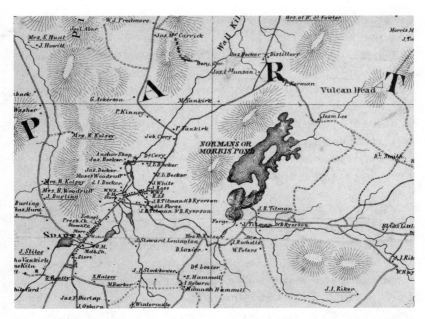

Figure 2.1. Map of Sussex County, New Jersey (detail). Peter Norman's farm is to the left of Vulcan's Head, top right. Job Cory's farm is at left center. The Kelseys (left) and Rochelles (lower center) were the families of the two beekeepers robbed by Amelia's brothers, Charles and Oliver. Griffith Morgan Hopkins Jr., 1860. Library of Congress, Geography and Map Division.

Charles, a blacksmith and farmer who was married and the father of four children in 1843 (one of whom, born in 1838 after his sister left for New York, was named Amelia), may have come to his senses by this time. His wife, Zeruziah Townsend, whose biblical name suggests roots in Puritan New England, may have pushed him back into line. Her childbirth history could be evidence of marital turbulence. After bearing children at regular two-year intervals up through the summer of 1842, she came to a halt, possibly a byproduct of whatever crisis led to Charles's night of crime with his brother the following year. In October 1846, after an interval of more than four years, Zeruziah gave birth to her fifth child, Theodore Frelinghuysen Norman (after the New Jersey Whig politician who was the vice-presidential candidate in Henry Clay's unsuccessful 1844 campaign). Over the next decade the couple had four more children, for a total of nine. It appears that Charles ultimately made his peace with his family and community.

Oliver's story is tougher and sadder. Over the next few decades he developed a full-fledged criminal career, engaging in assault, housebreaking, jailbreaking, attempted rape, and theft of more liquor and farm products, including more living, squawking fowls. He spent time in local jails and at least a few years in the New Jersey Penitentiary. His pattern of waging mayhem against his neighbors speaks of poverty, recklessness, and probably some form of emotional chaos. It also has a family resemblance to the violent rage that his sister displayed on the steps of the Astor House Hotel.

Charles, Amelia, and Oliver Norman were three of the eight children of Peter Norman and his first wife, Rebecca Chamberlin Norman. Rebecca may have first been married to Peter Norman's older brother, Oliver. In 1805 there appears to have been a family rupture, and Oliver took a group of family members, including at least one son, William, and left for Ohio, a target for western migrants in this period, leaving Rebecca behind. Peter took over his brother's farm on Sparta Mountain, his iron forge on nearby Norman Pond, and Rebecca, his wife. The same year Rebecca and Peter Norman had their first child, another William. This William was followed by Charles, Phebe, Jane, Harriet, Amelia, John, and, in 1825, their last child, Oliver, who was presumably named after his uncle, possibly as a gesture of forgiveness after the break that had occurred twenty years earlier.

After Oliver's birth, Rebecca Norman died. In 1826, when Amelia was about eight years old and Oliver still a baby, Peter married again. With his second wife, Ellen Ackerson Burr, he had eight more children: Peter Jr., Rebecca, Robert, James, Mary, Mahlon (who drowned at the age of twelve), and two final babies for whom no records exist, probably because they died in infancy or early childhood. Peter Norman, the father of sixteen children, and his wives kept their family together running a farm and, like many of their neighbors, an iron forge.

Lydia Maria Child, the abolitionist and author who would become Amelia Norman's principal supporter during the ordeal of her trial, often compared the sin and danger of city life to what she and other urban dwellers of this period thought of as the prelapsarian purity of the country. When Child first arrived in New York she was appalled by what she called "this great Babylon," with its "din of crowded life, and the eager chase for gain." The *Advocate of Moral Reform*, the semimonthly journal published by the American Female Moral Reform Society, similarly warned "mothers in the country" to keep their daughters from coming to New York City, where they would face a "moral pestilence" as dangerous as yellow fever. Journalist George Foster warned young women from the country to stay "calmly where you are, beneath your own pure skies, and amid the virtuous freshness of your home, no matter how humble it may be. . . . As you value your moral purity, and the welfare of your immortal soul, come not into the city, to lose yourself in the boiling, seething caldron of licentiousness that rages forever here." Child, Foster, and the moral reformers, shocked by the speed, danger, and disorienting complexity of urban life, had perhaps forgotten that rural life could be rough in its own way, and its inhabitants as criminal or demoralized as city dwellers.

John Norman, Peter Norman's father, was originally from Cornwall, in England. Born around 1735, he left England sometime before the Revolutionary War. John Norman was part of a large wave of Britons, most of them poor, who left for the American colonies at this time. Seeking economic advantages, some may also have been stirred by the rhetoric of liberty circulating in both England and America. John Norman's individual motivations are lost, but once he arrived in the colonies he served as a soldier on the American side in the Revolutionary War, a sign of his permanent alienation, for whatever cause, from his mother country.

After a short sojourn in Albany on the Hudson River north of New York City, John Norman migrated southwest to the Orange County village of Warwick, New York. He left his first mark in the records of Orange County when he married there in the mid-1760s, at around the time that Americans were starting to become restive under British rule. The impress left by the woman he married, identified in records only as Rachel, is much fainter. She was born, probably in Orange County, around 1741, but the surname of the family she came from is lost. During the Revolution John Norman served as a captain in Warwick's militia regiment under the command of Colonel John Hathorn. His service took place early in the war, during the discouraging period when the British occupied New York City and George Washington and the Continental army were in retreat. Colonel Hathorn and his regiment ranged around New York and New Jersey, skirmishing with British troops. Not enough records survive to know for certain what John Norman's own wartime experience was like, but Hathorn, in a letter to his commander, paints a picture of the sort of misery he may have shared in. In December 1776, Hathorn and his regiment were at Tappan, New York, and the men, worried about their families, "almost barefooted" and "nearly naked for Cloathes" in the cold weather, were threatening to disband and go home. "I use every Argument in my power, with them, to frustrate their Imprudent intention," Hathorn wrote desperately. He pleaded: "Pray sir, Use your Influence in obtaining Liberty for the people to return home. I am sorry to be obliged to declare that it will not be in my power to keep them more than three days longer." Seven of John and Rachel Norman's thirteen children were born before the Revolution; he may have been among those anxious, freezing men.

Sometime during the Revolution John and Rachel Norman and their children left Warwick for the village of Sparta, about twenty-four miles southwest in the adjoining New Jersey county of Sussex. The Wallkill River, which flows about nine miles to the west of Warwick village, runs directly through the center of Sparta, forming a natural link between the two places. When the Normans arrived, Sussex County was a wild, frontier area, still thinly settled. Mountainous, forested, and watery with rivers, streams, ponds, and the fens and cedar swamps the local people called "drowned lands," Sparta and the surrounding area was, and still is, ruggedly beautiful. After the railroad arrived in the area in the second half of the nineteenth century, city dwellers began traveling there in the summer to breathe the mountain air and appreciate the scenery; but the settlers who moved there a century earlier, pitted against wolves, bears, and snakes for their survival, did not have the luxury of appreciating Sussex County for its beauty.

These early settlers of Sussex County were religiously and ethnically diverse, as was typical of New York, Pennsylvania, and New Jersey in the eighteenth century. They were Dutch descendants of the original settlers of New Netherland, English Quakers, French Huguenots, Germans, Scots, Scotch-Irish, and other Britons, such as the Cornish Normans. Slavery persisted in New Jersey longer than in any other northern state, and there were also former slaves, which meant that a portion of the population had roots in Africa.

The stony, hilly landscape made large-scale farming difficult, so Spartans planted fruit orchards, grazed cows, kept bees, and grew wheat. They took advantage of the power provided by the area's rivers and plentiful streams to build water-driven sawmills, fulling mills, and gristmills. Because the roads were few and rough, settlers used the local waterways to carry produce to market and people from place to place. The absence of adequate roads also meant that most people traveled on horseback. Casper Schaeffer, a contemporary of Peter Norman from a family of German immigrants who grew up a few miles west of Sparta, remembered how when he was young "even the ladies, both young and old, were very expert" riders.

As was typical in frontier areas, people worked together to clear land and raise buildings. But as was also typical of American frontier societies, eighteenth-century New Jersey could be disorderly and violent. The whiskey that local people made out of their fruit and grains fed a scourge of alcoholism. Casper Schaeffer recalled how whiskey "seemingly flooded the whole land, every neighborhood, almost, having its distillery. Consequently intemperance prevailed to a fearful extent, slaying its thousands." Fighting accompanied the drinking, and Schaeffer remembered fights where "if the parties escaped without the loss of an eye or an ear, a finger or more bitten off, they were esteemed most fortunate."

John Chamberlin, the maternal grandfather of Oliver, Amelia, Charles, and their five full siblings, made his own contribution to the region's lawlessness. After Amelia Norman's trial a phrenologist who signed his report J.R.L. went to Sparta to snoop around for evidence that her violent behavior was inherited. Phrenologists claimed to be able to determine character by analyzing bumps on the head. They also placed great weight on inheritance. J.R.L. felt justified in his suspicion that Norman's heredity was at fault for her behavior when he found out about Charles and Oliver. He was then "rather surprised" to find out that neither of Amelia Norman's parents "was known to possess any thing like a thievish propensity, although the mother, I was told, was possessed of a somewhat revengeful disposition." Disappointed, he kept looking. "Believing, however, that the root of the evil must lie somewhere concealed in the family relation, I inquired into the character of the grandparents." There he found what he was looking for: "Their grandfather on their mother's side, had been sentenced at three different times to the states prison for stealing."

John Chamberlin does appear to have been a troubled and violent man with a criminal career similar in its senseless chaos to the one his grandson Oliver would later pursue. In 1792, when he was about forty years old, he was indicted for assaulting two relatives. For the next seventeen years Chamberlin managed to stay out of the courts, but then, when he was about fifty-seven, he set fire to stacks of wheat and rye belonging to Ephraim Wright, a neighbor. On November 5, he stole two horses and took off. He may have been attempting to flee before his trial on November 7 for the destruction of Wright's grain. But the theft of the horses, one of which belonged to his brother Benjamin, only landed him in more trouble. Before he could get very far he was captured and brought back.

Chamberlin was sentenced to seven years' imprisonment for destroying Wright's wheat and rye. He also received five years of hard labor for the theft of each horse. In 1814 he was in prison when he wrote Governor William Pennington to ask for a pardon. Now he was sixty-two, he told the governor, and "laboring under great bodily infirmity of the Dead Palsy," which made him "utterly incapable" of any more prison labor. The result is ambiguous: on the back of Chamberlin's pardon letter is the word "Postponed."

The violent behavior of Amelia, Charles, and Oliver Norman may have owed something to this heritage. It was probably also a product of the violence that was part of the rural neighborhood where they grew up. Sparta and its surroundings were not the bucolic paradise that nineteenth-century urban reformers liked to imagine had been lost with the rise of cities. Instead, their corner of New Jersey was penetrated by the coarse, turbulent atmosphere created by the local iron industry.

By the eighteenth century iron production was ubiquitous in New Jersey, especially in the mountains of the northwestern part of the state. During the American Revolution, George Washington, headquartered in nearby Morristown, concluded that "a great majority of the people" there were ironworkers, while in 1784 another traveler remarked that "it is impossible to travel across the Province without meeting with some little Iron-Forge." The area around Sparta was dotted with mines, forges, and furnaces. The mines and furnaces mainly used transient workers, and also slaves, but many local storekeepers, mill owners, and farmers, including the Normans, supplemented their incomes operating forges or working as blacksmiths. Peter Norman operated a forge at Norman's Pond on Sparta

Mountain, and two of his sons, Amelia's brother and half brother, Charles and Peter Jr., became ironworkers. The family's farm, where Amelia grew up, was called Vulcan's Head, a nod to the Roman god of metalworking and fire.

The iron industry enriched Sussex County, but it also brought danger and destruction. Ironworks were situated in forests, where there were plenty of trees out of which to make charcoal to run the furnaces, and near water to run their machinery and transport heavy bars of iron. The "forest factories" that produced iron in this region made a hell out of their surroundings. Furnaces burned for months at a time, spitting flame and smoke and adding heat to already hot summers. Their constant consumption of charcoal put wages in the pockets of local woodcutters, but also destroyed the forests. The pounding of giant hammers operated by water wheels obliterated the sounds of birds, wind, and water.

Extreme heat, the risk of fire, and the occasional rockfall, dam break, or explosion all endangered the lives of ironworkers. There were also human dangers. Ironworks, employing transient labor, located away from centers of civilization and the stabilizing force of family, were rough places, where drinking and fighting were common. The Ogden mine near Ogdensburg, located about two miles from Vulcan's Head, was originally known as "Sodom."

While the iron industry posed one kind of danger, the inequality endemic to the area posed danger of another kind. Even though the Normans owned a farm and a forge, they may have initially found it hard to set up for themselves, since large tracts of New Jersey land had long been monopolized by large, sometimes absentee landowners. The power that these men derived from their wealth, landholdings, and family and political ties allowed them to dominate the region. The mineral wealth in northwestern New Jersey consolidated the influence of these men and families even further; the ironmasters of Sussex County had since colonial times formed what one historian of New Jersey calls a "tight coterie." Because the large landowners of Sussex County often preferred to rent rather than sell, smaller farmers could be shut out.

In and around Sparta, the great family was the Ogdens, for whom the town of Ogdensburg was named. The Ogden who still sticks in national memory is Aaron Ogden, a Federalist senator from New Jersey during the presidency of John Adams who was elected New Jersey's governor in 1812, then became a steamboat entrepreneur. The family was further linked to state and national networks of power through marriages to members of the Morris and Burr families. The Ogdens, like the Normans, were among the original settlers of Sparta, but of much higher social standing—not only important local landholders and ironmasters, but founders of the Sparta Presbyterian Church in 1786.

The Normans appear to have been enmeshed with the Ogden family. Before his marriage Peter Norman was an Ogden tenant and farmworker. The Norman family attended the Sparta Presbyterian Church, where Ogdens remained leaders into Amelia's childhood and buried their members in its cemetery. The Ogdens would have shown the Normans and their neighbors what power looked like, and how everybody in the community stood in relation to that power. Amelia Norman would encounter power later on in New York in the person of Henry Ballard. On a smaller scale than the Ogdens she knew in her Sussex County childhood, Ballard, who operated an importing business in New York's waterfront business district, might have reminded her of the unequal gifts bestowed by the economic vitality of the antebellum United States.

During the years that Peter Norman's children were growing up, some of the region's rougher edges, both human and natural, were softened. In Amelia Norman's babyhood it was still possible to collect a bounty for a wolf or wildcat scalp in Sparta, but as she grew up the wilderness retreated, and Sparta village and the surrounding township of Hardiston developed from the frontier settlement her grandparents knew into a settled and prosperous community that was increasingly connected to the larger world. In 1834, the year Amelia left for New York, Thomas Gordon, author of a gazetteer, described Sparta approvingly as "a very pleasant village, having some very good houses, a neat Presbyterian church with cupola, a school house, two grist mills, two sawmills, four forges for making iron, in which there are, together, six fires; one tavern, three stores, and from thirty-five to forty dwellings." The natural waterways and the forest routes that Spartans traveled on horseback began to be supplemented by a thickening network of turnpikes that connected the village to other towns in New Jersey as well as to the cities of New York and Philadelphia. On them rattled wagons carrying iron, game, and produce, while stages carried travelers and mail to the growing number of post offices in Sussex County.

They also brought newspapers out from New York, which in the 1830s was home to the expanding penny press, along with local papers. The newspapers' practice of freely exchanging and republishing pieces from each other's papers meant that readers in even the most remote locations could learn about national and international news. They could also read poetry and serialized fiction and entertain themselves with tidbits of sensational gossip from around the country, such as Amelia Norman herself would one day be the subject of.

The reading matter trundled into Sparta on mail wagons might have tantalized a young woman into leaving her remote village for the big city, but only if she could read it. During Amelia's childhood there were common schools, classical schools, academies, boarding schools, and even schools for "young ladies" in Sparta and surrounding towns. This proliferation of schools for girls as well as boys, as elsewhere in the United States in this period, arose out of the enthusiasm for education that was generated by the American Revolution, since literate citizens were necessary for the operation of a republic. A resolution passed by a New Jersey township meeting held in 1827 to debate a revised state constitution made this point when it asserted that "it is solely by the knowledge and moral instruction of our citizens, we can preserve the purity of our republican institutions, and perpetuate the blessings of political and religious liberty." Educated girls were expected to grow up to raise sons who could participate in the republic as citizens. As a Virginia schoolmistress expressed it in 1777, "Nothing tends more to the Improvement of a Country than proper Schools for the Education of both Sexes"—even though women could not become full citizens themselves.

Another force that helped to smooth Sparta's rough edges was the evangelical revival movement known as the Second Great Awakening. The Awakening, characterized by emotional revival meetings where crowds gathered to hear charismatic preachers and renew their commitment to Christ, swept the United States in the first decades of the nineteenth century, reaching Sparta around the time Amelia was born. Robert Ogden Jr., an elder in the Sparta Presbyterian Church who was converted to Evangelicalism, described a revival meeting he attended in 1818 in the Sussex County village of Beemerville, north of Sparta. "The exercises of the day were solemn, impressive, edifying, comforting and consoling, and in the highest degree alarming to the impenitent," he recorded in his journal.

One minister looking back at his experience in Sparta in the 1850s remembered "the greatest display of the power of God in the conversion of sinners that I ever saw under my own ministry." Speculating on why this was, he concluded that the reason "the revival of religion moved with such power was that the people were many of them great sinners, and they knew it."

Sparta's evangelicals were particularly effective in pushing back the alcohol-fueled violence described by Casper Schaeffer. In 1835 an agent of the New Jersey Temperance Society was able to report that evangelicals had succeeded in convincing Sussex County farmers that they should feed their apples to their livestock instead of distilling them into liquor. There had been a shift in feeling, he reported, the number of distilleries was on the decline, and farmers were learning that "it is both morally wrong and impolitic to convert the fruitage of orchards into 'distilled death.'"

New Jersey's evangelicals organized Sunday schools, and they also promoted public education in the state. In 1827 the Nassau Hall Bible Society, based at the College of New Jersey in Princeton (now Princeton University), conducted a survey of literacy in New Jersey. The survey uncovered the poor quality of teaching in local common schools, high rates of illiteracy among adults, and large numbers of children who did not go to school. In Sussex County they found 831 such children. One result of the evangelicals' action was the passage by the New Jersey state legislature of a common school act in 1829. This act did not compel children to go to school—during the first half of the nineteenth century there were as yet no compulsory education laws in the United States—but it did fund township common schools, and it required school officials to report on conditions in the schools.

The Normans could not have been unaffected by the wave of religious fervor and the new ideas about education that pulsed through their village during Amelia's childhood. They attended the town's Presbyterian church, where the evangelical Robert Ogden Jr. was an influence. Nonetheless, Amelia must have been one of the unschooled children that the evangelicals' survey found in 1827, when she was about nine years old. When at twenty-five she was asked to sign the statement she gave at her indictment, she signed with a mark, demonstrating that she could not write her name. She may have been able to read, since a bare education sometimes included reading without writing. Things were changing in Sussex County during her girlhood, but evidently not rapidly or thoroughly enough to make a change for her.

In October 1834, when she was about sixteen years old, Amelia Norman left Vulcan's Head for New York City. A young girl who could not write could leave no diaries or letters to explain her decision. Her reasons, however, are not hard to guess. The household was crowded with children. Two younger brothers, Oliver and John, were probably still living at home. Ellen Ackerson Burr Norman, her stepmother, had produced three children since her marriage to Peter in 1826. By 1834 these step-siblings ranged in age from approximately two to eight.

There is not enough evidence to know what Amelia's relationship with her stepmother was and what role it might have played in her decision to leave home. In 1858 a New York doctor named William Sanger published the results of a study of two thousand New York prostitutes, young women whose trajectories were very similar to Amelia Norman's. Questioning them to discover why they had left home and turned to prostitution, he discovered that a little over half of them had lost either a mother or a father before they turned twenty. He heard stories about young women who had left their homes at around the same age as Amelia because of harsh treatment from stepmothers. There is, however, one clue that might counter this characterization for Ellen Norman: her first daughter, born around 1828, was named Rebecca, the name of her husband's first wife, Amelia's mother. Could Ellen Norman have been commemorating her stepchildren's mother? It is possible that in doing so, she was demonstrating her warm feelings for them.

Even without unhappiness at home, Amelia may have wanted to leave because of the limited prospects she saw for herself in Sussex County, which was improving, but still rough and remote. The experiences of her older sisters, Phebe, Jane, and Harriet, may have taught her that she could do better somewhere else. Phebe, the oldest, married her first husband in 1824 when she was around twenty. She subsequently married two more times and had a total of eight children. Her third husband was none other than Henry Bird, who had accompanied her brother Oliver on his 1843 raid of Sering Wade's poultry house. Bird, who appears to have been a farm laborer, died in 1900 and was buried in the cemetery of the Sussex County Welfare Home. Jane, born in 1810, married Peter Riker, a laborer, while Harriet, born in 1812, married shoemaker Silas Osborne. Amelia could not have known the later histories of her sisters and their husbands in 1834, but she must have been aware of the limited choices available to all of them. She may have wanted something different for herself.

The only reason for Amelia's departure for New York that can be known for sure is that she was offered a job there. The offer came from Eliza Meriam, a Sparta neighbor who had already left New Jersey to settle in New York City with her husband, Francis, and their children. Eliza's family, the Corys, and the Meriams, from Massachusetts, were prosperous, enterprising, and civic-minded. Eliza's parents, Job Cory and his wife, Jane Morrow, were, like Amelia's grandparents, John and Rachel Norman, early settlers of Sparta. Job Cory had begun as a blacksmith, distiller, and farmer and became a substantial landowner. In Sparta he served as a school trustee. His son, Eliza's brother David, was remembered by a local historian as of "sterling integrity, and sought to fulfill all the duties of the citizen." David's tombstone records his religious transformation during the Awakening. Born in 1791, "he lived thirty-four years without God, then was born of the Spirit and by faith and repentance obtained a true hope of eternal life." (The tombstone of his wife Mary, who survived him by six years, is more cryptic: "She hath done what she could.") Eliza's nephew, David and Mary Cory's son, another Job, born the same year as Amelia Norman, grew up to become an elder in the Sparta Presbyterian Church and a local officeholder.

Francis Meriam, whom Eliza Cory married in 1824, was born in Concord, Massachusetts, in 1799. He began his career as a butcher in Massachusetts and then went to New Jersey, where he met and married Eliza Cory. By 1827 Francis and Eliza had moved to New York, where Francis joined his older brother Ebenezer, who after youthful travels in the western wilderness of Kentucky and Ohio had established a business manufacturing soap. To make bath soap in the 1820s was to take a chance on a new industry. In the 1790s, when the Meriam brothers were born, few Americans thought it was necessary to wash their bodies all over on a regular basis, much less to wash with soap. By 1820, when a New York City directory described Ebenezer (who by this time had dropped the Puritan "Ebenezer" and adopted the more urbane "Eben") as a manufacturer of "fancy soap," or toilet soap, the middle class had begun to adopt more fastidious habits of personal hygiene. It took until the 1850s for Americans to adopt routine, all-over washing with soap as the norm. Eben, who also had a dry goods business, made candles, and expanded into other types of household soap, did well enough to need the help of his brother, whose early experience as a butcher may have given him some necessary experience with the animal fats used in soap making.

By the early 1840s Eben Meriam had amassed a comfortable fortune, retired from the soap business, and moved to Brooklyn Heights, where he developed a reputation as a wealthy, kindly eccentric. He began a new career as a meteorologist, contributing a column to *Scientific American*, and edited, published, and distributed a free weekly magazine, the *Municipal Gazette*, in which he expressed his views on science and local politics. By 1860 he was well known enough to rate a satirical poem in *Vanity Fair* magazine, "Meriam's Address to the Great Meteor," which began,

> Great spark that from the anvil of the skies
> Flew in the dazzled face of Friday night
> And even the ruby Mars grew pale with fright—
> I, a philosopher serene and cold,
> Holding sweet converse with each silent star
> From my tall tower on Brooklyn Heights, make bold
> To ask you mildly what the deuce you are?

The prosperity the soap business brought Eben Meriam bubbled over onto his brother and sister-in-law, enabling Eliza Meriam to hire Amelia Norman to help with her growing family. In October 1834, when Eliza brought sixteen-year-old Amelia back with her from Sparta to New York, she and Francis had four young children—three girls and a boy—the youngest an infant, the oldest age ten (a son born in 1827 had died in infancy). Amelia, coming from a household of siblings and half siblings, with several young nieces and nephews, would have had plenty of experience with babies and young children.

Eliza Meriam's offer was a chance for Amelia to leave home. In taking that chance she joined a wave of young men and women who left farms in New England and the Middle Atlantic states during the first half of the nineteenth century, trying for prosperity and independence either in the West or in the growing cities. Young, single women were particularly attracted to cities, where a rising middle class, people like the Meriams, provided both work and a home for them as live-in domestic servants.

When she decided to work for Eliza Meriam as a servant, Amelia Norman was doing what the great majority of women who migrated to cities did: domestic service was the largest employer of working women in New York in the first half of the nineteenth century.

So it was that one day in October 1834 Eliza Meriam and Amelia Norman would have gone to Hurd's temperance hotel—a tavern before its transformation in the Awakening—where the stages left Sparta for New York, traveled for up to a week along the stage route, alighted at Newark, caught one of the boats that ran daily from there to New York, and finally stepped onto Whitehall slip on the bustling edge of the big city.

Like Amelia Norman, Henry Ballard, born in Boston in 1812, was one of the many young migrants who came to New York in the first half of the nineteenth century, but in most other respects his background and history were different from hers. His earliest American paternal ancestor came to Boston in 1635, just five years after the town was established by the Massachusetts Bay Company. The family's Puritan roots lingered in their names. His maternal grandmother's first name, Wait, celebrated the Puritan virtue of patience; his own middle name was Standfast. Henry's parents, John and Hannah Greene Ballard, were known to Lydia Maria Child, who was from Massachusetts, probably through Boston connections. She described them as "worthy and highly respectable." They married in 1811 after the death of John Ballard's first wife and son; Henry was the first of his second wife's seven children. Unlike Rebecca Norman, whose short and tumultuous life left her young children troubled and motherless, Hannah Ballard, a doctor's daughter, accompanied her children throughout their lives, outliving all of them and dying in 1879 at eighty-seven.

Henry Ballard's father, John, was a merchant who began with a general store, then went into the carpet business in Boston with his brother Joseph. In the 1830s, Ballard family businesses clustered around Washington and Bromfield Streets in Boston's business district. Hannah and John Ballard and their children lived nearby at 49 Federal Street. A street adjoining Bromfield was called Ballard Place in the 1830s and 1840s. Like Norman's Pond in Sussex County, it was evidence of his family's active presence in the neighborhood.

By the time he was twenty-two, Henry Ballard, still living with his parents on Federal Street, was a partner in a dry goods company, J. H.

Figure 2.2. Washington Street in downtown Boston (entrance to Cornhill). The Ballard family's carpet and dry goods businesses were located on Washington Street near here. Pendleton's Lithography, 1835. Boston Public Library.

Bradford and Company, on Broad Street. In 1835, when he was twenty-three, he moved out of his parents' house to lodgings at Suffolk Place. The following year, still working at Bradford's, Ballard, who must have been prospering, left Suffolk Place and moved into the opulent Tremont House hotel. The Tremont House, located on Tremont Street, near the family's businesses, was large, new (it was completed in 1828), and notable for being the first American hotel to supply indoor plumbing to every floor. When the Astors built their great New York hotel, the Astor House, they looked to the Tremont House as a model, using its architect, Isaiah Rogers, and importing its manager, Dwight Boyden.

When Henry Ballard was twenty years old and still living in his parents' house, he defied his family's respectability and whatever Puritan scruples they retained and took a mistress, who for the next nine years would call herself Sarah Ballard, representing herself as his wife. Sarah was still a

Figure 2.3. The Tremont House on Tremont Street, Boston, ca. 1830. Boston Public Library.

teenager when she met Henry in Philadelphia, where, she later told Amelia Norman's lawyers, he seduced her away from her home—the same story Amelia would tell about herself and that her lawyers would repeat at her trial. During the years they were together, Sarah became pregnant several times. Each time Henry threatened to leave her unless she had an abortion. She complied, probably because she felt her status as a fallen woman had ruined her prospects for marriage or respectable work.

In 1837 Henry Ballard left Boston and moved to New York. He resettled Sarah in the city with him, perhaps openly for the first time, now that he was far from his parents. As New York became the country's premier commercial city, surpassing both Boston and Philadelphia, Ballard became only one of many New Englanders who, like the enterprising Meriams, were tempted away to the great city on the Hudson. New Englanders, whom Americans of this period called Yankees and liked to characterize as sharp businessmen (when Amelia Norman called Henry Ballard a "damned yankee" this is likely what she meant), became one of the city's most conspicuously numerous tribes. In 1828, three years after the Erie Canal opened the port of New York to the interior of the country, novelist James Fenimore Cooper noted that one in three New Yorkers "are either natives of New England, or are descendants of those who have emigrated from that portion of the country."

Perhaps it took a degree of Yankee shrewdness to start a business in New York in 1837, and for more reasons than one. The first was that only two years before, the city's wharf-side business district had burned to the ground. On the extraordinarily cold night of December 16, 1835, an errant coal from a stove started a fire in a store on Merchant (now Hanover) Street. With the temperature at an astonishing seventeen degrees below zero, water froze in hydrants, hoses, and wells, and in the nearby East River. Assisted by a wild northwest wind, the fire rushed through stores, warehouses, and slips. Embers blew across the river, where at least one roof was ignited but then quickly put out, sparing the city of Brooklyn. Trading ships in the slips were set alight; a sailor fell from his ship and was killed—one of the night's very few fatalities.

The flames were so high that they could be seen as far south as Philadelphia and as far north as Newton, New Jersey, just eight miles west of Sparta village. The *Newton Register* reported that "the flames of the great conflagration in New-York were distinctly visible in that village from 10 o'clock, throughout the whole night." The Normans and Corys, who had seen Amelia and Eliza off a little over a year earlier, would have seen, wondered, and worried. On Leonard Street, just a mile north of the fire, Amelia and the Meriams would have seen the flames and smelled the smoke. They also would have heard the explosions when firemen used gunpowder to blow up buildings in the path of the flames to deprive them of fuel, the tactic that ultimately stopped the fire's advance.

When the fire was finally extinguished the following afternoon—it continued to smolder for the next two weeks—674 buildings had been destroyed within the area bounded by Broad Street on the west, Wall Street on the north, Coenties Slip to the south, and the East River to the east. Stores and warehouses, all gone. The great Merchants Exchange building, just completed in 1827, with its columns, domed cupola, and statue of Alexander Hamilton, was destroyed. The sculptor who made the statue stood in the ruins and wept. Goods—mounds of coffee, barrels of spirits, heaps of fabrics worth "thousands upon thousands and tens of thousands of dollars"—lay ruined in the icy mud of the street. Clerks, cartmen, and porters woke to find themselves jobless. As for their employers, "many of our fellow citizens who retired to their pillows in affluence, were bankrupts on awaking," the *Commercial Advertiser* lamented. The paper gloomily reminded its readers that "those acquainted with our city will at once perceive that nearly the entire seat of its greatest commercial transactions has been destroyed." It also voiced optimism for the future: "We are warranted in the belief that the burden will principally fall in such a manner that it will be borne without shaking the credit of the city, or checking its prosperity for any considerable length of time," declared the *Commercial Advertiser*, even as the fire was still burning.

This belief proved correct. Leaders took action, business continued, the stock market quickly reopened, and before the year was over five hundred fireproof buildings had been built on new streets that were wider and better than the old ones. Just one year later a guidebook author noted the construction of a new Merchants Exchange to replace the old one and boasted that New York "ranks as the second commercial city on the

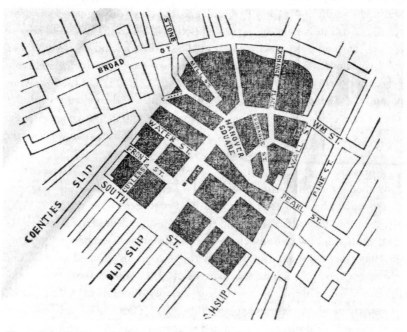

Figure 2.4. On December 22, 1835, the *New York Post* published this map showing the extent of the destruction caused by the business district fire. Library of Congress, Serial and Government Publications Division.

globe, and it must continue to grow with the growth of the rapidly advancing country, of which it will never cease to be the great commercial emporium"—just as if nothing had happened. The cheeky optimism of the city's businessmen was best expressed by James Gordon Bennett, editor of the *New York Herald*, whose office had burned in another fire, the summer before. "We are again in the field," he boasted just a month after his fire, "larger, livelier, better, prettier, saucier, and more independent than ever."

Very soon, however, the city and the country were in the grips of an even bigger financial disaster. Early in 1837 the economy began to falter, and in the spring, soon after the inauguration in early March of President Martin Van Buren, banks began to collapse. The Panic of 1837, as this event came to be known, was the product of a complex pileup of causes: rapid and uncontrolled speculation; the financial policies of Van Buren's predecessor, Andrew Jackson, particularly his destruction of the Second Bank of the United States; crop failures; and reverberations from financial instability in Britain. The result was a severe depression that lasted into the middle of the 1840s. Everyone was affected, but the rise in prices and loss of jobs affected the poor disproportionately. "The whole poor of the city are suffering," commented the *New York American* in February as the catastrophe approached. A month later diarist Philip Hone, observing the high prices of food in one of the city's markets, wrote anxiously, "What is to become of the laboring classes?"

Among those laboring classes, feelings ran high against those they perceived as wealthy extortionists. "Bread, Meat, Rent, Fuel! Their prices must come down! The voice of the people shall be heard, and will prevail!" read an announcement of a meeting in City Hall Park. When, following this meeting, a splinter of the crowd broke off and attacked the store of a merchant they believed was stockpiling flour to drive up prices, the conservative *Commercial Advertiser* raised the specter of the French Revolution. They translated what they saw into American terms, describing the flour rioters as a *canaille*, or crowd of rabble, led by "Jackson-jacobins," a reference to the working-class followers of Andrew Jackson. James Gordon Bennett also deplored the violence of the flour rioters, but at the same time he was on their side. "The terrible extortion of the landlords and the monopolists have driven the people to madness," he wrote; "*rents, food, & fuel*—all must come down," he insisted. Bennett, whose sentiments in this period were generally with the oppressed and against whoever was in power, would in a few years apply a similar perspective to the case of Amelia Norman.

By the time Henry Ballard arrived in New York, the business district was restored from the fire of two years earlier, proof of the commercial vitality that attracted him and so many others to the city and that would

Figure 2.5. James Gordon Bennett (1795–1872), editor of the *New York Herald*. Engraving by J. Ourdan from a photograph by Mathew Brady. Library of Congress, Prints and Photographs Division.

help him to flourish. His first address, combining home and business, was 29 Nassau Street, two blocks north of Wall Street, the burnt district's northern boundary. Two years later he moved his importing and dry goods business to 25 William Street, within the revitalized burnt district. As for the depression that followed the Panic of 1837, it evidently did not hurt him much, since in 1838, no longer living at the same address as his office, he moved to the city's showiest hotel, the Astor House.

The Astor House, which opened in 1836, was built by William B. Astor on land purchased by his father, John Jacob Astor, the millionaire fur trader and land speculator. The six-story granite building took up the whole block between Barclay and Vesey Streets opposite City Hall Park. Its columned entrance, where Amelia Norman later enacted her violent drama, was on Broadway. When Ballard moved in, the Astor House was the newest, biggest, and most luxurious hotel in the city. One visitor

Figure 2.6. Broadway, looking uptown. The Astor House is at upper right, next to St. Paul's Chapel. Bufford's Lith., ca. 1837. Museum of the City of New York, 29.100.1824.

reached deeply into his stock of superlatives to describe it as "enormous," "gigantic," "palatial," "mammoth." Charles Dickens, who was feted at the Astor House during his 1842 visit to New York, called it "this wilderness of an hotel," evoking the grandeur of the American landscape to describe this urban palace. The novelist Henry James, whose parents lived there after their marriage and whose older brother, the philosopher William James, was born in one of its rooms the same year Dickens visited, described it as "the great and appointed modern hotel of New York, the only one of such pretensions." Henry James, born in New York in the spring of 1843 (although not at the Astor House, which by this time the family visited only occasionally), had a child's recollection of its "massive image, that of a great square block of granite with vast dark warm interiors." It challenged City Hall across the street and a few blocks north, and by mimicking the older building's neoclassical architecture, demonstrated the ascendancy of commercial values over the republican ones that were current when City Hall was begun in 1803, when Thomas Jefferson was president.

The Astor House offered its guests and residents everything that was comfortable, convenient, and modern. It had 390 rooms, of which 308 were guest rooms; the rest included two dining rooms, a reading room, a smoking and conversation room, and no fewer than twenty parlors. There was indoor plumbing, with toilets and bathrooms on every floor and hot and cold baths all year. Circling the ground floor were stores offering "almost all things of which travellers have need," such as haircuts, shoe repair, umbrellas, drugs, postal services, and tickets to "theatres, balls, concerts, and other public amusements." All of this made the great hotel attractive not only to short- and long-term transients but also to New Yorkers: public dinners were held there, politicians caballed there, poets drank there, families, like the Jameses, on the move found respite there, and merchants and other prosperous men without wives or servants to cook their dinners, such as Henry Ballard, ate their meals there.

The very things that made the hotel attractive to many also attracted critics. Observers were amazed by the scene at the *table d'hôte* meals served in the Astor House dining room, where as many as one or two hundred well-dressed businessmen sat tightly together, their elbows pinned to

Figure 2.7. Men with newspapers in the Astor House reading room. Nicolino Calyo, 1840. Museum of the City of New York, 41.3.

their sides "like the wings of a trussed fowl." "Dollars and cents appeared to be the leading topic of conversation," an English observer wondered disapprovingly, and "the very few minutes they remain at the dinner-table, their hurried manner of leaving it to look after the beloved dollars, the way in which they bolt their food, and then bolt themselves, cannot fail to create in the mind of the stranger a feeling of astonishment." Lydia Maria Child, whose early fame as an author rested in part on housekeeping manuals, believed the Astor House and its dining room were a threat to domesticity. There, she argued, not only single men but "families exchange comfort for costliness, fireside retirement for flirtation and flaunting, and the simple, healthful, cozy meal, for gravies and gout, dainties and dyspepsia." A preacher with the American Female Moral Reform Society warned that the Astor House steps were where "lawyers, brokers, merchants, and villains of all kinds stand to look at girls and then follow them home." Despite, or more likely because of all this, the Astor House suited Henry Ballard very well. It allowed him to indulge the taste for luxurious living he had nurtured at the Tremont House, the Astor's Boston counterpart. And his establishment there was proof of the vitality of his business despite the fire of 1835 and the Panic of 1837. That is how he was situated in the spring of 1841, when he met Amelia Norman.

3

GO AND GET YOUR LIVING

The only way her guilt to cover,
(Since our criminal law won't nab him)
To give repentance to her lover,
And reach his bosom—IS—TO STAB HIM.

"A Clever Hit," *North American and Daily
Advertiser* (Philadelphia), February 16, 1844

During the almost six years that passed between the fall of 1834, when she arrived in New York as a girl of sixteen, and the spring of 1841, when she met Henry Ballard, Amelia Norman became part of a community. Number 109 Leonard Street, where the Meriams lived when Amelia Norman came to live with them, was in a dense, complex, urban neighborhood that contained examples of just about everything and everyone that, for better or worse, characterized nineteenth-century cities.

The house, on the corner of Benson Street (now Benson Place), a block east of Broadway, was in the Sixth Ward, which also contained the Five Points, the city's worst slum. Nearby also was City Hall and its leafy triangular park, often the site of political meetings, and the commercial bustle of Broadway. P. T. Barnum's American Museum and the Park Theater were just blocks away. During the years Norman lived on Leonard Street, the Tombs, where she would one day be an inmate, was rising just one block to the east, while the Astor House, where Henry Ballard would live, was going up a few blocks south and west.

Amelia Norman lived with the Meriams for four or five years, during which, Eliza Meriam testified at her trial, she impressed the family with her good conduct. Eliza may also have been the one who told one of Amelia's lawyers, John Morrill, that, as he told the jury, Amelia preferred going to church with the Meriam children rather than to "theatres and places of amusements." While living with the Meriams, Amelia made a friend, a woman named Isabella Hurley, who lived with her husband, Peter, on Allen Street. She also got to know another woman in the neighborhood, Mary Moore, who testified to the jury that before Amelia met Henry Ballard, she was a "free, light hearted woman."

Amelia left the Meriams at a time when they appear to have been struggling, probably as a result of the tough times that followed the Panic of 1837. That year the Meriams, still at 109 Leonard Street, where they had lived since 1834, started taking in boarders. In 1839 they moved to a larger house on Pearl Street near the seaport, one better suited for keeping boarders because of its size and its proximity to the wharves and the businesses that served them. The 1840 census shows them operating a household that included thirteen men between the ages of twenty and thirty, proof that by this time they were operating a boardinghouse and not simply taking in the odd boarder. In 1841 they moved again, this time to Beekman Street, where they were living (and still running a boardinghouse) at the time of Norman's trial. Eben Meriam seems to have made out better. He continued to run the soap factory until the early 1840s, when he retired to Brooklyn and started his new life as a prosperous retiree and weather enthusiast.

When Amelia left the Meriams, sometime in 1838 or 1839, she went to work in the household of a Mr. Ealer, who lived at 10 Duane Street, two blocks south of the house on Leonard Street. This arrangement may not have been a success, since after an unspecified period she returned to the Meriams. Throughout this time, Eliza later told the court, Amelia remained close to her and her family. Therefore it was probably the turbulence in the Meriam household and her own economic necessity, rather than a rupture with the Meriams, that caused Amelia to leave them a second time, in July 1839.

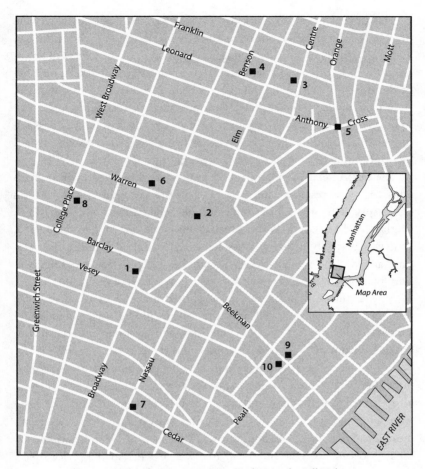

Figure 3.1. Amelia Norman's New York. Map by Bill Nelson.

Key: (1) The Astor House hotel; (2) City Hall Park; (3) The Tombs jail; (4) 109 Leonard Street, at the corner of Benson Street (now Benson Place), where Amelia Norman lived with the Meriams; (5) The intersection of Anthony, Orange, and Cross Streets, known as the Five Points; (6) 15 Warren Street, where Henry and Francis Ballard lived in 1843; (7) H. S. Ballard and Co., Importers, at 64 Cedar Street, where Henry Ballard was surprised by Amelia Norman and Sarah Ballard; (8) Joel Behrend's house at 53 West Broadway (called College Place); (9) Mary Moore's house at 100 Beekman Street; (10) 293 Pearl Street, where the Meriams moved in 1839 so they could take in more boarders.

This time she went to work for William Callender and his wife, who lived in the same Duane Street building as Mr. Ealer, and whom she had met when she lived there. Callender was a young police clerk with an office at the Tombs; his wife was the daughter of Samuel Sparks, a member of the Board of Assistant Aldermen, which, together with the Board of Aldermen, made up the city's legislature. William Callender would prove to be one of Amelia Norman's most stalwart friends, and his kindness, although not spread on the public stage as Lydia Maria Child's was, would be helpful to his young servant when she got into trouble later on.

The ties Amelia Norman formed in New York proved their strength when they were tested by illness; she had fits of some kind, possibly a form of epilepsy. "She was subject to fits all the time she lived with me," Eliza Meriam told the court. When Amelia's fits came on, Meriam explained, "she was perfectly helpless," they left her "weak and feeble," and, Meriam added, "she was always in delicate health." On one occasion, Meriam remembered, she was sent for when Amelia had a fit in church.

Amelia's fits continued when she worked for William Callender. He described how they came on suddenly: "She would be sewing, and would suddenly fall from her chair on the floor, and continue entirely unconscious for from two to five or six hours, and sometimes the whole night." Whenever he and his wife went out, he "stepped next door" to ask his father-in-law, Assistant Alderman Sparks, to keep an eye on her. Callender also recalled that Amelia frequently visited Eliza Meriam when she lived with him, and sometimes had fits during those visits. Despite Amelia's intimacy with the Meriam family, it was Callender the Meriams called for on such occasions. One time, when he was at work at the police office, they sent for him so that he could apply a "plaster that we had before used to relieve her."

In the spring of 1841, while living with the Callenders, Amelia Norman met Henry Ballard. At her trial, one of Amelia Norman's lawyers told the jury that Ballard met his client at the home of a "female acquaintance," a "young woman who has since turned out to be very bad," or one of Amelia's married sisters (the reporters at the trial disagreed about what they heard), and he afterward offered this woman a "present" to assist him in his "deliberate plot to seduce her." (Here, also, the reporters were confused: Amelia's married sisters were in New Jersey, while it was Henry Ballard who may have had a sister in the city.)

What followed looked at first like any courtship. Ballard, who abandoned Sarah, his longtime mistress, when he met Amelia, walked out with her publicly, going to "places of amusement" and stopping for refreshments. But like the introduction he engineered, Ballard's courtship turned out to be false. One day, after telling her that he would take her to "a more private place" for refreshments, he took her instead to a house of prostitution on Mott Street. There, in the words of one of Norman's lawyers, "he succeeded in accomplishing her seduction." Like the heroine of a seduction novel, Amelia had been cajoled, convinced, tricked, and, finally, possibly, raped.

At her trial Norman's lawyers could count on their audience in the courtroom and readers of the press accounts of the trial to recognize and understand this narrative. As the subject of Ballard's predation, Norman must be his innocent victim, and so they presented her at her trial. For obvious reasons they did not explore what may have been her own possibly equally calculated decision to take up with a prosperous merchant who could support her at a time of economic uncertainty. She had taken a chance before, when she left Sparta to come to New York. Possibly she did so again when she met Henry Ballard, even up to the point of offering her body in exchange for security. But even if she did enter her relationship with Ballard in a calculated manner, she would not have welcomed the violent contempt with which he treated her.

In May 1841, after this catastrophe, Amelia left Callender's house. She went to stay with Mary Moore, who, presumably on the basis of their friendship, took her in not as a servant but as a boarder, even though Moore did not keep a boardinghouse. During the two or three months she stayed at Mary Moore's she was uneasy, sullen, and silent, sitting for hours at a time without speaking. Moore thought she was suffering from "lowness of spirits." Amelia confided little to Moore, but Moore drew her own conclusions. She saw Henry Ballard passing outside her house, and she saw Amelia go out to meet him. Amelia "complained of being unwell" and took "one or two boxes" of pills. She suffered from several severe fits while at Moore's. "I formed an opinion," Moore later told the court, "that she had been promised something that had not been performed; that she had been promised to be married or something like that." When Moore asked her directly what was the matter, Amelia replied that she "would know one day." Amelia must have realized by then that she was pregnant.

That August, probably around the time she left Mary Moore, Amelia presented a similar picture of despair to Isabella Hurley. "She came to my house and sat upon the back stoop crying," Hurley later told the court. When Hurley asked her what was wrong, Amelia replied that she had neither home nor work. Hurley offered to help her. She suggested that Amelia go see if her sister had any work for her and, if not, to come back, and Hurley would help her find another place.

Isabella Hurley's sister lived on Ninth Avenue near West Forty-Second Street. Setting off on a streetcar, Amelia got off at West Thirty-Third Street, either by mistake or because that was as far as the streetcar went, and got lost. She told Hurley, when she returned to her a few days later, that she "could not find the place." In the 1840s the Manhattan landscape above Fourteenth Street, where the city still had not reached, was as if in a state of suspended animation. Markers at projected intersections showed where streets would advance to realize the grid plan that already shaped development on the southern tip of the island. Poet Edgar Allan Poe, who lived on a farm on West Eighty-Fourth Street in the mid-1840s, described how old houses with no future in the advancing metropolis were being allowed to decay. They were "doomed," Poe wrote, withered by the "acrid breath" of "the spirit of Improvement."

Margaret Fuller, who came to New York in 1844 to write for the *New York Tribune*, lived with Horace Greeley, the *Tribune*'s editor, and his family in the sort of crumbling house that Poe described, in a rural grotto on the East River in what is today midtown Manhattan. Lydia Maria Child visited her there in 1845, and in a letter to a friend she described its setting. Traveling on a horse-drawn omnibus, probably similar to the one Amelia Norman rode to find Isabella Hurley's sister on the West Side, she endured roads that were "one mass of mud." Arriving at East Forty-Ninth Street, she found "instead of a street" a "winding zigzag cart-track. It was as rural as you can imagine, with moss-covered rocks, scraggly bushes, and a brook that came tumbling over a little dam and run under the lane."

When Amelia Norman reappeared at Isabella Hurley's house after wandering fruitlessly in the wilderness of the West Side of Manhattan, Hurley gave her the directions a second time, but then "never saw her at my house again." Based on what she had seen of Norman's behavior, and without having learned very much from Norman herself, Hurley "formed an opinion that she was in trouble."

Between the summer of 1841 and the fall of 1842, when Ballard left for a long trip to England, Norman began a wandering life as Henry Ballard's mistress, moving fitfully from one boarding arrangement to another, decamping each time her landladies discovered that her relation with Ballard "was not such as it should be." After her unsuccessful effort to find work with Mrs. Hurley's sister, she went to Brooklyn, possibly to conceal her pregnancy, then, with Ballard's assistance, and possibly at his insistence, had an abortion. Next Amelia boarded at a house on Twenty-Sixth Street, on the city's northern margin. After that she boarded with a Mrs. Adams on Delancey Street, then with a Mrs. Prentice on Oliver Street, then out to Newark, New Jersey, where it was possible to catch a stage for Sparta, as maybe she was intending to do. Ballard, still living at the Astor House, visited Norman at all these places, representing himself as her husband or her uncle, calling himself Mr. Norman, Mr. Brown, Mr. Williams, and once, Francis Ellenly. Francis was the name of the brother who came to New York to join him in business; Ellenly could have been a reference to Helen, sometimes called Ellen Jewett, the prostitute whose murder in 1836, the year before Ballard came to New York, filled the newspapers.

While Amelia was at Stewart's Hotel in Newark, Ballard, calling himself Mr. Williams, wrote her letters, addressed to Mrs. Williams, "containing strong feelings of love and affection." (These letters may be proof that Amelia could read, even if she could not write.) By August or September 1842, Amelia was back in New York, boarding at the house of Mrs. Grey on Canal Street and pregnant again. Henry Ballard, no longer playing the affectionate lover, visited her there with his lawyer, Edward Sandford, and "by threats and expostulations" forced her to go to the house of Margaret Bird, a "female physician." Ballard and Sandford may have intended her to have another abortion, or they may have wanted her to give up her baby after it was born; "female physicians" provided both of these services. Instead, Amelia gave birth to a child who was still alive and in her care at the time of her trial in January 1844. Curiously, none of the accounts of Amelia Norman's trial in the press or elsewhere ever gave the name or even the sex of her baby. That this child was at the center of her own concerns is clear. But in the mid-1840s, before the child welfare movement that would begin to develop a decade later, New Yorkers had not yet learned to care about the welfare of poor infants born to unmarried mothers.

The birth of Amelia's baby in the fall or late summer of 1842 was a moment of crisis. Henry Ballard tried to make Amelia go to the police to swear that the baby was not his, and he demanded back the letters he had written her when she was in Newark. Into this crisis stepped William Callender, who lodged a complaint of seduction against Ballard.

Seduction was the term used in the nineteenth century to describe a man's sexual enticement of a single woman. It was also a concept in common law. The seduction tort (a tort is an act that causes harm, and for which the person who caused the harm is legally liable in civil law) allowed the father or master of an unmarried woman to sue her seducer for damages on the basis of his loss of her services, usually because of the pregnancy and motherhood that resulted from the seduction. The tort was rooted in seventeenth-century English law, and it can be understood in the context of a family structure dating back to Roman times in which male household heads legally owned the labor and, to varying degrees, the bodies of wives, children, apprentices, indentured servants, and slaves. In the 1840s in the United States significant vestiges of this structure still stood—especially in the institution of slavery—although it was eroding under the assaults of the abolition movement, the decline of indentured servitude, the retreat of apprenticeship and the corresponding rise of free labor, and, by the late 1840s, the movement for women's rights.

Callender may have learned about the seduction tort as a result of his daily immersion in government, the court system, and the police. The police office, where he worked as a clerk, was located in the complex of courts and jails that made up the Tombs. His father-in-law and neighbor, Assistant Alderman Sparks, may have been a further source of information about law and government. This web of connections may have supplied Callender, a young man in his twenties, with the knowledge and the confidence to lodge a suit against Ballard.

Callender's understanding of the tort, however, was imperfect. Since Amelia Norman was his employee, and technically not a dependent in his household, he did not have the same standing to sue that a father or master would. His suit, then, looks more than anything else like a gesture of friendship and concern, a sense of responsibility toward his servant, and an effort to grasp at whatever legal redress he could find. Callender ultimately abandoned his seduction suit when Henry Ballard and his lawyer, Edward Sandford, persuaded him to back down, promising him that Ballard would provide Norman with "money for all necessary purposes" and "obtain rooms for her to remain in comfort." Then, instead of fulfilling these promises, Ballard repeated his first trick, placing Norman in what he claimed was a "respectable house" that turned out instead to be what one of Norman's lawyers described as an "infamous house on Green Street"—a brothel. In the 1840s, brothels clustered on Green Street, with some blocks containing as many as eight. His ruse accomplished, Ballard left on a trip to England, abandoning Amelia and their child.

The year that followed these events is a blank. In the statement Amelia gave at her indictment she said that she was a dressmaker. That may be how she supported herself and her child during that year. It is likely that she also worked as a prostitute, a baggy category that in the nineteenth century encompassed kept women as well as streetwalkers. Amelia's lawyers were careful to represent Norman's virtue as unquestioned before she met Ballard, but they did concede that she followed a "vicious course of life," a phrase used to imply prostitution, after she met him. The *Advocate of Moral Reform* used the same phrase, describing how Amelia had been "comfortable and happy in the employ of a respectable private family, until she was robbed of her virtue by Mr. Ballard, who first seduced and then deserted her, leaving her alone in the world, compelled to resort to a vicious course of life for a subsistence, refusing to do anything for her after the ruin he had brought upon her."

Sometime before the summer of 1843 Henry Ballard returned to New York. Rather than live again at the Astor House, he reestablished himself in new lodgings in a five-story townhouse at 15 Warren Street, close to Broadway and just two blocks north of the big hotel. He was joined on Warren Street, and in partnership at his store, now on Cedar Street, by his younger brother, Francis. Francis Ballard's trajectory in business was similar to his brother's. Born in 1818, he was living with his parents on Federal Street when, in 1840, along with another brother, Charles, two years older, he set up a dry goods business at 25 Kilby Street in Boston. By 1841, having shed Charles, Francis was operating on his own as Francis G. Ballard, dry goods, at the same address. By 1843, when he was twenty-five, he had packed in his Boston business and come to New York to join Henry, then thirty-one.

The bachelor household that Henry and Francis set up on Warren Street was not unusual in a city full of young migrants who valued the rapid accumulation of wealth more than they did the perpetuation of family, community, and tradition. Asa Greene, author of *A Glance at New York*, an 1837 guide to the city that delineated the distinctions between its many groups of young men on the make, with chapters devoted to "rogues," "dandies," and "mobs," described the bachelor culture that New York nurtured. "Every year doth celibacy more and more increase in New York," he remarked. By celibacy, of course, he meant not abstinence, but indulgent bachelorhood. Antebellum New York was home to an underground culture of sex that was a playground for such bachelors, and it tempted married men as well. Prostitutes, the racy "flash" press, and such entertainments as "model artist" exhibitions, in which thinly clad women took "artistic" poses, all sold their goods to young men like Henry and Francis Ballard. Prolonging youthful "celibacy" by living with a brother rather than a wife, taking meals in the male crush of the Astor House dining room, and keeping a mistress—all of these were very much a part of the sporting culture the Ballard brothers found in New York.

It seems that when Henry Ballard returned to New York, he took up with Amelia Norman once again, and he may have pressed her to have another abortion. On Tuesday, August 8, 1843, frustrated and angry, Amelia showed up in a cab at the Ballard brothers' door on Warren Street. The cab driver rang the bell for her. When Francis answered the door, the driver asked for Henry, who was either not at home or else refused to appear. Francis dismissed the driver, closed the door, and returned upstairs, but when the driver rang again, he came down, walked out to the cab, and found Norman, whom he identified, when he told this story at her November indictment, as "a girl of the town [a prostitute] called Amelia Norman." When Francis told Amelia that she could not see Henry, she replied, according to Francis, "in nearly the following language that if she could not see him there she would see him at his store for she was determined to ruin him, and if she could not do it in one way she would in another, and that she would either send him to the Devil or to Hell." "Ruin," surely on Amelia's mind because of her own status as a "ruined" woman, and because of the financial depression from which so many, but evidently not the Ballard brothers, were suffering, must have seemed like the most potent, the most deeply felt of epithets to hurl at the man the *New York Herald* called her "destroyer."

Either then, or sometime within the next day or two, Amelia went to confront Henry at his store. With her, astonishingly, was Sarah Ballard. The two women had crossed paths and, on learning of their common experience with Henry Ballard, joined forces. When they arrived at H. S. Ballard and Co., Importers, on the corner of Cedar and Nassau Streets, Ballard was not in. When he walked in soon after, he must have been startled to see his two cast-off lovers in league and in his store. Amelia tried to speak to him, but he turned and walked out the door. Then she gave him a taste of what she would deliver in November. She attacked him, first with her fists, and then with her parasol, which she broke over his head. Ballard fled, taking refuge in a nearby store.

After this incident, Norman and Ballard each took their grievances to the law. Ballard went to the police and made a complaint, but not for the assault. Instead he swore that Norman was a prostitute, probably to humiliate her and to spare himself the embarrassment of admitting that he had been hit over the head with that most feminine of implements, a parasol. There was no law against prostitution in New York in 1843, but laws against vagrancy and disorderly conduct had long been routinely used by the police to pick up streetwalkers. The previous week a prostitute named Emma Richardson had attacked a man in the street with a knife. In response, the acting mayor, an alderman and Tammany Hall figure named Elijah Purdy, ordered the police to "arrest all the loose women found in the streets." This incident may have made the police particularly eager to honor Ballard's claim. On Friday, August 11, Norman was arrested and jailed.

The following day, a Saturday, while still in jail, Norman made a counterclaim. She filed a seduction complaint against Ballard, stating that she had been "torn from a comfortable home and forced against her will into a house of prostitution." Mayor Purdy was sympathetic enough to dismiss Ballard's complaint and let her out of jail, sparing her the possibility of conviction and six months in jail. But when her accusation against Ballard was taken up on Monday, it too was dismissed. As had happened a year earlier when William Callender attempted to sue for seduction on her behalf, Norman discovered that she had no standing to sue—the seduction tort granted this only to fathers and masters. And the mayor felt that because she had "accepted a compromise after the alleged seduction" and continued as Ballard's mistress, he was "forced to have no jurisdiction in the case." The next week the press accused her of worse, stating that her claim was nothing but "a fabricated charge to extort money." "We hope," the *New York Sun* opined, "the affair will be brought before the tribunals of justice, and all the facts made public." Instead, both sides dropped their claims, and for the next two months both Henry Ballard and Amelia Norman stayed out of the notice of the press.

Had Norman followed the script established by the authors of the seduction novels, popular poetry, and the stories in the *Advocate of Moral Reform* whose protagonists she so resembled, she would have thought herself irredeemably "ruined," a "fallen" woman. The notion of ruin, which would be repeatedly used by her lawyers at her trial to describe her plight, was used in the nineteenth century to describe the total and permanent moral and physical destruction that a woman was supposed to suffer when she had sex, willingly or not, outside the boundaries of marriage. According to the popular script, a woman fell inevitably into prostitution after her first sexual indiscretion and from there into a downward spiral toward madness and death. Instead, facing material ruin, Norman wrote her own story. With herself and her child to support, she retrieved herself when she took the job with Joel Behrend in August 1843, after her stint in jail. In doing so she was not so different from other working-class women (particularly during the depression years that followed the Panic of 1837) whose standards of sexual morality may have been earthier than those of their middle-class sisters and who were at least as interested in saving themselves and their children from destitution as they were in protecting their sexual reputations.

To separate herself from the parasol-wielding avenger of Cedar Street, Amelia told Behrend that her name was Mrs. Ballard. During his testimony at her trial, Behrend made no mention of her child, so Norman may have placed the baby, by this time almost a year old, with a round-the-clock caretaker of young children, as so many live-in domestic servants had to do, and as she may have already been doing.

Despite the humiliations of the August confrontation, Ballard and Norman continued to struggle with each other through the fall of 1843. Sometime that fall, possibly on the very evening of the crime, Norman again pleaded with Ballard for support. For herself and the child she wanted "but twelve shillings a week, and she would work for her clothes." Ballard refused, instead telling her spitefully to "go and get her living as other prostitutes did." Thus the scene was set for the violence that took place on November 1 and the chilly months in jail that followed.

4

AN AWFUL PLACE

What is this dismal-fronted pile of bastard Egyptian, like an
enchanter's palace in a melodrama!—a famous prison, called The
Tombs. Shall we go in?

CHARLES DICKENS, *AMERICAN NOTES*, 1842

The city jail, where Astor House driver William Crummie took Amelia
Norman on the night she attacked Henry Ballard, was a massive, gloomy,
stone structure known popularly as "the Tombs." Covering the block
bounded by Franklin, Leonard, Centre, and Elm (now Lafayette) Streets,
it was on the site of what had once been a bucolic picnic spot near the
Fresh Water, or Collect Pond. The area had been encroached upon by city
streets and gradually ruined by the waste emitted by tanneries, slaughter-
houses, and breweries; by 1813 the pond was gone. The neighborhood
that arose on the swampy ground that resulted was the Five Points, the
city's worst slum. The Tombs, completed in 1838, hulked on its border, a
stony reminder of the forces of order.

The Tombs was not a single building but a complex surrounded by a
high, thick granite wall. The main entrance, on Centre Street, was raised
above street level by a bank of stone steps that narrowed as they rose, sug-
gestive of an Egyptian pyramid. A portico over the entrance was supported
by four massive columns topped with palm leaves. The architrave was
decorated with a carved Egyptian motif: a winged globe surrounded by

Figure 4.1. The Tombs, also known as the Halls of Justice, opened in 1838. Johann Poppel, 1850. New York Public Library, Wallach Division Picture Collection.

serpents. All these elements were in keeping with the structure's Egyptian Revival style, which was used in this period for cemeteries and prisons and was a gloomy counterpart to the columned neoclassical buildings—the United States Capitol is one example, the Astor House Hotel is another— that reminded Americans of the republics of the ancient world.

The building was meant to awe, and it did. Charles Dickens, who toured the Tombs during his 1842 visit to New York, called it "a dismal-fronted pile of bastard Egyptian, like an enchanter's palace in a melodrama!" British journalist Henry Cooke, who, like Dickens, visited the Tombs in the early 1840s, believed that "a more gloomy abode can hardly be." Journalist George Wilkes, who spent a month in the Tombs at the same time as Amelia Norman, described it as the "sepulchre of the characters, hopes, and purses of all . . . who enter." Novelist Ned Buntline described the effect the Tombs' solemn stone assemblage of steps, columns, palm leaves, and winged, snake-surrounded sphere had on one of his characters: "We looked upon its massive pillars, its dark and heavy front, and a feeling of awe stole over him, as the shade of a rising storm cloud gathers over a sunny meadow. 'It is an awful place,' said he."

This Dickensian rhetoric (some by Dickens himself) was part of the melodramatic nineteenth-century literary and journalistic style that celebrated the titillating horrors of the slum. Dickens's invitation, "Shall we go in?" in his 1842 travelogue, *American Notes*, which documented his trip to the United States, was typical of this genre of urban writing, in which the author served as a tour guide for his readers. Amelia Norman needed no literary introduction to the Tombs, since during the years she lived with the Meriams on Leonard Street the massive structure was under construction less than a block away. Still, as she approached in the cab with William Crummie, the prospect of being imprisoned there must have made the sight of this familiar landmark as chilling to her as it was to Dickens's readers.

The Tombs complex and its components had multiple official names that expressed its various functions: City Prison, Halls of Justice, House of Detention. It housed the Court of Sessions, where Amelia Norman's trial took place; the office of the district attorney, sheriff, and other court officials; the police office, where William Callender worked as a clerk and George Washington Matsell worked as a police justice; a watch station (the "watch," with roots in New Amsterdam, preceded the establishment of the professional police force in 1845), and cells to temporarily house people arrested overnight. Amelia Norman spent the night of November 1 in one of these cells. A reporter for the *New York Weekly Express* imagined for his readers what her night there might have been like, together with the poor wandering souls the police picked up on the streets, "in one of the cages, with a raised plank for her couch, a block of wood for her pillow, and her companions in the adjoining boxes the alarmed shrieking wretches who frequently are made the unwilling inmates of a watch house."

The jail where the men were housed was a separate structure that stood inside the wall along Elm Street. It was a long, narrow, stone building, almost the length of the block and four stories high, connected to the courtroom by a bridge. Inside, 148 cells ran around the walls of each floor. At the top was a skylight meant to bring in light and air. The skylight and other features, including piped-in water, water closets, heat provided by a hot water pipe, and windows (albeit with a view of the gibbet in the courtyard), provided more comfort than was generally available in the slum dwellings in the surrounding neighborhood.

These innovations were evidence of the city's interest in prison reform, a movement that was transforming prisons from places of punishment to penitentiaries—asylums for prisoners to repent and remake themselves into virtuous citizens. The Tombs was designed by architect William Haviland, an innovator in prison reform. It was intended to loosely follow the "separate," or Pennsylvania system in which prisoners remained entirely apart from the contaminating influence of other prisoners, living and working in their cells, meeting only with prison officials, lawyers, and family members. The goal of this system and the competing "silent" system, in which prisoners worked together but were not allowed to speak to each other, was to impose soothing and restorative order on the minds of prisoners who had been damaged by the disorderly forces of modern urban and industrial life. Dorothea Dix, the investigator of conditions in American insane asylums and prisons, explained that the social disorder that was increasingly coming to define urban life in the mid-nineteenth century was due to "the defects of our social organization, to the multiplied and multiplying temptations to crime, in fact, it is to our wealth and prosperity, and to our very civilization, that we chiefly owe the increase of evil-doers."

Since the Tombs was not for convicted criminals serving long sentences, but rather a city jail for people serving short sentences, people awaiting their trials, and witnesses, it was not a true penitentiary. Instead, its planners hoped to use the separate system to keep the innocent, including the witnesses and children who were locked up along with the adult criminals, apart from the guilty. But even with this hopeful (if limited and never fully realized) goal, and despite the idealism of the city officials who planned it, the Tombs acquired its fearsome reputation soon after opening. The architecture, meant to be impressive, was depressing. The building quickly became crowded. Sited over the filled-in Collect Pond, it was damp. In 1845 Dorothea Dix described it as "that most corrupting city-prison, the Tombs, where hundreds congregate, and communicate and receive evil influences continually," where "the moral miasma is diffused throughout" and "free association neutralizes all efforts to instruct and reclaim."

As if to prove Dix's point, George Wilkes bragged that "the range of the whole *Hotel* is allowed me," and boasted about the luxuries he had delivered to his cell: "Roast duck and a bottle of wine for two? Ah ha! There are a good many ways of dodging the irksomeness of confinement!"

Figure 4.2. George Wilkes (1817–1885), author, publisher, adventurer. Wilkes was in jail at the same time as Amelia Norman and wrote about her in *The Mysteries of the Tombs: A Journal of Thirty Days Imprisonment in the New York City Prison for Libel* (1844). Library of Congress, Prints and Photographs Division, Brady-Handy Photograph Collection.

Wilkes, born in New York's Sixth Ward in 1817, was just a year older than Amelia Norman. As a smart, handsome, working-class boy, he made a career as a journalist at a time when expanding literacy and a booming press created opportunities for writers who lacked access to education and influence. In 1841 he helped found and began coediting the *Sunday Flash*, one of the first examples of the "sporting," or "flash," press. Directed at men, the flash press laughingly enlightened its readers with news and gossip about sports, theater, and sex. The three editors assigned themselves the pseudonyms Scorpion, Startle, and Sly. Wilkes was Startle. In 1843 Wilkes was spending a month in jail for violating the terms of the suspended sentence he had received after pleading guilty to the charge of publishing an obscene paper—the *Sunday Flash*—which had since closed under pressure of a citywide crackdown on obscenity.

When Wilkes arrived at the Tombs after his sentencing in November 1843, he was placed in the cell just vacated by his boyhood friend and fellow radical Democrat Mike Walsh. This was the same Mike Walsh who was editor of the *Subterranean* and leader of the radical Spartan Association, who spoke in City Hall Park of his commitment to the "elevation of the downtrodden masses" on the same day that Norman attacked Ballard across the street. Walsh, like Wilkes, lived with bravado in the Tombs, ordering in food and meeting with his friends.

Walsh, who lost the race for state senator he was nominated for on November 1, had been convicted on five charges: four for libel and one for assault and battery. For these he was fined $175 and sentenced to two months in the penitentiary on Blackwell's Island. Before he left for Blackwell's—giving up his cell to his friend Wilkes—and after his incarceration on Blackwell's, Walsh spent time at the Tombs, where he came to know and sympathize with Amelia Norman. He expressed his views on her plight in two editorials in the *Subterranean*. Walsh, who described Norman as an "unfortunate but high-minded girl," understood her to be no less crushed and disregarded by the city's monied and powerful, as represented by the person of merchant Henry Ballard, than its workingmen were by the forces of industrialization that threatened their independent livelihoods and their self-respect as men. He slandered Ballard colorfully and at length: he was a "dastardly, base, mercenary, miserly dog," a "beggarly dog," an "abject craven wretch," a "scurvy wretch," a "pitiful wretch," a "villain," a "miserable poltroon," and "paltry, pusillanimous."

The raucous political culture Walsh belonged to associated a "warm blooded" manliness with republican independence and partook of an urban version of the violence the Normans knew on the New Jersey frontier. James Gordon Bennett imaginatively personified Walsh's Spartans as a "full grown babe with its fists doubled up, and ready to strike at any-body and everybody." The same year as his conviction for assault and battery, Walsh posed as a pugilist for a political print that he signed and handed out to supporters.

There was no place for women in this culture. Walsh made light of the damage Norman did Ballard as a "scratch" and wondered, "Has she no male relative to avenge the wrongs which she has suffered at his hands, and which nothing short of his worthless blood will wash out?" Even though Walsh believed Norman's situation "called forth a feeling of pity for her, and of indignant contempt for him, in the breast of every chival-rous and high-minded man in the community," he did not condemn her for acting on her own behalf. If names mean anything, he may have rec-ognized her as a fellow Spartan.

Walsh, Wilkes, and the other male inmates found other ways to escape the grim environment of the Tombs, or at least to defiantly demonstrate that they would not be brought down by it. Wilkes describes how they sang, chatted, and played practical jokes through the water pipes. One night Walsh screamed into the pipe: "Look out! Look out! The pipes are bustin'!" causing, according to Wilkes, "an uproar" among the frightened inmates.

As an effort at reform, as even a nominal example of the "separate" system, the Tombs was a failure. When Dickens visited in 1842, just four years after the complex opened, he noticed that the skylight in the men's jail was closed and the two wind sails that hung from the roof to bring fresh air into the building were "limp and drooping," as if to signify that even sunlight and fresh air had given up.

Amelia Norman would not have shared in the defiant roistering that Wilkes and Walsh participated in. Women prisoners at the Tombs were housed in a two-story row of cells along a curved corridor inside the exte-rior wall around the corner of Centre and Leonard Streets, separated from the men's prison by the yard. These cells, built to accommodate thirty or forty inmates, were originally meant for debtors, an often genteel group of inmates who were thought to require comfort, physically apart from the potentially threatening inmates of the House of Detention. Since New York no longer imprisoned debtors by the 1840s, these cells were repur-posed for women prisoners. The lower level was for poor women, many from the surrounding slum, whom George Wilkes called the "refuse and

Figure 4.3. Mike Walsh (1810–1859) posed as a pugilist on the frontispiece of his book, *Sketches of the Speeches and Writings of Michael Walsh* (New York, 1843). He signed himself "I remain as usual—Mike Walsh." Library of Congress, General Collection.

off-scourings of the body social." Dickens saw them "peep anxiously" through the square openings in their cell doors. As was the practice at many city institutions, prison officials used these women inmates for labor, letting them out of their cells each day to scrub, sweep, and work in the kitchen.

Amelia Norman, possibly because of the attention she had already received from influential reformers, was spared this treatment. She lived in a cell on the second floor of the former debtor's prison, where, according to George Wilkes, female "criminals of better caste" were stowed. Despite this privilege, they were not spared—and some participated in—the jailhouse conversation that Wilkes described as "continually ribald and indecent . . . coarse, profane, and obscene in the highest degree." He told the story of a young Irish woman, a servant, who was arrested for stealing sugar "from her mistress to give to her poor relations." When she made the mistake of rejecting the advances of one of the inmates and expressed disgust at the "frequent profanity and vulgarity of the conversation of her companions," she was made the "mark for all the ribald indecency and low ridicule" of the group of prostitutes she had to live with. Witnessing this scene were two little girls, ages nine and eleven, vagrants waiting to be taken to Long Island Farms, a public institution for children located on the Queens shoreline.

Wilkes was sympathetic to the women he saw at the Tombs, including Amelia Norman. Citing the "ruin" that could lead a woman to prostitution and then to jail, he lamented: "Alas poor woman! . . . let her have been through every hour of her previous life the paragon of all that is sweet and amiable in nature; the charm of all eyes and the pride of every circle; faultless, sinless, stainless; let her have been all this, and yet for yielding in an evil hour, to an overflow of the very qualities that make her this, she is damned forever."

Wilkes observed that the inmate community formed "a little world within itself, and has all the attributes of a world." In describing the inmate society he witnessed during his month in the Tombs, Wilkes was influenced not only by what he saw, but also by Eugène Sue's popular novel, *Mysteries of Paris*, whose title he borrowed for his prison memoir, *Mysteries of the Tombs*. Sue's *Mysteries* arrived in New York just as Amelia Norman's performance on the Astor House steps brought her into public view in the fall of 1843, and the story of its heroine, the reformed prostitute Fleur de Marie, entangled itself with that of Amelia Norman in the minds of those who followed Norman's trial. The same newspapers that brought Norman's trial to their readers day after day simultaneously printed advertisements for Sue's *Mysteries*, published excerpts from it, reviewed it, and editorialized about it. Margaret Fuller followed her assertion about the importance of Norman's case with a digression on Sue: "In this connection," she wrote in *Woman in the Nineteenth Century*, "I must mention Eugene Sue, the French novelist, several of whose works have been lately transplanted among us, as having the true spirit of reform as to women." Sue's history of Fleur de Marie, Fuller wrote, demonstrated that he had the "heart of a reformer" and saw what women "need, and what causes are injuring them." Even Lydia Maria Child, who knew Norman better than did any of her other supporters, equated Sue's fiction with Norman's story: "I sometimes fear that like poor Fleur de Marie, she will never be able to wash from her mind the 'stern inexorable past.'"

Sue's novel was originally published in France, at first serially in the *Journal des Débats* from June 1842 to October 1843 and later as a massive book in nine volumes. It was a sensation, first in France and then around the world. "Nearly all of France was occupied for more than a year with the adventures of Prince Rodolphe before going about its work," commented French poet and critic Théophile Gautier about one of the work's central characters. It was translated into many languages and traveled even to the Russian Pale of Settlement, where young Jews yearning for a taste of modernity read it in Yiddish. When it arrived in the United States, almost immediately after its run in the *Journal des Débats* came to an end, two New York publishers, Harper and Brothers and the New World Press, raced each other to translate and publish it. Mike Walsh excerpted it in the *Subterranean*. It became, according to an Ohio newspaper, "all the excitement of the Eastern cities at present." According to the *New York Herald*, its story was "familiar with every person in the community who reads." It was immediately dramatized, appearing at the Chatham Theater in New York in November 1843, and it was widely marveled at and criticized by, among others, Karl Marx, Edgar Allan Poe, Lydia Maria Child, and the *Advocate of Moral Reform*. George Wilkes was only one of many authors who modeled his work on Sue's *Mysteries*.

Sue's novel was set among the workers, beggars, criminals, and prostitutes of the Paris underworld, and like Charles Dickens, to whom he was often compared, Sue created a sympathetic picture of the lives of the urban poor. As the *Boston Daily Atlas* commented, "It is the book of the people, and eloquently pleads the cause of the oppressed and humble classes." Its frankness and realism may have appalled the editors of the *Advocate of Moral Reform*, but it impressed Wilkes, who, reading it in jail, thought "the descriptions of the author are masterly and the effects of imprisonment are depicted with an almost omnipotent pencil." At the same time the gothic excitement of the labyrinthine plot kept readers breathless from one installment to the next. Central to that plot is the story of Fleur de Marie, a noblewoman who is abandoned by her mother in infancy, then raised as a prostitute in the Paris underworld. Even after she is retrieved by her father, Rodolphe, and restored to wealth and aristocratic comfort, she dies of shame, unable to forget the sexual dishonor of her past.

The stories of Fleur de Marie and Amelia Norman, cross-pollinating in the press, infusing fiction with fact and fact with fiction, entranced the public and filled publishers' pockets. An editorialist for the *Boston Post*, writing after Norman's trial, noted that "since the Mysteries of Paris was first given to the American world, there has not been such a universal swallowing of literary doses as people of all classes have partaken . . . down to the hour" of Amelia Norman's trial. The editor added: "As for the news-boys, I never saw them look happier or more impudent: The exposure of crime keeps them warm and comfortable;—murder, seduction, arson, and defalcation are the fruitful sources from whence they derive their amplest revenue!"

If Fleur de Marie was a fantasy brewed in Eugène Sue's imagination, it was the flesh-and-blood Amelia Norman whom George Wilkes saw in the Tombs and described in his *Mysteries*. In Wilkes's telling, the prisoners in the Tombs could be rough, but they could also be generous to each other. Norman, despite the desperate misery she experienced in the Tombs, was evidently a participating member of this society. One of her neighbors in the women's prison was a German immigrant, a Mrs. Lechner. Lechner, along with her husband, another German immigrant, had been arrested for their involvement in a widely publicized theft in December from an Albany-bound steamboat of a trunk containing more than $40,000 of currency belonging to Wall Street banks and brokers. The Lechners had already been arrested and were in the Tombs when on

Sunday, January 14, 1844, the day before Amelia Norman's own trial was scheduled to start, the mayor and the police discovered the stolen trunk at the Lechners's house on Rivington Street. When they went to the Tombs to confront Mr. Lechner in his cell in the men's prison, they discovered that he had turned his bunk on end, attached a handkerchief to it, and hanged himself.

Fearing that Mrs. Lechner might try to do the same if she learned about her husband's suicide, the prison keeper, Malachi Fallon, enlisted the help of Amelia Norman, whose cell was nearby. Fallon left the doors of both cells open so that Amelia could keep an eye on the still-unsuspecting new widow, who had been married just a month earlier. With her own trial the next morning, Norman kept watch over her neighbor through an unsettling night. In the morning Mrs. Lechner was still alive and still in the dark about her husband's fate. If Norman knew the secret, she had evidently kept it. The experience, however, shook her own equilibrium badly, as would become clear on the Monday morning when her trial was to begin.

Norman also helped eighteen-year-old Jane MacDonald, originally a servant like Amelia, who had been lured into prostitution and was then arrested for robbing a client. On the morning of her trial in January, Amelia lent her a dress to wear in court. MacDonald was quickly convicted and sentenced to three years in Sing Sing Prison, north of the city. Lydia Maria Child met Jane MacDonald while visiting Sing Sing under the auspices of a prison reform society. Jane's trial had lasted only an hour, and she had had no counsel. She told Child, "There were a great many strange faces; and one gentleman talked a good deal. It seemed to be all against me. They did not ask me anything, and nobody said anything for me; and then they told me I must go to Sing Sing for three years." MacDonald was later saved by Amelia Norman's dress. At the trial, the victim of the robbery swore that the dress he saw her wearing in court was the same one she had on during the crime she was accused of committing—impossible, because MacDonald had borrowed the dress from Norman on the day of her trial. When the source of the dress became known after the trial, MacDonald's supporters successfully petitioned the governor for a pardon.

Wilkes saw Amelia Norman's cell at the Tombs, and he described it by comparing it to that of another of her neighbors, a prostitute and pickpocket named Melinda Hoag. In Hoag's cell, according to Wilkes, "everything indicated comfort and many things, luxury." Hoag had pictures, "costly satin and linen articles of dress," "fancy baskets," a bed "ornamented with a ruffled pillow case," and a shelf with crockery and shining copper utensils. He described Norman's cell as "similarly but more simply furnished."

Wilkes's description suggests that Norman, like Hoag, had friends who remembered her and, now that she was in trouble, supplied her with comforts. These friends included some of her old employers, all of whom would later come to her trial to testify on behalf of the kind young woman they had known in better times. Joel Behrend, her last employer, went to the Astor House after her arrest to see Ballard, and he visited her in jail. He may also have been the anonymous "B" who wrote the *Tribune* to insist that Norman had been "greatly wronged by the epithets bestowed on her" and "that she was a virtuous and happy girl until seduced to her ruin and then deserted by Ballard." William Callender, who had cared for Norman when she had fits during her stint in his home, did not visit her while she was in jail, which is surprising, since he worked at the police office in the Tombs. But he showed his concern when at her trial he vouched for her good character.

Another friend was the tenderhearted prison doctor, Benjamin McCready, who later told the court that he took an interest "in her situation" and visited her frequently. As a doctor he was attentive to her illnesses, including the fits she was prone to, but he also noted her state of mind, which he characterized as "despondency, amounting almost to despair," and worried that she might attempt suicide. He got permission for her to walk around outside her cell.

George Wilkes, who, like his colleague Walsh, saw Norman as a victim of the merchant class that Ballard represented, expressed his support for her when he retold her story in his *Mysteries*. He described how Ballard "repulsed her with disdain" when she asked him for help for herself and her child, repeating Ballard's cruel suggestion that she " 'get a living like other prostitutes.' " In a passage that suggests the saintly Fleur de Marie more than the pragmatic, assertive, and violent Amelia Norman, he sympathetically described "the suffering meekness, which, till this hour had bowed submissively beneath every cruel stroke, blazed into madness, and drawing a weapon from her bosom, she sought with her little strength to inflict the great revenge which Omniscience had overlooked." If "the matter rested only in the hands of Justice," Wilkes argued, Amelia would not be in jail: "the penalty would be reversed, the heartless seducer sent to prison and she set free."

5

A Great Heart

Yes, a great heart is hers, one that dares to go in
To the prison, the slave-hut, the alleys of sin,
And to bring into each, or to find there, some line
Of the never completely out-trampled divine

James Russell Lowell, "Lydia Maria Child," in
A Fable for Critics, 1848

During her time in the Tombs, Norman attracted new and influential friends who became more important to her than any of her fellow inmates proved to be. These not only fortified her with their attention and material support, but they also began to read moral and political meanings into her ordeal that went well beyond the sensational interests of the press and even the boundaries of her own experience. First among this new set of allies was the popular author and reformer Lydia Maria Child, who became her chief protector throughout her trial and afterward.

Lydia Maria Child, born the daughter of a baker in Medford, Massachusetts, in 1802, was a prolific author of novels, stories, works for children, household advice manuals, political tracts, newspaper and magazine articles, biographies, histories, poetry, and reviews. This flood of literary output, which began with the publication of her first book, *Hobomok*, a historical novel published in 1824 when she was only twenty-two, made Child, then Lydia Maria Francis, into a widely read author and public

Figure 5.1. Lydia Maria Child (1802–1880). John A. Whipple, ca. 1865. Library of Congress, Prints and Photographs Division.

figure. Of this flood, all that has survived to the present in popular memory is her "Over the River and through the Woods." Eventually set to music, it was originally a poem, first published in 1844.

Child was also a committed, if conflicted, reformer who by the early 1830s was deeply embroiled in abolition. Like many reformers of this era, she was committed to more than one cause and to the interlinked community of reform. The Quaker poet and abolitionist John Greenleaf Whittier wrote that Child "was by no means a reformer of one idea, but her interest was manifested in every question affecting the welfare of humanity. Peace, temperance, education, prison reform, and equality of civil rights, irrespective of sex, engaged her attention." It was through her involvement in prison reform that she met Amelia Norman in the Tombs.

In May 1841, Child left Massachusetts, where she moved in intersecting abolitionist and Transcendentalist circles, and came to New York to edit the *National Anti-Slavery Standard*, a weekly newspaper published by William Lloyd Garrison's American Anti-Slavery Society. Child credited her conversion to the abolitionist cause, and to reform more broadly, to a meeting with Garrison, who was a founder of the American Anti-Slavery Society and one of the most influential leaders of the nineteenth-century abolition movement. She later remembered how Garrison had "got hold of the strings of my conscience, and pulled me into Reforms."

In the eighteenth century and the first few decades of the nineteenth, efforts to stop or limit slavery on the part of white Americans were generally gradual, limited, paternalistic, and respectful of the financial stakes of slaveholders. Even those who worked to end slavery generally did not contemplate the possibility that former slaves might be incorporated into society as full and equal members. Garrison's ideas were a radical departure from these earlier tepid efforts. He took what came to be called an "immediatist" position, arguing that since slavery was a sin, there was no excuse for it to go on a minute longer. Garrison and his followers, including Lydia Maria Child and her husband, David, believed something that very few other white Americans at the time believed—that slaves were entitled to claim full equal rights as citizens. These were startling, even dangerous views to hold in the early 1830s in the North as well as in the South, and Garrison and other abolitionists, including Child, were made to suffer for them. Anti-abolitionist mobs attacked abolitionists in New York, Philadelphia, and Boston. Garrison himself was seized by a mob from a meeting of the Boston Female Anti-Slavery Society, where he had gone to speak, and hustled roughly through the streets of the city with a rope around his waist, the mob tearing at his hat and clothes as he went.

The chief casualty of Child's abolitionist activities was the sudden collapse of her reputation and with it her income when in 1833, the year that Garrison founded the American Anti-Slavery Society, she published *An Appeal in Favor of That Class of Americans Called Africans*. The *Appeal* was a significant departure for her, and some of her readers were shocked by its outspoken radicalism. The Boston Athenaeum, which had rewarded the precocious young author with a reader's card after the publication of her first book, now took that valuable prize away. The *Juvenile Miscellany*, a journal for children that she edited, lost subscribers and closed in 1834. Her abolitionist colleague Wendell Phillips recalled how "almost every door shut against her." The British author Harriet Martineau described Child as "a lady of whom society was exceedingly proud before she published her Appeal, and to whom society has been extremely contemptuous ever since." Despite all this, the *Appeal* sold. If it shocked some people, it also inspired a small but growing group of others. Author and abolitionist Thomas Wentworth Higginson wrote of its influence: "As it was the first anti-slavery work ever printed in America in book form, so I have always thought it the ablest; that is, it covered the whole ground better than any other. I know that, on reading it for the first time, nearly ten years after its first appearance, it had more formative influence on my mind in that direction than any other." Child bravely continued, publishing three more antislavery works between 1835 and 1836.

The *National Anti-Slavery Standard*, which Child came to New York to edit in 1841, was born in 1840 out of a crisis in the American Anti-Slavery Society over the question of whether women could hold leadership positions in the organization. The Society split over this issue, and the faction that opposed women's participation left, taking the Society's newspaper, the *Emancipator*, with them. This event was a symptom of the restiveness that began to overtake some abolitionist women whose work to restore civil rights to slaves made them look more critically at the "civil death" to which they were condemned themselves.

At the time she took up Amelia Norman's cause, Child had conflicted feelings about the emerging movement for women's rights. When in 1839 Angelina and Sarah Grimké, two sisters who broke with their South

Carolina slaveholding family and went on the abolitionist lecture circuit, urged her to "say and do more about women's rights" and rebuked her for her "want of zeal," she argued: "It is best not to *talk* about our rights, but simply go forward and *do* whatsoever we deem a duty. In toiling for the freedom of others, we shall find our own." She balked at the idea of all-female reform organizations. In 1839 she told Quaker abolitionist Lucretia Mott, who would be one of the organizers of the first American women's rights convention, at Seneca Falls, New York, in 1848, "I never have entered very earnestly into the plan of female conventions and societies. They always seemed to me like half a pair of scissors." In the years surrounding Norman's trial, Child described herself as pro-"rights-of-woman" while at the same time declaring that "much of the talk about Women's rights offends both my reason and my taste. I am not of those who maintain there is no sex in souls." She was painfully conflicted.

Her abolitionist comrade Thomas Wentworth Higginson suggested that Child may have been made uncomfortable by the anti-domestic rhetoric and in some cases scandalous sexual behavior of the early advocates for women's rights, women such as Mary Wollstonecraft, Frances Wright, and her own Transcendentalist friend, Margaret Fuller.

Child, who never, not in her motherless girlhood, not in her married life, lived the sort of domestic life she wrote about in her advice books for wives and mothers such as *The Frugal Housewife* and *The Mother's Book*, yearned for domestic life and love and valued them above all things. "Domestic love is the only rose we have left of paradise," she wrote; and it was "*Home*—that blessed word, which opens to the human heart the most perfect glimpse of Heaven, and helps carry it thither, as on an angel's wings." On top of these scruples, Child was a romantic individualist who was never comfortable as a cog in the machinery of reform. In 1870, after weathering a lifetime of internecine reform politics, Child wrote a friend with heartfelt emphases, "*Reform* always seemed something *outside* of me, something belonging to the *external* of my life; but the *love of beauty* is my *inmost*."

Notwithstanding everything that made her uncomfortable with the methods and behavior of women's rights advocates, Child adamantly believed that men and women were equal, if different, and that women should not be subordinated to men. Men have "vanity and ambition," she wrote a friend, "and so have women." Yet men can "gratify theirs in a thousand ways," while society shuts women out from "business, politics, art, and literature." Women deserved the same right to "moral and

Figure 5.2. Margaret Fuller (1810–1850), author of *Woman in the Nineteenth Century* (1845), in which she commended Lydia Maria Child for helping Amelia Norman. Wilson & Daniels, ca. 1855. Library Company of Philadelphia.

intellectual development" as men did, she argued. "True culture, in them, as in men, consists in the full and free development of individual character, by their *own* perceptions of what is true, and their *own* love of what is good." Child's domestic vision was part of what lay at the heart of her beliefs about women. If women had equal rights and opportunities, they would make better wives and mothers, they would become "more rational companions, partners in business and in thought, as well as in affection and amusement."

Even better, she believed, would be a world in which the same standards of sexual purity that were expected of women were also expected of men—if men would behave more like women. "Would it not be an improvement for men also to be scrupulously pure in manners, conversation and life?" she asked. "Whatsoever can be named as loveliest, best, and most graceful in woman, would likewise be good and graceful in man." Men would benefit from this change. They would be "ennobled and refined" by sharing household duties with their wives, and they would receive "co-operation and sympathy in the discharge of various other duties, now deemed inappropriate to women."

Coexisting with Child's utopian vision of gender relations was anger at what she called the "false structure of society," which encompassed the subjection of wives to husbands, women without a means to earn a sustaining living to men who did, and the laws and customs that buttressed that structure. Enforcing this "false structure," she believed, was violence. "That the present position of women in society is the result of physical force, is obvious enough; whosoever doubts it, let her reflect why she is afraid to go out in the evening without the protection of a man," she wrote, noting the paradox that to be safe from the violence of men, a woman needed a man to protect her. That Amelia Norman had used violence to protect herself seems to have stimulated Child's ambivalent admiration.

Child's willingness to consider that Norman's violence might have been justified is surprising, since in this period she had explicitly declared her opposition to violence. She was in agreement with "nonresistance," a viewpoint then circulating among some abolitionists. Nonresistants opposed any use of physical force, and participation in any organization that supported its goals with violence, including government. They opposed military service and punishment for crime. They hated the federal Constitution for the compromises its framers had made with slavery, even calling for "disunion"; but they also opposed the use of violence by slaves seeking to escape their bondage. As Christians they hoped that love and "moral suasion" would be powerful enough to make change. As the most "ultra" of the "ultraist" reformers in the 1830s and 1840s, the most "perfect" of the "perfectionists," nonresistants occupied a position that was extreme and ultimately short-lived. By the 1850s, the period of the Fugitive Slave Law, "bleeding Kansas," and John Brown's raid at Harpers Ferry, and ultimately with the outbreak of the Civil War in 1861, they came to accept that violence had become an unavoidable part of the movement to free the slaves. Lydia Maria Child was as uncomfortable with organized nonresistance as she was with organized abolition and organized women's rights efforts, but she sympathized deeply with it. "The non-resistance society is as distasteful to me as it possibly can be to you," she wrote an abolitionist friend in 1843, "but I every day become more and more enamored of the principles, and see in them, more and more clearly, a sovereign cure for all the ills that flesh and spirit are heirs to."

Child was also opposed to violence in the form of capital punishment, a viewpoint she expressed in 1842 in two "Letters from New-York." Watching the crowds gathering to witness an execution at the Tombs, she observed that even she was morbidly excited by her proximity to violent death: "Society had kindled all around me a bad excitement, and one of the infernal sparks fell into my own heart. If this was the effect produced on me, who am by nature tender-hearted, by principle opposed to all retaliation, and by social position secluded from contact with evil, what must it have been on the minds of rowdies and desperadoes? The effect of executions on all brought within their influence is evil, and nothing but evil."

Adding to Child's anger about the "false structure of society" was the reality that men often failed to provide the support and protection that was the prize women were promised in exchange for their subordination. Beneath the chivalry that Mike Walsh, for one, believed "warm blooded" men naturally offered to women, Child saw the threat of violence. She believed that "gallantry" was governed by a "gross chattel principle" that made wives into "household conveniences, or gilded toys." Husbands, she suggested, were not so different from "the most inveterate slave-holders." "This taking away *rights*," she argued, "and *condescending* to grant *privileges*, is an old trick of the physical-force principle; and with the immense majority, who only look on the surface of things, this mask effectually disguises an ugliness, which would otherwise be abhorred." Here Child was in agreement with Sarah Grimké, who wrote, "Ah! How many of my sex feel in the dominion, thus unrighteously exercised over them, under the gentle appellation of *protection*, that what they have leaned upon has proved a broken reed at best, and oft a spear." Henry Ballard's behavior toward Amelia Norman was an example of such a betrayal, albeit one that took place outside of marriage, in the forbidden arena of prostitution. Another was Child's marriage.

Lydia Maria Francis first met David Child in 1824, long before she developed her acidic perspective on gallantry. She was dazzled by the handsome, well-educated David, just back from a brief diplomatic assignment in Portugal and an impulsively undertaken military interlude in Spain. David, the twenty-two-year-old Maria (as her friends called her) told her diary, "needs nothing but helmet, shield, and chain armour to make him a complete knight of chivalry."

After the Childs married in 1828, Maria came to realize that the attractive, warm, idealistic, yet hopelessly feckless David would never be able to make a living, nor would he ever be able to make a full commitment to their household. He tried careers in teaching, diplomacy, law, politics, and journalism, but nothing stuck. In 1838 the Childs began farming beet sugar in Northampton, Massachusetts, another of David's idealistic yet unremunerative projects. Like his wife, David Child was an abolitionist, and beet sugar was initially developed as an antislavery crop, grown to provide an alternative to slave-grown sugar from the Caribbean. The Northampton farm, where Maria spent a "terrible year of toil and discord," opened a rift in the Child's loving yet difficult marriage. As she later wrote despairingly, "My husband's deficiencies in business matters are *incurable*"; he "can no more help having them than he can help the color of his eyes." The offer of the *Standard* in New York gave her an excuse to leave David and set out on her own.

In New York Child boarded with Quaker abolitionist and prison reformer Isaac T. Hopper and his family. The household of the septuagenarian but vigorous Hopper included his second wife, Hannah Attmore Hopper, the couple's young children, and Isaac Hopper's grown son from his first marriage, John Hopper, a lawyer. All of the Hoppers, including Isaac Hopper's daughter Abigail Hopper Gibbons and her husband, James Gibbons, were reformers and abolitionists who, like Child, were early associates of William Lloyd Garrison, standing with him when it was unpopular, even dangerous to do so, and sticking with him after the split in the American Anti-Slavery Society. John Hopper was twice attacked by anti-abolitionist mobs, once in his father's bookstore on Pearl Street after a rumor spread that an escaped slave was hiding there, and a second time in Charleston, South Carolina, when a "gang of intoxicated men" led by a New York marshal, in the city to help capture runaway slaves, found that he was carrying abolitionist pamphlets. Isaac and Hannah Hopper were Child's good friends, but it was John Hopper, twenty-six to her thirty-nine when she arrived in New York, to whom she became the closest, conducting with him a passionate friendship, what appears to have been a kind of chaste love affair.

John Hopper was a sparkling character. One friend described him as "a miracle of fun and drollery." Another remembered his "earnest and ardent and fervid nature." He was a jokester, once clearing a crowded horse-drawn omnibus pretending to be mad. He was an obsessive lover of the theater, despite the sobriety of his Quaker upbringing, which mandated plain dress and abstention from popular entertainment. His infatuation with the English actress Fanny Kemble generated the story among his friends that he saw her onstage no fewer than sixty-seven times, stopping to wriggle out of his Quaker clothing in an apothecary shop on his way to the theater.

When Lydia Maria Child arrived in his father's household, she and John went together to plays, concerts, and art galleries, to picnics, and on country expeditions. Most nights they went walking on the Battery, the park at Manhattan's southern tip overlooking New York Harbor, until midnight. John called her "little Zippy Damn"—probably the punch line of some intimate joke, possibly a reference from the theater, unrecoverable now. Child chastely described John to her friends as her "adopted son," but she fooled neither them nor herself. When one friend expressed concern, she replied self-effacingly: "My charms were *never* very formidable, and at this period I think can hardly endanger a young man of 26, passionately fond of the beautiful." (Edgar Allan Poe, who knew Child, tactlessly seconded her modest self-evaluation, writing that she was "anything but fashionable" and that "one would pass her in the street a dozen times without notice.") But, she added, "if there is danger in being absolutely necessary to each other's happiness, for the time being, we are both in great peril."

The Hopper family's great cause, along with abolition, was prison reform (a family friend remarked that the Hoppers had a "natural love for sinners"). In Philadelphia, Isaac Hopper, who earned a bare living as a tailor, had been a prison inspector. This work, in which he visited prisoners, heard their stories, acted as their advocate, and assisted them after they were released, was of a piece with his work helping runaway slaves, exploited children, and anyone else whose oppression he found out about. After the family moved to New York in 1829, he operated a bookstore that sold Quaker and antislavery literature, became active in Garrison's American Anti-Slavery Society, and continued working with individual slaves and prisoners.

In November 1844, Isaac Hopper founded the Prison Association of New York. John Hopper was a member, and Abigail Hopper Gibbons helped organize the Women's Prison Association of New York. The goals of the Prison Association of New York, and of the movement for prison reform in the United States in this period, were the reduction of violent treatment of prison inmates, the restructuring of the prison environment to enhance health and comfort and, as with the separate and silent systems, impose order, and to reform criminals with these environmental measures and with religious teaching. The Prison Association, as well as the Women's Prison Association, was also concerned about the welfare of prisoners after they were released, and worked to help them find employment and adjust to life on the outside. (The reformers and missionaries who haunted prisons were not necessarily welcomed by the inmates. George Wilkes enjoyed taunting a group that peeked around the door of his cell one day and asked what he was in for. " 'Murder!' " Wilkes lied. " 'My God!' exclaimed both of the ladies." Then they "went downstairs after having doubtless detected the impress of vice upon every lineament of my countenance.") It was through the Hoppers' long-established practice of prison visiting that Child and John Hopper met Amelia Norman in the Tombs.

Child described the impression Norman made on her when she first saw her in her cell: "In prison, her despair was most painful to witness. . . . I shall never forget her pale and haggard looks, and the utter hopelessness of her tones, when I first saw her in that tomb-like apartment." She describes a struggle between Ballard's lawyers and Norman's supporters over bail. The bail set for Norman's release, $5,000, was high, and Norman's supporters tried to have it lessened, but Ballard's lawyer fought back, trying to get affidavits that showed that Norman was continuing to make threatening remarks against Ballard in the Tombs. Child remonstrated that "the worst thing they could report of her was, that in one of her bitter moods, she said, 'she sometimes thought turn about was fair play.' "

While Amelia Norman was in jail, John Hopper used his legal contacts to help her. Soon after she arrived at the Tombs, Norman acquired a lawyer, Thomas Warner. Warner may have been one of what George Wilkes described as "the legion of heartless desperate and talentless pettifoggers" who "infest" the Tombs, bribed the keepers to find them clients, then abandoned them if it turned out that they did not have "friends outside who are good for more." Some later behavior of Warner's made it "wise for him to settle as far off as the vicinity of Botany Bay," according to a chronicler of New York's courts. When Warner abandoned Norman for another client on the Saturday before the Monday her trial was to begin, Dr. Benjamin McCready, the physician who worked at the Tombs, notified John Hopper. Hopper went to the jail to see Norman and offered not only to find her another lawyer, but also to pay for her defense. He was helped in this by a man Lydia Maria Child described as a "noble-souled, warm-hearted stranger, a Mr. Carney of Boston," who, although "a man of limited means," offered fifty dollars, and went with Hopper to seek out a new lawyer.

The client Warner abandoned Amelia Norman for was Henry Leitga, a tailor (and like the Lechners, a member of New York's German immigrant community) accused of murdering his wife, then burning down their house where she lay in bed. The "Broadway tragedy," as one newspaper called it, took place only a few days before Norman's encounter with Ballard at the Astor House, and the two cases ran parallel in the court and in the press. Wilkes, who encountered Leitga in the Tombs, described him as a "pallid faced, repulsive looking ruffian in a profusion of oakum colored hair, and a cold, stony expression of the eye," who was hated by the other inmates. Maybe Warner thought that Leitga's case would be more lucrative than Norman's. If, however, he believed she lacked "friends outside who are good for more," he was wrong.

Lydia Maria Child became the first among Norman's friends in her time of need. At the time Child met Norman, she was ready for a new cause. In May 1843, less than a year before Norman's trial, she gave up the editorship of the *National Anti-Slavery Standard*, just two years after she started. At the same time she detached herself from the organized abolitionist movement, if not from the cause itself. Even before she took on the *Standard*, the squabbling within the movement made her, she wrote, "sick at heart, discouraged and ashamed." When she agreed to be the editor of the American Anti-Slavery Society's paper, she did so "expressly on conditions that I would have nothing to do with fighting and controversy." The column she originated at the *Standard*, called Letters from New-York, had been an effort to step outside the hothouse of abolitionist politics, broaden the paper's audience with a wider range of subjects, and introduce new readers to the cause.

During her years as editor, the *Standard*'s circulation doubled, from twenty-five hundred to five thousand (in the early 1840s abolition was still a marginal cause, and abolition papers had small audiences). But she struggled with officers of its parent organization, the American Anti-Slavery Society, when they tried to dictate the *Standard*'s editorial positions, feeling that they were coercing her "individual freedom." "The parting hour has come between me and the anti-slavery organization," she told her friend Ellis Loring; from now on "I will work in my own way, according to the light that is in me." In a column in the paper headed "Farewell," she told her readers that she was asserting her independence: "The freedom of my own spirit makes it absolutely necessary for me to retire. I am too distinctly and decidedly an individual, to edit the organ of any association."

Child's sympathy for Norman may also have owed something to her splintering marriage and her extramarital attachment to John Hopper, both of which put her outside the sexual and marital norms. In February 1843, just under a year before Norman's trial, Child took a step to liberate herself from David, from whom she was still living apart. To preserve her earnings, and to try to escape a system that made incapable men like David masters of capable women such as herself, she separated her money, which as her husband he was entitled to use, from his. "I have come to be *afraid* to lean upon David in all matters connected with a *home* and *support*," she wrote Loring, and "I hardly care what happens to me, if I can only manage not to be separated from John." John, she wrote ambiguously, "supplies to me the place of a real son, and my affections have got so entwined around him that it would almost kill me to have to leave him. I do hope things will so happen that David and he and I can live together, and bless each other."

Child's choice of Norman as a cause in 1843 was also a figure in a pattern she had established of rescuing wounded people—often, but not always, poor, young children, and young women who had been wronged by men. "The fallen woman, the over-tempted inebriate, she could take to her home and watch over month after month. . . . Prison doors were no bar to her when a friendless woman needed help," John Greenleaf Whittier wrote of her.

In December 1843, less than a month before Amelia Norman's trial, Child sent her husband to pluck a ten-year-old orphan boy out of the Tombs, where he had been committed for vagrancy, then she gave him a bath, bought him new clothes, and found him a home. In later years she would help escaped slave Harriet Jacobs publish her memoir, *Incidents in the Life of a Slave Girl*. More spectacularly, in 1859 she offered to go to Virginia to nurse abolitionist John Brown in jail after his attack on Harpers Ferry. When Brown suggested she help his family instead, she threw herself into action. She explained, "When God lays a forlorn fellow creature in my arms, and says There! take her and warm her! I cannot otherwise than do it."

As a popular author Child also surely recognized that Norman's plight made a deeply compelling story. After she left the *Standard* in the spring of 1843, she returned to her interrupted career as a writer. In August 1843 she published a collection of her "Letters from New-York," paying for the publication herself. This edition sold out rapidly, went through two more editions by 1845 and a total of eleven by 1850. At the end of 1843 she restarted the column, this time publishing it in the *Boston Courier*. These later "Letters from New-York" were published in a second series in 1845, even as the first continued to sell in edition after edition. Child devoted one of these columns, "Letter from New-York No. V," to Amelia Norman, publishing it in the *Courier* in February 1844. An edited version was reprinted in the *Standard* a few weeks later, the cuts probably made by Child herself. She did not include this column in any of the editions of the collections, possibly because she felt its tone of anger against men, law, and society would repel the general readers she was trying to attract with her books.

Around the time that she was involved with Norman, Child returned to writing works for children, and stories, poetry, and journalism, much of it in the *Columbian Lady's and Gentleman's Magazine*. She was haunted by the theme of the wronged woman and used it in her stories, including details that she gleaned from Amelia Norman's circumstances. Child's stories, according to Thomas Wentworth Higginson, were "mostly based upon the sins of great cities, especially those of man against woman." He added, "She might have sought more joyous themes, but none which at that time lay so near her heart."

The leadership of the American Female Moral Reform Society also understood the power of Amelia Norman's story. Founded in 1834 by followers of the evangelical preacher Charles Grandison Finney, the Society had as its original mission saving the city's prostitutes; but when the women of the streets proved intractable, the Society shifted its focus to preventing prostitution by guiding, warning, and protecting young women who came to the city on their own. The Society's semimonthly journal, the *Advocate of Moral Reform*, regularly published stories about young women who came to the city from the country, met predatory rakes, succumbed to sexual temptation, and were lost forever to respectable society with nothing but shame and death to look forward to. "Mothers," they warned in an 1840 issue of the *Advocate*, "keep your daughters away from the city—from every city. There is a moral pestilence in this city with which it is dangerous to come in contact. . . . We announce to the mothers in the country that they cannot with safety send their daughters to the city, to learn any trade, or to be employed as domestics. Hundreds have been induced by fair prospects and specious promises, to come to New York, and have died in some pest house of sin, unknown, unpitied, and unmourned."

Lydia Maria Child was not a member of the American Female Moral Reform Society. But she showed her alliance with their cause when she wrote, in her "Letter from New-York" devoted to Amelia Norman, "Seduction is going on by wholesale, with a systematic arrangement, and a number and variety of agents, which would astonish those who have never looked beneath the hypocritical surface of things. In our cities, almost every girl, in the humbler classes of life, walks among snares and pit-falls at every step, unconscious of their presence, until she finds herself fallen, and entangled in a frightful net-work, from which she sees no escape."

The moral reformers, who were less open to joy than Child, saw danger for young women everywhere. They warned against novel reading, because of its "direct tendency to paralyse the moral sensibilities" (Child, the author, certainly would not agree). They were incensed by Sue's *Mysteries of Paris*, reprinting an outraged critique of the "infamous book" that trafficked wholesale in "mental and moral poison." They were leery of theaters because of their "immorality," ballrooms were places of "infamy and death," and the waltz was "a whirling movement" whose "personal familiarities" an "unsophisticated American girl" would shrink from if not for the judgment-clouding influence of "*fashion*." Even the circus was a danger: "The *circus*—that hot-bed of profanity, debauchery, and crime."

The Society's focus on moral perfectionism was a legacy of its roots in the evangelical movement, the Second Great Awakening, in which its founders participated; but after years of working in the slums, especially during the hard times that followed the Panic of 1837, its members had few illusions about the effects of poverty and inequality on the lives of the women and children they worked with. Even as they maintained their commitment to the "cause of moral purity," they developed a more tough-minded understanding of the structural causes of the "sin" they observed. They came to understand that the pitiful wages earned by seamstresses and servants could make the higher earnings of prostitutes seem tempting, and they wrote in favor of higher wages for working women, pointing out "the injustice of withholding from the laborer her hire, and driving her, menaced by want, to seek the wages of iniquity."

Amelia Norman's story appeared to the moral reformers as a fulfillment of the warnings they regularly published in the *Advocate of Moral Reform*, and they assembled on her side as soon as they learned her story. During the two weeks between Norman's attack on Ballard and the publication of the next issue of the *Advocate*, representatives of the Moral Reform Society visited Norman in jail, heard her story, and digested and shaped it for the benefit of their readers.

"The girl who gave the wound," an anonymous member of the Society wrote in the *Advocate*, "says that until a little more than a year past she was comfortable and happy in the employ of a respectable private family, until she was robbed of her virtue by Mr. Ballard, who first seduced and then deserted her, leaving her alone in the world, compelled to resort to a vicious course of life for a subsistence, refusing to do anything for her after the ruin he had brought upon her." Like the heroine of a seduction novel or Eugène Sue's Fleur de Marie, "her mind was rendered miserable and herself wretched on account of her degradation," to the point "that she would rather die than live."

At the same time that the moral reformers were following Norman's story, they were petitioning the legislature of the state of New York to make seduction a criminal offense. As soon as they heard about Amelia Norman's attack on Henry Ballard, they moved to associate her crime with their campaign. Like Lydia Maria Child, they demonstrated ambivalence about Norman's use of violence, reporting not unsympathetically that she was "bent on revenge." They worked this threat of future violence into their appeal to the legislature. "It begins to be obvious," an article in the *Advocate of Moral Reform* warned, "that if our law-makers are obstinate in refusing to punish seduction and kindred crimes, these crimes will be pretty certain to punish themselves—far more severely and notoriously than if the law took hold of them—we prefer Statute law to Lynch law."

All the allies Amelia Norman acquired during her months in the Tombs understood the value of her experience as a story they could shape to fit their own ends. Chief among these were Lydia Maria Child, the women of the American Female Moral Reform Society, and the press. Even those who were nothing more than sympathetic bystanders were tempted. George Wilkes figured her into his *Mysteries of the Tombs*, taking advantage of the craze for Sue and making her a character in his *Mysteries*.

George W. Matsell, the police official who had rushed to the Astor House on the night of the crime to interview Henry Ballard and the witnesses to the crime, was also interested in Norman's story. He was a connoisseur of language, a shaper of tales, at various times a bookseller, lexicographer, editor, publisher, and a skilled and colorful writer in the Dickensian mode, even if his only literary outlets during his early years in the police were his official reports. In 1843 he was an ambitious police justice who organized a detective corps, taking part himself, sometimes in disguise, in the capture of thieves. In 1845, when New York's first professional police force was formed, he became its first chief.

Matsell interviewed Norman in jail after she had been there for several weeks. She answered his questions about her name (revealing her real

name, in place of the alias she gave when she was arrested, Lydia Brown),
age, birthplace, address, and occupation ("I am 25 years old, was born at
Sparta in the State of New Jersey, live at no 51 West Broadway, am a dress
maker by profession which I follow for a living"), and then, on the advice
of Thomas Warner, then her lawyer, refused to say any more. She signed
her statement with a mark.

Matsell may have been disappointed by Norman's terse responses,
since he was interested in the language of what he called "the rogue fraternity." In 1859, after his retirement from the police department, he wrote
and published *Vocabulum; or, The Rogue's Lexicon*, a dictionary of the
language of the criminal underworld. Dealing with criminals in his police
work, he explained, "I was naturally led to study their peculiar language."
"To accomplish this task was no mean undertaking," he continued, "as
I found that it required years of diligent labor to hunt up the various authorities, and these when found proved only partially available, as much
of the language in present use was unwritten, and could only be obtained
by personal study among first-class thieves who had been taught it in their
youth."

Norman may have failed to supply Matsell's literary imagination with
source material, but in January she would enter the place that rivaled
the theater as the principal arena of the city's master storytellers—the
courtroom—and she would not fail there.

6

THE TRIAL BEGINS

A woman, who in a fit of phrenzy stabs the man who has ruined her
by the basest treachery, must answer for it to the law, though hers is
only an attempt; but for the *man*, whose long career of perfidy and
brutal lust has *effected her* ruin, and whose cowardly selfishness has
several times placed her life in extreme jeopardy, the Law has no
penalty! Such is now the law of New-York! Such is Human Justice!

"A HARD CASE," *NEW YORK TRIBUNE*, JANUARY 18, 1844

Amelia Norman's trial was set to start on Monday, January 15, 1844, in
the Court of Sessions in the Tombs, but that morning Norman tried to
hang herself in her cell. The day before, Lechner the robber had fatally
suspended himself from his upturned bunk with a handkerchief. Amelia, who that night had been keeping an eye on Mrs. Lechner to prevent
her from copying her husband, copied him herself, turning her bunk on
its end and using a cord made from a ripped-up petticoat. She was saved
when another prisoner heard "some strange and unusual noise" coming
from her cell and alerted the deputy keeper, who rushed in and stopped
her. Lydia Maria Child believed that the defection of Norman's lawyer,
Thomas Warner, on Saturday may have "proved the drop too much for a
spirit that had so long been under the pressure of extreme despondency."
Amelia was brought into the courtroom Monday morning looking "extremely pallid and much care worn," and the trial was postponed until
the next day.

After this near catastrophe and false start, the trial began again on Tuesday morning. The courtroom was crowded "almost to suffocation" with spectators. To get inside from the street, spectators had to climb the tapering, pyramidal stone steps and enter the lobby, a huge space, twenty-five feet high, with floors tiled in an Egyptian mosaic and eight massive stone columns standing in two rows. Child found the Egyptian style oppressive, but she liked the lotus-topped columns. The "graceful palm leaves, intertwined with lotus blossoms, spoke soothingly to me of the occasional triumph of the moral sentiments over legal technicalities, and of beautiful bursts of eloquence from the heart," she told the readers of "Letters from New-York," voicing the skepticism of the law she had learned in the abolition movement.

The courtroom was equally grand. Entered through a door in the lobby, it was an immense domed space, with more tall columns and a gallery that seated three hundred spectators. The three judges who made up the Court of Sessions sat on the top tier of a high platform, where, framed by massive columns, they dwarfed the lawyers who performed beneath them. It was meant to intimidate the public with the grandeur and power of the law, but it was also a kind of theater, and the crowds that thronged the

Figure 6.1. The Court of Sessions in the Tombs, where Amelia Norman's trial was held. New York Public Library, Wallach Division Picture Collection.

Court of Sessions, daily filling and often spilling out of its three hundred seats during popular trials, were the same ones that contributed to the growth of the theater in this period.

The Court of Sessions, which met at the Tombs on the first Monday of every month, was composed of three city officials. At Norman's trial these were the city's recorder, Frederick Augustus Tallmadge, who served as the presiding judge, and two aldermen, Elijah F. Purdy and David Vandervoort. Amelia Norman and Elijah Purdy had seen each other before. He was the acting mayor she had unsuccessfully appealed to the previous August with a seduction complaint against Ballard after Ballard had her arrested for prostitution.

If Purdy remembered Norman, he never said so during the trial, and in fact neither he nor Vandervoort said much. Purdy, who represented the tenth ward, an area that encompassed a portion of today's Lower East Side, was a player in New York City's Democratic Party. He was active from the 1830s, when the party was associated with the populism of president Andrew Jackson, until his death in 1866, when the city was led—and robbed through a scheme of large-scale embezzlement—by Tammany Hall and its leader, William M. Tweed. *Harper's Weekly*, no friend to Tweed and his cronies, remembered Purdy's long-term, unconditional devotion to his party when it described another politician as "a thick-and-thin Democrat of the Elijah F. Purdy . . . school." David Vandervoort, also a Democrat, although one whose career left a fainter imprint, had represented the Eighth Ward, west of Broadway, intermittently since 1841.

As recorder, Frederick Augustus Tallmadge was the leader of the three judges that made up the Court of Sessions, and it was his judicial voice that dominated at Amelia Norman's trial. Born in Litchfield, Connecticut, in 1792, he was the son of Benjamin Tallmadge, who as "John Bolton" and "721" had worked directly for General George Washington during the Revolutionary War operating the Culper Ring, a group of spies active around British-occupied New York City and his native Long Island. By the time of his son's birth, however, he had put away his cloak and daggers and settled in Litchfield, where he became a wealthy merchant and town postmaster. A Federalist, he was elected to Congress in 1801 and served eight terms.

Frederick Tallmadge, raised in his father's prosperous Connecticut household, a world away from the working-class Jacksonian politics he

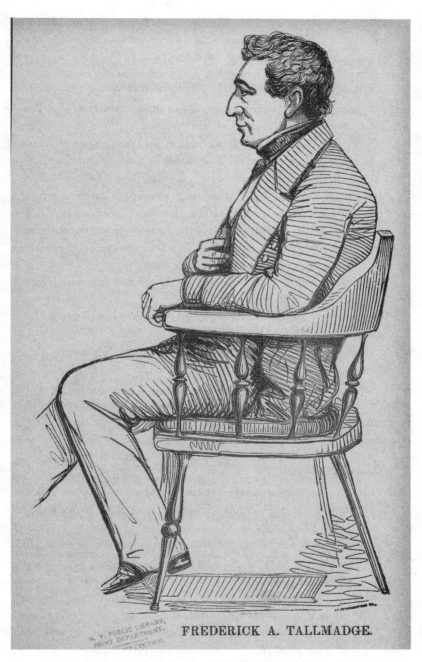

FREDERICK A. TALLMADGE.

Figure 6.2. Frederick Augustus Tallmadge (1792–1869), 1843. Tallmadge was the city recorder and the leading judge of the Court of Sessions at Amelia Norman's trial. New York Public Library, Wallach Division Print Collection.

would know later in New York City, graduated from Yale in 1811 and studied at the well-regarded Litchfield Law School in his home town. Then, like many other New Englanders (including Henry Ballard a generation later), he left Connecticut for the commercial dynamism of New York. Tallmadge began practicing law in New York in 1813 and continued for more than half a century. He was a member of the Whig Party, which had been founded during Andrew Jackson's second term as president to oppose Jackson's policies and those of his Democratic Party. In the 1830s and 1840s Tallmadge was a legislator in the city and the state of New York. He served two terms as city recorder, from 1841 to 1846 and then again from 1848 to 1851. During the interval between those terms he served in Congress. When anti-immigrant sentiment flared in New York in the 1840s and 1850s, a vicious response to the massive immigration from famine-stricken Ireland in the mid-1840s, Tallmadge joined in, becoming a leader of New York's Native American Party.

The prosecutor in the case was the acting district attorney, Jonas B. Phillips, who had been a playwright before he turned to the law. He was a member of a prominent and accomplished Sephardic Jewish family from Philadelphia that included authors and actors as well as businessmen like his stockbroker father. His cousin Mordecai Manuel Noah was, among other things, a playwright and, before Norman's trial, one of the three justices on the Court of Sessions. After arriving in New York from Philadelphia in 1828, Phillips began writing a stream of plays, reportedly as many as seventy, that were produced on New York stages in the 1830s. His dramas and melodramas, with titles like *The Evil Eye*, *The Polish Wife*, and *The Cross of Death*, were popular with working-class audiences. By the 1840s he had given up the theater, studied law, was admitted to the bar, and became an assistant district attorney, where one judge he worked under remembered him as "an honest, a most industrious and an efficient public officer."

Assisting Phillips was Henry Ballard's personal lawyer, Edward Sandford. Prosecutors that were privately hired and paid by plaintiffs, as Sandford was, were a phenomenon in the nineteenth-century United States. As population and territory grew, the legal system was stretched thin, and competent public prosecutors were sometimes in short supply. Privately paid prosecutors were commonly used, and the practice was legal, but those who felt that prosecutors ought to be responsible foremost to the public and the law frowned upon it. During Amelia Norman's trial her lawyers frequently reminded the jury of Sandford's morally questionable status as a privately paid prosecutor.

Sandford was not only Ballard's lawyer, but also his friend and slightly older contemporary. He had been present at key moments in Ballard's affair with Amelia Norman, a fact that emerged in the arguments made by the defense. He and Ballard had together compelled her with threats to go to Margaret Bird, "female physician," where she gave birth to her child; he had helped Ballard persuade William Callender to drop his seduction suit against Ballard; and he was with Ballard in his store on the day that Norman, accompanied by Sarah Ballard, confronted him there. The defense wielded these facts in order to reveal Sandford's complex and, they suggested, morally unsustainable position.

Edward Sandford was born in Ovid, New York, in 1809, the son of a doctor. As a young man in the 1830s he had been buffeted and bruised by the era's political and financial turbulence. After catching the "contagion of speculation," as the antebellum enthusiasm for speculation in the wide-open markets for land and money was disapprovingly called by some, he went bankrupt in the Panic of 1837. Initially a Democrat, he lost faith in the party of Andrew Jackson after the crash and turned toward conservatism. Known for his "indomitable industry," he recovered both his wealth and his reputation. Still, he had suffered. Lydia Maria Child referred to his "obvious ill-health," which may have been a by-product of his recent hard luck. The emotion that flashed through his argument during the trial may have owed something to the personal battering the defense subjected him to but possibly also to the pain of his own recent experience.

Sandford did most of the talking for the prosecution, outperforming the former man of the theater, Jonas Phillips. Even though few in the courtroom agreed with the points he would make during the trial, the press agreed that he was an impressive enough lawyer. The *Tribune* thought he spoke with "great energy and ability," and even Lydia Maria Child conceded that he carried out his job "with great ability."

Defending Amelia Norman was a team of three lawyers assembled for her by well-wishers, including John Hopper, and the court. One of the three was David Graham Jr., the lawyer whom Hopper and the mysterious Mr. Carney rushed to hire after Amelia was abandoned by her original lawyer, Thomas Warner. Graham was everything the shady and unreliable

Warner was not. Thirty-four years old at the time that he took Norman's case, Graham was a busy, brilliant criminal lawyer, known for his skill, tenacity, and precocious erudition. He was also a promising if ultimately minor player in Whig politics in New York, and a legal reformer.

Graham was born in London in 1808 as his family emigrated from Ireland to New York. In Ireland David Graham Sr. was a Presbyterian minister with ties to the Irish republican movement that had manifested itself a decade earlier in the uprising of 1798. Once in New York, the senior Graham used the oratorical powers he had honed in the pulpit in a new and successful career as a lawyer. David Graham Jr. and his brother John both followed their father into the law. David studied at Columbia College, trained with his father, then was admitted to the New York bar at twenty-one. At twenty-four he published his first book, *A Treatise on the Practice of the Supreme Court of the State of New York*, which became a standard text for the next twenty years. In 1838, just thirty, he became a professor at the newly opened law school at the University of the City of New York.

In the fall of 1843 one of Graham's clients was Mike Walsh, whom he represented in a libel case against a rival newspaper editor. But the case that had established Graham's reputation as a criminal lawyer by the time of Norman's trial was that of Ezra White. According to Philip Hone, a former mayor of New York and the foreman of the jury that had convicted White, Ezra White was one of the "hardened wretches" who "infest" the city, patrolling "the grog-shops in the Bowery, Corlear's Hook, Canal Street, and even some in Broadway, where drunken frolics are succeeded by brawls, and on the slightest provocation knives are brought out, dreadful wounds inflicted, and sometimes horrid murder committed." That is what happened on a February night in 1839, when in a bar where dancing had spiraled into fighting, White "thrust about him right and left" with a knife.

One of these random thrusts killed Peter Fitzpatrick, a man who happened to be standing nearby. White was convicted of murder and sentenced to death, but in the spring of 1841 Graham won him a conviction of manslaughter instead of murder and a term of four years of hard labor instead of the noose. Graham's tenacious determination to save his client from death, which White had so casually dealt out to Fitzpatrick, caused one newspaper to fume that "if ever [a] community was disgraced by its legal proceedings towards any great criminal, that of New York was by the case of Ezra White. . . . And this mighty consummation [White's final conviction for manslaughter] is reached through every possible technical quibble." Or, as another writer put it, Graham had "shown black as white."

Graham achieved such results with a courtroom presence that was a mesmerizing mixture of legal skill, oratorical power, coolness, and charm. Abraham Oakey Hall—another New York legal figure who, like Jonas Phillips, had a foot in the theater, in his case as a playwright and sometime actor—who wrote a memoir of the three legal Grahams, recalled that David Graham Jr. had an "insinuating manner and method. He was a native diplomatist. He never lost his temper." In convincing judges and juries he made use of his "musical voice, choice emphasis, harmony of intonation, language of the eye, grace of gesture, fervid utterance." His eyes "were peculiarly lustrous and full of frankness. When they looked upon judge, juror, or witness, it was impossible to gainsay their truthfulness or charm of expression." Aaron Vanderpoel, a New York judge when Graham was practicing in the city, joked that "Graham's eyes are in their gaze as strong as affidavits." Adding paradoxically to Graham's power was the impression he made of delicacy, partly the result of the ill health that had manifested itself by 1843 and would cause his early death within a decade, and also of his "slight, slender build." Hall thought he was "almost effeminately graceful" and that he "suggested a man who could be effective with foils." "Woe be to the witness," Hall warned, "who was deceived into the play of prevarication by the smooth glidings and snakelike charm of David's manner under cross-examination."

Alongside his practice as a criminal lawyer, Graham also had a career in New York politics, initially as a National Republican and then as a Whig. These parties came successively into existence to oppose the policies of Andrew Jackson, whose election as president in 1828 was understood by some to have ushered in an era characterized by excessive democracy and corruption. The National Republican Young Men of the United States, whose 1832 Washington convention Graham attended as a delegate, characterized Jackson as an "individual whose ignorance and imbecility has already spread a blight and mildew over the hopes of our country." The coalition of urban workers, western settlers, and southern farmers who supported Jackson read his presidency another way, characterizing it as an era of the "common man."

For about a decade beginning in the early 1830s, Graham held leadership positions in local National Republican and Whig Party organizations. At the national level he participated in Whig politics as a supporter of Henry Clay during his presidential candidacies of 1832 and 1844 and his failed attempt at the Whig nomination in 1848. According to an admirer, Graham's popularity was such that he "might have had any nomination within the gift of his Whig brethren of this city."

Maybe so, but his political activity was limited and, except for his support for Henry Clay in Clay's multiple attempts at the presidency, local. In 1831 Graham ran unsuccessfully for the New York State Assembly; in the 1830s and 1840s he was a New York City alderman; in 1842 he was corporation counsel (the city's lawyer); in 1846 he was a member of a committee organized to revise New York's city charter; and the following year he became a member of a commission to revise New York State's legal procedures. In 1840 the Whigs nominated him for mayor, but he turned the nomination down.

For a period in the mid-1840s, he appears to have retreated from politics, possibly partly because as the son of Irish immigrants he had become uncomfortable with the nativist turn in Whig politics that attracted Frederick Tallmadge. During this time Graham, a Whig, contributed twenty-five dollars to a fund organized by the Democratic Tammany Hall to relieve "the famished and suffering Irish." He resurfaced in 1848 to support Henry Clay's failed effort to get the Whig nomination for president, then agreed to support Zachary Taylor, ultimately the Whig nominee. The same year he named a son Henry Clay Graham.

When Graham refused the mayoral nomination in 1840, he was probably being sincere when he pleaded his "paramount duty to my private and professional relations." The exhausting pace of his career as a criminal lawyer was dictated by the requirements of his "numerous and expensive family," which included his wife, Cornelia Matilda Hyslop Graham, and five children. Along with the expense of raising five children, Graham may have had to cope with a difficult marriage. According to A. Oakey Hall, Cornelia Graham was "one of New York's famous belles, of high family connection." The opinionated lawyer and diarist George Templeton Strong suggested that her careless extravagance may have helped erode the family finances.

Graham's fragile health may also have prevented him from having a larger political career. At the Whig meeting of October 31, 1843—held the day before the parallel Democratic meeting in City Hall Park where his client Mike Walsh spoke—Graham concluded his speech, to applause, with, "I know I am unable to add anything, even if I were in better physical frame to do it." A reporter from the *Herald* watched as he took his seat soon after this, "apparently much exhausted." He was much changed from what he had been in 1840, when a newspaper reporting on his mayoral nomination noted his "ruddy and youthful appearance." Yet despite pressures that were literally killing him, Graham agreed to take on Amelia Norman's case when John Hopper and Mr. Carney arrived at his office on the corner of Beekman and Nassau Streets in the winter of 1844. He also refused to take a fee, returning the fifty dollars they gave him to Lydia Maria Child. The money was enclosed in what Child described as "a noble letter" in which he offered the money to Norman, asserting that "this trial involved considerations higher and holier than the relations of lawyer and client."

The other lawyers assembled to defend Norman were John A. Morrill and James S. Carpentier. Both were assigned to Norman by the court. Morrill was already known to the public because of two notorious clients he had recently represented. One was the abortionist Madame Restell, who was convicted for abortion, then a misdemeanor, on a woman named Mary Ann Purdy, in July 1841, in the first of many trials Restell would undergo in her career. At the time of Amelia Norman's trial in January 1843, Morrill was still representing Restell in a series of appeals that continued until February 1844, when the case was finally dropped.

Morrill's other infamous client was John Colt. In the fall of 1841, bookkeeper John Colt murdered printer Samuel Adams in what he claimed was an act of self-defense after a dispute. In a maddened effort to hide what he had done, Colt cut Adams's body into pieces, packed them in a wooden crate, and had the crate hauled to the dock and onto a ship headed for New Orleans. The press and public responded with a mixture of horror and titillated excitement to Colt's trial, which began, after several postponements, in January 1842, exactly two years before Amelia Norman's. Walt Whitman, then in his early twenties and editor of the *Aurora*, was disgusted by the attention Colt's story attracted, remembering later how Colt "was hunted by an unrelenting public appetite for blood!" James Gordon Bennett of the *Herald*, meanwhile, exulted, "Never was such an intense excitement exhibited." Herman Melville and Edgar Allan Poe each borrowed elements from the story of John Colt for their fiction, Melville in "Bartleby the Scrivener," and Poe in "The Oblong Box."

David Graham and Lydia Maria Child were also connected to Colt's case. Graham felt that despite its horror, Colt deserved a lesser sentence because, Graham believed, the murder was not premeditated. He was one of a group of lawyers who pleaded unsuccessfully with New York governor William H. Seward to pardon Colt.

Child, like Whitman, was appalled by the "corroding excitement" Colt's trial caused. Like Graham, she believed "that the murder committed by John C. Colt, awful as it was, was not premeditated, but done under the sudden excitement of violent rage," much as, two years later, she would sympathize with Amelia Norman. She devoted a "Letter from New-York" to the Colt case, and it was evidently this that attracted the attention of Colt's brother, the Connecticut gunmaker Samuel Colt, who had been paying his brother's lawyers. Samuel Colt asked Child to help Caroline Henshaw, his brother's mistress, and her child. Child bustled ardently into action, as she did for lost souls throughout her life. She wrote a friend at Brook Farm, the utopian community outside Boston, to ask if he could find a place for Henshaw there. "Oh here is a rare chance to teach the world a noble lesson! Will you forego the opportunity?" she wrote. "Somehow or other, though a stranger to me, God has laid her upon my heart."

Of Amelia Norman's three lawyers, James S. Carpentier is the one for whom the least information survives. Unlike either of his cocounsels, he had not made a name for himself in any important trial. At the time of Norman's trial he was an associate of Thomas Warner, the lawyer who had abandoned her. Nonetheless, they trusted him enough to make the opening statement for the defense on Tuesday, when the trial finally began.

When Amelia Norman appeared in the courtroom on Tuesday, the opening day of the trial, she was a picture of neatness and modesty, sorrow and silence, a contrast with the noisy and excited crowd. After the crisis of the previous day, she was composed, if still sad. The *Herald* reported that she "was very neatly dressed with a black cloak, hat and veil of the same color and a white linen Byron collar turned from her neck in a very neat manner, with wristbands of the same material." A woodcut portrait in the *Herald* that appeared the following day shows her in this outfit with her simple collar, modest veil, and firm, if sorrowful, expression. Her hands, however, are buried in a large muff with a handkerchief dangling, as on the night of November first. This portrait, according to a *Herald* reporter in Newark, New Jersey, caused such "a rush among the ladies" who were following the trial that the paper sold out, and the *Herald*'s Newark agent had to send for more copies.

Ballard, who lurked uneasily in the courtroom, was also scrutinized by the reporters. A *Herald* reporter described his large, blue eyes, light brown hair, sandy whiskers, and high cheekbones "with a flush of red extending on the upper part." Ballard's "genteel" appearance, however, confused the reporter, who felt his face was "any thing but such as would appear to become a gay seducer." His editor, James Gordon Bennett, disagreed. He saw a "long heavy face," "small head," "large aqueline [*sic*] nose," "cold grey eyes and thin lips," a description that owed something to the principles of phrenology, according to which character could be determined by the structure of the head. Bennett also recognized in Ballard a familiar urban type, concluding that he was "nowise distinguishable from the thousand smartly-dressed, commonplace looking individuals, with whom you meet as you walk down Broadway about the hours when the counting houses and dry goods stores discharge their clerks and salesmen for dinner."

With Norman in the courtroom was Lydia Maria Child, accompanied by John Hopper and his stepmother, Hannah Hopper. Also present were several representatives of the American Female Moral Reform Society. If any members of the Norman family were there, the newspapers did not notice them. Henry Ballard's courtroom support consisted of his brother Francis. Henry himself was there only because he had been subpoenaed by the defense, even though neither the defense nor his own counsel ever called on him to testify. In his closing statement at the end of the trial David Graham said that Ballard had not dared to testify, "as there were witnesses in abundance in Court to contradict and stamp with falsehood and infamy his accusations." And, Ballard was probably afraid.

Figure 6.3. Amelia Norman as she appeared in the *New York Herald* on January 18, 1844, during her trial. Library of Congress, Serial and Government Publications Division.

He was right to be afraid. Lydia Maria Child thought that his reticence to show himself in the courtroom was "perhaps, a prudent measure, for the populace were in that excited state, that it might have been unsafe for him to have been generally recognized." The tumultuous crowd in the courtroom repeatedly stamped, clapped, and shouted its support for Amelia Norman and its disdain for him. Court officers had trouble quelling "the outbreaking of the deep sympathy that was felt for her by the immense and deeply excited multitude in attendance." As he left the courtroom each day, Child reported, the people who crowded around the door called to him: " 'Don't come too near us! It is as much as we can do to keep our canes and umbrellas off your shoulders' "—a frightening reminder to Ballard of his encounter with Norman and her parasol in his store on Cedar Street. Mike Walsh was "astonished" that the "scurvy wretch" could "come out of a courtroom without being tarred and feathered." In an editorial in his *Herald*, Bennett explained the source of the "irrepressible expression of public indignation against Ballard" and the widespread sympathy for Norman, who had so evidently tried to kill him. It was because Ballard represented a "numerous class" of men who, even as they pass for "highly respectable, moral, reputable, worthy men," use their power to "betray and ruin virtuous females of the humbler grades of society," who seek out poor women, among whom "the work of ruin is less expensive and less dangerous." To combat the work of men like Ballard, Bennett supported the criminalization of seduction. But he also suggested that the ruin they spread went beyond women to everyone harmed by a society that was becoming increasingly impersonal, transactional, exploitative, and mystifying. Ballards are everywhere, he warned, "in Wall Street—in the warehouses down town—lounging about the hotels—at the club-rooms—behind the scenes at the theatres—even at the house of God—you find these men."

To evade the danger, Ballard hid himself in the courtroom: behind the stove, on the stairs in back of the bench, in a corner where the jury couldn't see him. Amelia's lawyers took his hiding as an invitation to hound him, to declare him a "coward seducer, who dared not show his face." As the jury was being called on Tuesday morning, David Graham asked Henry Ballard to identify himself. When he did not answer, "all eyes" in the courtroom turned mistakenly toward Francis. Only when Graham called his name a second time did Henry finally rise and identify himself. This was the first of many times that the defense would try to force Henry Ballard out of hiding and into the teeth of the hostile audience.

The jurors were sworn. There were two grocers; a baker; a "marketman," who must have operated a stall at one of the city's food markets; a man who sold "fish tackle"; and a broker and a merchant, who could have been men of means. One juror, James C. Coleman, might have been one of the men of this name listed in the city directories as a sawyer, a cooper, or a foundry worker. No occupations are listed for jurors Joseph H. Horton of East Broadway and Gilbert Hatfield of Elm Street, but both lived at the margins of the Five Points slum. Two more jurors, Russell Dowd and Mark B. Markwald, do not appear in the city directories at all. There were no women on the jury; for almost another century, no woman would serve on a New York jury.

The first speaker was Edward Sandford, the counsel for Ballard and the prosecution. Sandford told the jury that he would have nothing to say about Norman's and Ballard's history but would instead focus only on what happened on the evening of the crime. That evening, he related, Amelia Norman, a prostitute Ballard had met at a brothel, followed Ballard through the streets until they reached the Astor House. There, after "parlying [*sic*] with him for a short time, she caught him by the collar and plunged a dirk knife into his breast." To make the jury understand how narrowly his client had escaped from death, he produced the knife and showed it around the courtroom. At the sight of it "a murmur of applause ran through the Court room."

The crowd's reaction to the display of Norman's knife proved Lydia Maria Child's belief that "two thirds of the community, nurtured and trained as they are in the law of violence, needed to summon all their respect for law and order, to keep from openly expressing sympathy with" Norman's act of violence. In an era when federal legislators caned one another in Congress, when newspaper editors attacked each other in the street, when violence on the frontier was routine, when slavery, which was inherently violent, persisted, and when a still-living former president, Andrew Jackson, was an enthusiastic duelist, the crowd was primed to regard violent behavior as normal, even justified.

Sandford turned next to his three witnesses, the men who had witnessed the crime: Astor House driver William Crummie; Samuel Floyd, the merchant who happened to be near the hotel entrance as the crime occurred; and hotel doctor Alexander T. Watson. Their testimony made it clear that Henry Ballard had been stabbed and Amelia Norman had done the stabbing, even though not one of them had seen everything.

Crummie and Floyd each described how they saw the conversation between Ballard and Norman on the Astor House steps, and had run and grabbed Norman when they heard Ballard cry out. Crummie told how he saw Norman when she "made a plunge into" Ballard, but did not see the knife, even though he saw something glance in the evening light. On cross-examination by John Morrill he admitted that he could not tell if it was a knife or a breast pin. Shown the knife in the courtroom he admitted that Ballard's wound "must have been made with this knife; it couldn't have been made with nothing else." Samuel Floyd was able to identify the knife more confidently, since even though he had not seen Norman "make the plunge," he took the knife from her after he and Crummie restrained her. He described seeing Ballard in the Astor House afterward, standing at the bar in his bloody coat. Crummie told the jury about his conversations with Amelia Norman at the Astor House and then in the cab on the way to the Tombs, and the language—she wished she had killed the "damned yankee"—that contradicted the demure appearance of the veiled defendant in the dock.

Dr. Watson, the third witness of the day, confirmed Floyd's description of a freely flowing wound and described how after examining Ballard in his room at the Astor House he determined that the sharp knife had been blocked by a rib from penetrating Ballard's heart. Watson then added details about the knife, which Samuel Floyd had brought to his office in the Astor House: "There was grease upon the hinge of the knife; it opened with so much facility that I was induced to examine it." The sharpness of the knife, the greased hinge: these factors meant that "a very slight degree of force was sufficient to produce this wound." Watson's implication was that this was a wound that could have been made by a woman.

David Graham took advantage of Watson's assertion to ask Ballard to stand up, this time to demonstrate the contrast in size between him and Norman. Again, Ballard, seated in a spot out of sight of the jury, refused. The prosecution objected to Graham's request, Graham appealed "to the common sense of the court," but he was overruled; Ballard remained in his seat. John Morrill then tried another tactic, asking Watson to describe Ballard's weight and height. "He is a man of middling stature," replied Dr. Watson—a response that the defense may have found frustrating. The prosecution, with no more witnesses to call, rested its case.

The jury heard next from James S. Carpentier, who delivered the opening statement for the defense. The strategy of the defense was just the opposite of that of the prosecution. While the prosecution wanted to focus only on what had undoubtedly happened on the night of November 1,

Norman's lawyers wanted to show that her suffering at Ballard's hands was what drove her to do what they could not deny she had done. They sought to convince the jury that even though Amelia Norman was on trial, it was she, not Henry Ballard, who was the victim.

The result was a series of clashes between the lawyers that created just the kind of drama that people crowded courtrooms to see. Lydia Maria Child, indignant at Sandford's efforts to suppress Ballard's and Norman's history, described the "perpetual fighting with witnesses, to keep the truth out of court." But, Child asserted, even though "Mr. Sandford sprung every way, to stop up any crevice through which the impertinent light might enter, enough did get before the jury, to satisfy them that Amelia Norman had been a virtuous, discreet, amiable, and quiet girl, before her acquaintance with Ballard; and that the history of her wrongs was no fiction of romance."

Carpentier began with a swift sketch of Amelia Norman's early life, eliminating the criminal history of the Normans. He also obfuscated her age, telling the jury that when she met Henry Ballard she was sixteen, although she was actually around twenty-three in the spring of 1841. He claimed that before Norman met Ballard she was virtuous and chaste, her character was "beyond reproach," she had a "kind and mild disposition," and she was "loved by all who knew her." He described how she and Ballard met after Ballard "deliberately formed the purpose of seducing her," and how after he had succeeded in falsely establishing himself as a suitor he took her to the house of assignation on Mott Street and there "finally succeeded in accomplishing her seduction." Carpentier traced their movements from one boardinghouse to another in New York and Brooklyn and to Stewart's Hotel in Newark. He described how Ballard "induced" Norman to go to Madame Restell for first one and then another abortion, and then the birth of her child with the help of "female physician" Margaret Bird. He described how Ballard left for England, leaving Amelia and their child "destitute." He told how after Ballard returned, Amelia went with Sarah Ballard to his store and in her rage broke a parasol over Ballard's head. He told the jury that Sandford "might have told more about it if he chose, for he was present at the time." And finally, just before the night of November 1, when Norman implored Ballard to "make some provision" for her and the child, he told her to "go and get her living as other prostitutes do." According to Carpentier's narrative it was Norman's encounter with Ballard and the resulting loss of her "character and virtue" that had so "phrenzied her mind, that the offence was committed under such circumstances as would justify it."

When Carpentier claimed that Ballard's treatment of Norman had frenzied her mind, he was signaling that he and his colleagues intended to try to use the insanity defense. The insanity defense, as it was understood in common law in the United States in 1844, stated that persons who were deranged to the extent that they could not tell the difference between right and wrong at the time they committed a crime were consequently not culpable. The insanity defense in American law did not hold when the perpetrator had had a chance beforehand to think and plan. In the days to come, the defense would repeatedly ask witnesses to describe Norman's state of mind before and after she met Henry Ballard. Each time Edward Sandford protested, and the judges frequently, but not on every occasion, supported Sandford.

Norman's lawyers also invoked a principle known as the "unwritten law." The "unwritten law," an extralegal courtroom phenomenon, was the idea that a husband had the right to kill a man who had cuckolded him (and the man was conceived of as necessarily the seducer, not an equal partner with the wife in a betrayal) if he caught the couple in the act. The all-male juries of the nineteenth century sympathized with the uncontrollable frenzy a husband would be expected to feel when not only his feelings but also his sexual property rights in his wife were violated. Because of this understanding, men who killed their wives' seducers were usually acquitted.

While it was unusual for women to stand up for themselves and attack their seducers, when they did, they too were usually acquitted. When Carpentier asserted that Norman's "offence was committed under such circumstances as would justify it," as he did in his opening statement, he was taking a chance, counting on the all-male jury's willingness to regard Norman's defense of her honor in the same way that they would understand their own defense of a wife, daughter, or sister.

Lydia Maria Child struggled with the validity of the "unwritten law," which she described as "the universal teaching, which endorses retaliation and violence under the name of the law of honor." She thought that in the case of Amelia Norman, it might be justified: "If revenge is ever to be excused, what circumstances can be imagined so extenuating, as those which exist in the case of a virtuous girl seduced, deserted, and insulted? Man cannot inflict on man any injury, any provocation, to be compared with hers." She assured the readers of her newspaper column that she believed that "all revenge is crime, all violence is of the devil," but, she challenged, "Let them ask themselves what they would have said and done, if they had been situated like her, with all those terrible wrongs eating into her heart and brain, like fire. May this consideration lead no one to excuse or palliate the dreadful crime of murder, but may it teach them, to reflect well on the false structure of society."

Another element in the strategy of the defense was to create precisely the "fiction of romance" that the romantic tale-spinner Lydia Maria Child paradoxically argued Norman's case was not. Norman's lawyers understood that the audience in the courtroom expected to be entertained in the same way that they were in the theater. During Amelia Norman's trial, as in other trials in New York in this period, the audience acted in the courtroom as they did in the theater, applauding, stamping their feet, cheering their heroes, taunting villains. The careers of politicians, preachers, actors, and lawyers all rose or fell based on their ability to interest, even thrill, an audience with speech. A. Oakey Hall, the New York mayor and playwright who knew David Graham and his family, observed that "the fame of a great lawyer is as evanescent as that of an actor" and believed that the ability to magnetize an audience was as important in the courtroom as it was on the stage. A lawyer's oratorical abilities, he wrote, "fairly compelled verdicts."

Carpentier closed his opening statement with an invitation to the jury to regard Ballard as a coward and a villain: "The counsel for the prosecution will pretend that, unless she is sent to the State Prison, Mr. Ballard cannot live in this city. What, Henry S. Ballard cannot live in this city on account of this girl! Then, in God's name, let him leave it—we have plenty of such villains in the city now." He brought the case home to the men of the jury by reminding them of their own wives and daughters, exhorting them "to guard them against the approaches of such a villain."

When Carpentier sat down, members of the courtroom audience applauded and stamped their feet in approval of his performance. Court officers worked to quiet them down, and one arrested a "poor man" for stamping. When the man was charged with contempt of court he apologized, saying that he did not know he was doing anything wrong, since he had never been in a court before. The judges discharged him with a warning, and the court adjourned for the day.

By Wednesday morning, news of the court's performance of the day before had spread, so that long before the business of the day began, the "halls, vestibules, passages and steps of the Tombs, swarmed with an anxious and excited multitude." As soon as the doors opened the crowd packed in, leaving many disappointed would-be spectators behind to mill among the Egyptian columns. Inside the courtroom a "busy hum of voices discussing the character of the offence" created an excitement "so great that it was difficult to preserve order."

The defense had arranged to bring in a crowd of witnesses to testify on behalf of Norman. "There stand *our* thirty witnesses," said David Graham, "ready to prove every word we have stated, and a good deal more, if the court will only allow them to be heard." But of the thirty they found, the court allowed them only thirteen: Norman's employers Eliza Meriam, William Callender, and Joel Behrend; friends Mary Moore and Isabella Hurley; landladies Ann Pierson and Mrs. Gray (who did not appear); the Tombs' doctor, Benjamin McCready; Sarah Ballard, Henry Ballard's previous mistress; Edward Stewart of Stewart's Hotel in Newark; the abortionist Madame Restell; and John Liston, the lawyer who happened to be leaving the Astor House just in time to see William Crummie restraining Amelia Norman in his arms. The thirteenth witness, William Knight or Knapp, is a mystery. His name is never mentioned anywhere else, and he did not appear at the trial.

On Wednesday two of these witnesses were scheduled to appear: William Callender and Madame Restell. It may have been Restell's name on the court calendar in the lobby outside the courtroom that listed what jailbird-journalist George Wilkes called the "most amusing daily performance" that helped draw the crowds. If so, they were disappointed, since she failed to appear that day. Callender was there, but almost as soon as he began to speak, the prosecution, wishing to exclude the history of Norman and Ballard prior to her attack on him, cut his testimony short after one of Norman's lawyers asked him "What was the conduct of Amelia Norman while she resided in your family?" Then, with no witness testimony to hear, the jury instead spent the day listening to wrangling between the defense and the prosecution over whether or not testimony describing Norman and Ballard's relationship before the evening of November 1 could be admitted. Sandford spoke for more than two and a half hours, arguing that no grievance Norman might have against Ballard excused her from her responsibility for attacking him. Only proof of her "delusion and lunacy" could do that, and he did not believe there was any evidence of insanity at the time of the crime.

John Morrill countered, arguing that Norman had been "seduced, blasted, and ruined, by Ballard"; he had "destroyed her body, her character, and her mind." He contended that the defense "had a right to introduce every particle of testimony showing the intercourse and acquaintance between Ballard and the accused," and that only this evidence could demonstrate to the jury what Norman's state of mind was at the time she attacked Ballard. And, Morrill proposed, Sandford himself had opened the door to a discussion of the couple's past when he asserted that Norman had been a prostitute at the time she met Ballard. Ballard, furthermore, "had been ashamed to publicly show himself in this court, but had skulked behind the stove pipe, where he now stood." This dig was rewarded with "great applause" by the audience, which had to be quelled by "the instant calling to order of all the officers and criers of the Court."

The press enjoyed the spirited back-and-forth, and remarked on the skill of the lawyers. They noted that Sandford spoke with "great force and ability" (the reporter for the *New York Evening Post*, always in a rush to make the evening deadline, admitted that he left the court before Sandford finished speaking). Lydia Maria Child was also impressed, but with qualifications. "It was an adroit game," she told her readers, "as exciting to watch, as a skillful game of chess. I never before felt so much intellectual respect, and so much moral aversion, for the legal profession."

In the debate over whether Norman and Ballard's past relationship could be admitted as evidence, both sides cited for comparison a case that had been tried in New Jersey the previous spring. This was the trial of Singleton Mercer, a twenty-one-year-old Philadelphian who in February 1843 had shot and killed another young man, Mahlon Hutchinson Heberton, for the abduction and rape of Sarah Mercer, Singleton's sixteen-year-old sister.

The judge at Mercer's trial had admitted testimony about the actions of Heberton and both Mercers, including Singleton Mercer's madness, prior to the murder. Norman's defense had signaled that a comparison with the Singleton Mercer case would be part of their strategy when on Tuesday, the first full day of the trial, they brought copies of *Herald* extras with

Figure 6.4. Singleton Mercer as he was portrayed in the *New York Herald* on April 1, 1843. Library of Congress, Serial and Government Publications Division.

reports of the case into the courtroom, brandishing them so the reporters could see; and they brought them again on Wednesday. The press, taking their cue from Norman's defense, noted the similarities between these two much-publicized cases, occurring within the space of less than a year.

The experiences of Amelia Norman and Sarah Mercer were alike in some details; more often, Sarah Mercer's experience really was what Amelia Norman's lawyers inaccurately represented their client's to have been. The teen-aged Sarah, who was living at home with her comfortable family, was led by Heberton, without her family's knowledge, on what turned out to be a false courtship. When he had her trust, he forced the young girl, who several witnesses at her brother's trial testified was intellectually limited, into a brothel and raped her at gunpoint. Amelia Norman was more like Sarah Mercer's brother than like Sarah herself: like him, her lawyers asserted, she had committed a justifiable act of violence in a moment of madness.

Like Ballard, Heberton was presented by Mercer's lawyers as a heartless rake who preyed on women whom he regarded as socially beneath him. Although the Mercers and the Hebertons were both wealthy, Singleton Mercer, the son of an Irish immigrant who had earned his wealth running a grocery and tavern, worked as the principal clerk in a Philadelphia importing house. Mahlon Heberton, in contrast, was a rich, idle man-about-town. His deceased father had been a wealthy and well-connected doctor, and his widowed mother was "highly respectable." Mercer's lawyer painted Heberton as "an abandoned libertine by profession and practice. He was not only a practised, but an accomplished one, too. He followed no business or occupation for a livelihood; his counting house was a brothel—his companions libertines and harlots—his merchandize, lust—the only commerce he followed was seduction." Heberton felt superior to Singleton Mercer and his family and let Mercer know it. When Mercer challenged him to a duel, Heberton haughtily declined, claiming, the press reported, "social inequality."

Singleton Mercer's insanity began to manifest itself after Sarah Mercer returned home and told her family what had happened. Eliza Mercer, their mother, summed up for her son the disaster that had crushed their family: "My dear son, Heberton has ruined your sister." Singleton, one of his lawyers asserted, "became bewildered—reason tottered, and fell from its throne—and Singleton was an insane man—totally unconscious of right or wrong." He "raved about the room," he threatened to kill his sister, he heard voices telling him to " 'kill him! kill him! kill him!' "

Two days later, as Heberton tried to leave town, Mercer shot and killed him on the Trenton ferry. As with Amelia Norman, witnesses saw the crime committed, so there was no doubt about his guilt. He immediately turned himself in and was taken to jail in New Jersey, where he was tried. But even though Mercer purposefully pursued Heberton across the Delaware River two days after learning of his sister's rape, his lawyers were able to persuade a jury to acquit him on the grounds that his insanity at the time of the crime so clouded his mind that he could not tell the difference between right and wrong.

In raising the example of the Mercer case, Norman's lawyers hoped to persuade the court to follow the example of the judge in that trial and allow the jury to consider that Norman, like Mercer, had been driven mad by loss of sexual honor—in her case, her own—and to hear about the events that brought her to that state. Recorder Tallmadge admitted that the question of admission of evidence was of "considerable importance" and agreed to think about it and give his opinion the next day.

The newspapers also offered their opinions. A small notice in Horace Greeley's *Tribune* titled "A Hard Case" protested: "A woman, who in a fit of phrenzy stabs the man who has ruined her by the basest treachery, must answer for it to the law, though hers is only an attempt; but for the *man*, whose long career of perfidy and brutal lust has *effected her* ruin, and whose cowardly selfishness has several times placed her life in extreme jeopardy, the Law has no penalty! Such is now the law of New-York! Such is Human Justice!" Bennett's *Herald* made a more self-interested observation: "If the testimony for defence is admitted, the details will be of the most peculiar and racy character ever presented in a court of justice."

7

VERDICT

Women to cards may be compar'd: we play
A round or two; when us'd we throw away;
Take a fresh pack: nor is it worth our grieving
Who cuts or shuffles with our dirty leaving.

George Granville, Lord Lansdowne, "Women"

Thursday began with the opinion that Recorder Tallmadge had promised
the day before. It was his view, he told the courtroom, that evidence about
Henry Ballard's behavior toward Amelia Norman during the two years of
their acquaintance could not be admitted as evidence. According to the
law, he said, all that mattered was whether or not Norman was in "that
deluded state of mind that deprived her of the power of distinguishing
right from wrong" at the moment she stabbed Ballard. How she came to
be in that state ought to be of no concern to the jury. The law had to make
a distinction between assailants who were deprived of their reason at the
time of an attack and those who "had brooded until sorrow and despondency had ripened into revenge." Society, this son of a Revolutionary War
officer continued, could not "allow an injured party to seek revenge upon
his oppressor, at his discretion, for real or supposed wrongs, instead of
appealing to the laws of his country for redress." To do so "would break
the ligaments that bind society together, would destroy the ability of our

institutions formed for the preservation of peace and order, and justify popular violence and anarchy."

Tallmadge, however, was willing to leave the door open, just slightly. When David Graham quickly countered, arguing for the right to admit evidence about the state of Norman's sanity at the time she stabbed Ballard, Tallmadge agreed that that was proper. And, he added, "if the fact of the insanity were established, they might *then* proceed to show by testimony the *causes* that led to that state of imbecility or insanity of mind of the prisoner" that led her to attack Ballard.

On Thursday the jury heard all the remaining witnesses for the defense, including Eliza Meriam, William Callender, Mary Moore, and Isabella Hurley, each of whom could speak about Norman's behavior before and after she met Henry Ballard. Repeatedly testing the boundaries that Tallmadge had defined, Norman's defense worked to prove that Norman's encounter with Ballard had changed her from a virtuous, happy young woman to one who was in desperate trouble, miserable, and out of her mind. Each time the defense entered into the territory of Norman and Ballard's history together, the prosecution objected; most of the time the prosecution's objections were supported by the court. Several times there were eruptions of showy anger between the two sides that the audience noisily appreciated and the court struggled to calm.

The first defense witness of the day was John K. Liston. He described how after Norman stabbed Ballard, she "appeared very pale and languid, and prostrate from some cause." "What did you see in her conduct that induced you to draw a conclusion as to the state of her mind?" asked one of the defense lawyers. Liston answered: "She appeared prostrate from past excitement."

The next witness was Madame Restell, the trial's celebrity witness, who, after refusing to show the previous day, finally came to testify. Appearing in the witness stand "most elegantly attired" and causing "great excitement" in the courtroom, Restell answered the question put to all the witnesses about their identity and occupation and described, with great circumspection, what she did: "I am a midwife and female physician," she told the room. She received pregnant women at her house on Greenwich Street, but only "in cases of malformation," the term she used to describe birth defects. When asked if it was her "practice to take females to board with you to be delivered of children?" she answered, "It is in cases where I receive a certificate from [her] physician that they cannot bear children." This seemingly contradictory reply only makes sense when "delivered of children" is read not to mean that Restell was delivering live babies, or not only, but was providing abortions. If the question seems as circumspect as the answer, it may be because of her relationship with John Morrill. Maybe he and his colleagues agreed to deal with her gently in exchange for her presence at this trial of his other client, Amelia Norman. In any case, he did not challenge her obfuscating answers.

When asked how many women she had at any one time, she replied, "I decline answering." When asked if "persons sometimes have assumed names," she answered, "I do not know—my object is to cure." When the defense asked her if she sold pills, she opened up a bit, perhaps proudly. "Yes I do," she replied. "We sell them from ten to fifteen boxes per day sometimes." She expanded: "These pills are for irregularity." When the defense asked if she had ever seen Amelia Norman or Henry Ballard before, she claimed never to have seen either of them, even though Carpentier had earlier told the jury that Ballard had compelled Amelia Norman to go to her for an abortion. Of Amelia she said, "I think I can say positively I never saw her before; I know she never boarded with me." Of Henry: "I don't think I ever saw that gentleman before; don't think he ever called at my house, am quite sure he never did." The excitement Restell's appearance caused in the courtroom was the result of the notoriety she was starting to acquire as a target for opponents of abortion. In 1841 the anonymous author of a pamphlet publication of the Mary Ann Purdy trial, the trial at which Restell was represented by John Morrill, described her as "a monster in human shape." Also in 1841, her name was raised, with not much evidence, in connection with the case of Mary Rogers, a young cigar store clerk who had been murdered, possibly after an abortion, and whose body was found floating in the Hudson River. In 1847 the *National Police Gazette* published an image of a scowling Restell hovering, as if by black magic, over a winged demon devouring a baby.

Without attention from the law, American midwives had long provided abortions or abortifacients to women who had not yet "quickened," or felt the first fetal movement. Recognizing "quickening" as the start of

THE FEMALE ABORTIONIST.

Figure 7.1. Madame Restell (1812–1878), whose real name was Ann Trow Lohman, as depicted in the *National Police Gazette*, March 13, 1847. NewsBank Inc. and the American Antiquarian Society.

pregnancy, they understood, or claimed to understand, the dilemma of the women they served as no more than a "blockage," "interruption," or "irregularity" of menstruation that could be relieved. The first statutory abortion laws, passed by states between 1821 and 1841, were directed not at pregnant women but at suppliers of potentially poisonous abortifacients and were essentially poison control laws. By the 1850s, however, an anti-abortion movement in the United States had taken on significant force, signaling a shift in attitude.

Several factors contributed to this shift. These included the emergence of abortion from a quiet, private practice among women to one that, as it became increasingly commercial, was made visible in advertisements placed in the newspapers by such prominent "female physicians" as Madame Restell and Margaret Bird, both of whose names came up at Amelia Norman's trial. That an increasing number of married, middle-class women used these services heightened alarm, particularly among the traditionally trained doctors who increasingly found themselves in competition with "irregulars," or "quack doctors," the wild assortment of untrained medical practitioners—sellers of pills and potions, practitioners of "cures"—that flourished in the antiauthoritarian atmosphere of the antebellum United States. Madame Restell's 1841 arrest was her first, even though she had been practicing in New York since the 1830s. Her advertisements, her success, and the wealth she flamboyantly displayed all contributed toward making her one of the earliest and most vilified symbols of the anti-abortion movement in the United States.

To follow the scandalous Restell, the defense called Isabella Hurley, the neighborhood friend Amelia had made while living with the Meriams. Hurley told the jury that during those years Norman often visited her and her husband Peter at their home on Allen Street. "What was the conduct of the accused before her acquaintance with Mr. Ballard, as to virtue and amiability?" asked David Graham. Sandford objected, the court overruled the question, and Graham continued. "Have you had any reason to note any particular disposition of mind of the accused, and when was it?" Hurley described how in August of 1841 she found Amelia crying on her back stoop. "I formed an opinion that she was in trouble," Hurley said, but "I did not form any opinion at that time that her mind was shattered; nor any opinion as to the state of her mind." When cross-examined by the prosecution, Hurley explained, "I consider every person who is troubled in mind or spirits, as partially deranged."

William Callender, whose testimony was cut short the previous day, came next. Defiantly, David Graham asked him the question he had tried to ask the day before: "What was the conduct of Amelia Norman while she resided in your family?" The result was the same: Sandford protested, and the court overruled the question. Graham continued, this time asking

Callender to describe Norman's fits. Callender did so, but he insisted with what sounds like emotion that "I never saw any thing out of the way as to her temper in my life."

After the court refused to allow Graham permission to ask Callender if Norman had received letters from Ballard while she was in his house, Graham continued: "Was the accused not a woman of more than ordinary self possession of mind and evenness of temper?" Callender, who described Norman as "a member of my family," stated firmly, "While she was with me she was of a very even state of mind." Now, however, she was changed: "I have not seen her while she was in prison; her appearance at the present time is not the same as when she was with me; she is more emaciated and broken down; I never saw any thing out of the way with her in my life; she was as still, modest, retired, quiet female, as I ever knew."

Like William Callender, Benjamin McCready, the doctor at the Tombs, whose testimony came next, had also witnessed Norman's fits. When the defense asked him to describe "the nature of her illness," Sandford once again objected, and an argument broke out between the prosecution and the defense. Graham asserted that the defense would fight to have the testimony of their witnesses heard and was applauded by the audience. McCready sat down, the audience was quieted, the court took a short break to cool down, and court officers were stationed around the room.

When the proceedings began again, McCready remained seated, and Sarah Ballard, Ballard's prior mistress, was called. According to the *Herald*, Sarah looked to be about twenty-five years old, had "dark brown hair and dark blue eyes, ruddy complexion. She was neatly dressed in a black cloth cloak, black velvet hat and feather, with lace veil. She appeared much composed, and responded with great readiness." Her composure made a contrast with Amelia Norman's stricken appearance. Norman's eyes, the *Sun* told its readers, beamed "with silent tears, exhibiting evidence of the desolation of feeling that reigned within her breast." James Gordon Bennett noticed a "crowd of painted harlots" that appeared in the courtroom that day. Who were they? There is no other mention of them. Possibly these women visibly identifiable as prostitutes came to hear the testimony of one of their own.

Introducing herself, Sarah told the jury that she met Ballard in 1832. "Did you live with him?" asked Graham. Sandford objected to the question, and Tallmadge upheld his objection. But Graham, arguing "in a most powerful burst of Eloquence" for his witness's right to speak, told her story himself, thus ensuring that the jury heard it, regardless of Tallmadge's prohibition. Thus the jury learned from Graham that Henry Ballard had lived with Sarah Ballard from 1832, passing her off as his wife, until the spring of 1841, when he abandoned her for Amelia Norman, "leaving her penniless and wholly destitute."

Turning again to his witness, Graham asked, "Did you go to the store of Ballard with the accused?" "Yes," Sarah replied, "I went in August; she told me that he had agreed to do for her; I told her how he had treated me." "That is all," said Graham, "unless the prosecution wish to hear the rest." Sandford replied: "No, we do not wish any more." As she left the witness stand, Sarah responded cheekily to Sandford, "No, I do not think you wish to hear any more, sir." The audience was delighted with this bold response and laughed and applauded.

Mary Moore, whom Norman boarded with after she met Henry Ballard and left William Callender's, came next. She described Norman's transformation from a "very free, light-hearted woman" to one who was "very uneasy and low of spirits," sometimes sitting alone in her room half a day without speaking. "From these particulars did you form any opinion as to the state of her mind?" asked the defense. Moore, who had seen Norman go out to meet Ballard, thought that she had been promised something "that had not been performed," possibly marriage. The defense did not make anything of Moore's suggestion that Ballard had offered to marry Norman, potentially exposing himself to a breach of promise suit, probably because they knew that he had not.

Moore told the jury how when Norman boarded with her she had "very often" had "fits and spasms." She told of how Norman had complained of being "unwell," and about the boxes of pills she took. Moore, perhaps out of delicacy, did not ask Norman what the pills were for, but she did ask what was troubling her, to which Amelia replied that Moore " 'would know some day.' " This reference to a possible pregnancy prompted a juror, who may have remembered the boxes of pills Madame Restell sold and was less constrained by delicacy, to ask, "Was the box labelled or not?" Moore replied, "I cannot tell." When Moore was finished, a young man was charged with contempt of court for encouraging the crowd in the lobby to break down the door of the courtroom—a clue to the pandemonium that was the backdrop to the proceedings.

Even though the room was no calmer than when he first tried to speak, McCready was brought back to finish his testimony. As a doctor, McCready was able to bring his medical training and experience to the question of Norman's madness. Asked by the defense what her condition was while in jail, he described how he often found her ill, suffering violent headaches, despondent, and in tears. He feared she might commit suicide and told the keeper so. He described Norman's fits: "She has several times had hysterical paroxism. I have found her lying on the floor of her cell, crying as if her heart would break, in a manner so violent as to lead me to believe that the attack was hysterical." Her paroxysms and headaches, he observed, were accompanied by a "peculiar troubled expression about the eye, characteristic of such attacks." Her physical illnesses, he felt, were due to "the state of her mind or mental condition" and also, he felt, owed something to her gender: "Like every feeble female, she appeared to be particularly excitable," he said.

What looked to Norman's friends simply like "fits" was to McCready's sharper medical eye a recognized if poorly understood disease: hysteria. Over the centuries hysteria had been associated with a wandering uterus, supernatural forces, emotional upset, unidentified internal lesions, and especially with the sexual and reproductive problems of women. In Benjamin McCready's time, as in Sigmund Freud's later on, hysteria manifested itself in many ways, often mimicking other diseases. Hysterical patients had fits and tics, bouts of laughter and crying, outbursts of odd language, depression, hallucinations, unexplained pains, blindness, paralysis, and many other physical and mental symptoms. Freud's experiments with hysterical patients at the end of the nineteenth century led him to believe that its many baffling physical manifestations were psychological in origin, but in the 1840s doctors were unsure whether its cause was physical, emotional, or both. Sellers of patent medicines included hysteria in the long lists of afflictions they claimed they could cure. It was not until the end of the nineteenth century, and especially by the twentieth, that doctors, by this time armed with expanded medical knowledge, were better able to sort these grab bags of symptoms, including most of the ones attributed to hysteria, into identifiable diseases.

On cross-examination Dr. McCready described another symptom: constipation. When Norman first arrived at the Tombs, he related, "I understood that constipation of the bowels had existed for three weeks; it was twenty-four hours before she was relieved by medicine." Dr. McCready did not explain, perhaps because he may not have felt the need to, that there was an association between madness and constipation. Singleton Mercer, whose story everyone at Amelia Norman's trial knew, was also constipated. As a child, Mercer's lawyers claimed, he was "of a fragile frame—of bilious temperament—highly nervous—much afflicted with constipation—which leads directly to insanity."

McCready's testimony was followed by further scuffling between the lawyers, leading one of the judges to implore them to "temper their remarks and not indulge in personalities. . . . Come, come, gentlemen—these personalities will not answer." By then it was five o'clock, and the judges, presumably exhausted by the excitement, decided to take a break. When the court reassembled at seven that evening, the defense called two witnesses who did not appear, Mrs. Gray, the boardinghouse keeper on Canal Street where Norman stayed in the fall of 1842 around the time her child was born, and William H. Knight or Knapp. Then they heard from Eliza Meriam.

Of all the witnesses who testified at Norman's trial, Eliza Meriam was the one who had known her the longest and was best able to describe her character and state of mind in the years before she met Henry Ballard. She told how she had brought Norman with her from New Jersey to New York in 1834 when she was fifteen or sixteen years old, thus matter-of-factly destroying Carpentier's assertion that she was sixteen when she met Ballard in 1841. She could have said something about the behavior of some members of the Norman family, whom she knew. She might, for example, have said that Sering Wade, who was robbed of his poultry by Oliver Norman the previous fall, was her own brother-in-law, but she did not, nor did she mention Charles and Oliver Norman's other exploits, which she surely knew about. Instead she said only that Amelia had a stepmother but no mother and that her father was a "respectable farmer in New Jersey," "in comfortable circumstances," and about sixty years old. During the four years Norman lived with her, Meriam said, her conduct was "very good" and she had "no male visitors." After Amelia left to work first for Mr. Ealer and then for Mr. Callender, Meriam kept in touch, remaining "intimate with her all this time." Asked by both the defense and prosecution to describe Norman's fits, she described how Norman was "perfectly helpless" when she had them and they left her "weak and feeble."

Following Eliza Meriam's testimony on Thursday evening were three more witnesses. Ann Pierson, the Thompson Street boardinghouse keeper with whom Amelia stayed in the fall of 1841, and Edward Stewart, the proprietor of Stewart's Hotel in Newark, New Jersey, had little to say. The third witness was Joel Behrend, Norman's last employer. His testimony was perhaps the most important of the day, since he and his wife were the last to see Norman before she left their house to follow Henry Ballard to the Astor House.

Behrend described how Norman's behavior deteriorated over the fall of 1843 from pleasant and "ladylike" to distracted and crazy. He told of how on the afternoon of November 1 he saw Norman eating cakes in the street while pacing back and forth. On cross-examination Behrend gave his definition of insanity: "A crazy person is one not in her right mind," he explained. Unlike Dr. McCready, Behrend did not believe that Norman was hysterical. "I have seen persons in hysterical fits; her laughing was more like mad laughing; it was not hysterical, as I think that arises more from a contraction of the nerves." Behrend had observed Norman's symptoms closely: "She appeared to laugh involuntarily, not knowing it; she appeared to know when she cried, as she was then conscious." Whether Norman was hysterical or not, Behrend was in no doubt that she was insane on the evening of November 1.

At nine o'clock on Thursday both sides rested their cases. Norman's defense had struggled to show that their client was insane, taking advantage of Frederick Tallmadge's permission that morning to try. But none of the descriptions their witnesses gave of hysteria, despondency, "mad-laughter," constipation, or "fits" added up to a definition of insanity that might have excused her action. On the subject of her own state of mind, however, Amelia Norman privately had something to say. She told Lydia Maria Child: "'God alone can judge me, for he alone knows to what a dreadful state of agony and desperation I was driven.'" Like all of the very few statements of Norman's that survive, this one is filtered through somebody else's telling. What she really knew, what she really felt, has vanished.

When the court reassembled on Friday morning, all that was left was for each side to present its closing statement and for the jury to deliver its verdict. The courtroom again was "crowded to its utmost capacity by anxious and attentive auditors," while "a thousand or more were literally packed together in the vestibule, awaiting an opportunity to enter." Recorder Tallmadge, hoping to prevent the outbursts of the previous days, warned the audience to preserve order or risk arrest. After the unruly room settled down, John Morrill rose to give his closing statement for the defense.

Morrill's statement alternated between legal arguments, emotional declarations, Shakespeare, and poetry in a performance that drew tears and applause, and that must have reminded the audience of the variety programs they knew from the theater. At the heart was his effort to convince the jury that Norman was insane on the evening she stabbed Henry Ballard, that Ballard's villainy was the cause of her insanity, and that Norman's trial, as a means of flushing out a rake such as Ballard, was more cause than case.

To prove Norman's insanity, Morrill invoked medical authorities, the testimony of Dr. McCready, and that of the other witnesses. He took advantage of the *frisson* provided by the appearance of his other client, Madame Restell, to link Amelia's insanity to her first abortion, induced by what he asserted—regardless of Restell's denial—were pills bought for her by Henry Ballard from Restell. Using the same phrase used by Singleton Mercer's lawyer, he said: "It was at this period that her mind began to be affected. Reason at that time had abdicated its throne, and it did not reassume its sceptre except at the visits of this Ballard—this insect who polluted the community with his presence, and poisoned whatever he touched."

He acknowledged that feelings for the "poor unfortunate woman" had operated on his own heart. "I entered upon this cause with feelings of virtuous indignation," he told the jury. "I made up my mind to leave family, office, professional duties, and neither to sleep nor to eat until I had given her deliverance to the people, who are looking now anxiously for the result. I have looked at the circumstances of this case, from the time I started with it to the present moment, I repeat, with feelings of virtuous indignation at the being who has laid this indictment against her."

About Ballard, Morrill asked: Who was this "being"? "What was he? One of your vapid fashionable merchants, who enter into the lower classes of society, thinking that because they are merchants there will not be much noise made if they seduce a poor unfortunate girl." He was an "abandoned profligate, who, after having destroyed the virtue of an unhappy woman, left her; threw her off, a prey to want, in poverty and in distress." He asked the jury to imagine Ballard on the Astor House steps, speaking to his acquaintances after he rebuffed Amelia at the door. At that moment he must have "felt as the poet says":

> "Woman to cards may be compared; we play
> A round or two—when used, we throw away—
> Take a fresh pack; nor is it worth our grieving,
> Who cuts or shuffles with our dirty leaving"

Norman, Morrill told his audience, had been "plucked" by Ballard "like a flower in the bud; and she now stood before the Court the weed that he had made her!"

When Edward Sandford objected to Morrill's characterization of his client, Morrill jeered: "'Let the galled jade wince: our withers are unwrung!' We care nothing for the interruptions of this paid counsel! We care nothing I say for his interruption; we shall place our cause before this jury; and if he is fearful of the name and conduct of Mr. Henry S. Ballard being commented upon, why, according to the language of my associate, 'let us have an acquittal of the prisoner, if you are fearful of comment!'" This New York audience, which never had to wait long to see a Shakespeare performance, applauded Morrill's attack on Sandford and his client with its line from the scene where Hamlet subjects his mother and the king to a play in which the murder of his father is reenacted. They understood his reference to the usurping king wincing like a spurred horse, and with their "great applause" they signaled that they agreed with Morrill that Henry Ballard, like King Claudius, was guilty.

Morrill also made one of the very few mentions at the trial of Henry and Amelia's child, and the only substantial one: "For a moment let the jury look at her as a woman, the mother of children, with a little child yet alive, thirteen months old, the offspring, the illegitimate offspring of her coward seducer, who dared not show his face! Let them remember her child—her child now, waiting to be returned to the arms of its poor mother, and she broken down in her heart, destroyed in her peace, but not yet thank God, utterly blasted in her hopes!" This child who is never named, whose sex is never identified, whose age is important only because it establishes a fact in the relationship of its parents, was very much a minor player at the trial where most people, in keeping with the apathy typical of the time about the welfare of the young children of the poor, believed that larger matters were at stake. Morrill did not say where the child was during Norman's period in jail and during her trial, nor did anyone else.

Reminding the jury that "virtue was upon its trial now" and they were the judges, he closed with another poem, "two couplets from a work which everybody knew," Oliver Goldsmith's "Song," on the fate of the fallen woman:

> "When lovely woman stoops to folly
> And finds too late that men betray,
> What charm can sooth her melancholy?
> What art can wash her guilt away?

> "The only art her guilt to cover,
> To hide her shame from every eye,
> To give repentance to her lover,
> And wring his bosom—is to die!"

Morrill sat down "amidst considerable applause from all parts of the court."

Acting district attorney Jonas Phillips was next, but the restrained performance of this former playwright could not compete with Morrill's. According to the *Tribune*, Phillips spoke for more than an hour with "calmness and argumentative ability," but his cool recounting of the evidence and his assertion that he would not "wander in the regions of romance to influence the minds of the community or jury" meant that his argument attracted little space from any of the newspapers. He meant, he said, just to "contend for the punishment for a crime that had been committed," and he urged the jury to find Amelia Norman guilty.

Phillips was followed by David Graham. Reiterating the defense argument introduced by John Morrill, Graham dwelled on Amelia Norman's derangement at the hands of Henry Ballard. He told the jury that Ballard had found Norman, Ophelia-like, "in the bud and beauty of innocent and engaging womanhood. He found her lovely in body and easy and cheerful in mind. He left her body a wreck and her mind a ruin—a mind laughing, while playing in its madness with its own broken fragments." ("On this part of the summing up," the *Tribune*'s reporter commented admiringly, "the counsel was magnificently eloquent.")

He also worked, as Morrill had, to impress the jury with the baseness of Ballard's character. Ballard, Graham said, "was marked in his character by a brand more deep and damning than that of Cain." He was a coward, "skulking" in the corners, afraid to testify since there were "witnesses in abundance in the Court to contradict and stamp with falsehood and infamy his accusations." Graham declared that he would defend his "riven and broken-hearted client" from the slanders of Ballard's counsel, and he appealed to the "honest and enlightened jury" to join with him and save Norman from the "final ruin and destruction prepared to overwhelm her."

Graham linked Norman's case to a larger cause, specifically the campaign then actively in progress around the state to criminalize seduction, a campaign led by the American Female Moral Reform Society whose representatives were in the room. There was, he said, "a lamentable want of law to protect female virtue, and the absence of all criminal enactments to punish the base and villainous seducer—while property and every other thing of value, were protected by laws." He did not condone violence, he assured the courtroom, but Amelia Norman had attacked Henry Ballard because of "the absence of any guard whatever thrown by the law around female virtue, and the want of any punishment whatever for the ruthless destruction of that virtue and its concomitant peace, other than in an action for damages," by which he meant the seduction tort.

In this statement, as throughout the trial, Graham used every bit of his charm and power to dazzle. The *Tribune* was awed by his "great ability and power" and "unsurpassed eloquence." Lydia Maria Child, in her "Letter from New-York" on Norman exclaimed, "The blessing of God be with him! During four weary days, he exerted himself with watchful vigilance and untiring zeal. His appeal on behalf of outraged womanhood, was a noble burst of heartfelt eloquence, which I shall forever remember with gratitude and admiration."

Graham's statement took almost two hours; when he finished it was four o'clock. The court took a break, and when it began again at 5:30,

Edward Sandford stood up to speak. Lydia Maria Child felt sorry for him. He was up against the "almost total want of sympathy to sustain him in his trying position," and even though it was David Graham who had the claim on a seductive frailty, she thought Sandford looked ill.

Sandford began by batting helplessly against Graham and Morrill's persuasive power with the crowd. He promised he would not do what they had done and "excite the sympathies and mislead the judgement of the jury." Instead he would address himself to the jury's "sound reason and sober judgement." As he had done throughout the trial, he protested the "vituperation and abuse" the defense had visited on his client, and he denied their representation of Ballard as a seducer. He argued that Amelia had not been insane at the time she stabbed Ballard. If she had not rationally planned to meet and attack Ballard, how did she come to have a knife, "so unusual for a female to have?" Once again, as he had done on the first day of the trial, he displayed the knife. If she was really out of her mind, why didn't she stab "the first man she met in the street"? Why didn't she attack the cabman? Why did she follow Ballard to the Astor House rather than strike him impulsively "on their first meeting"? He rummaged through the witnesses' testimony and found that Behrend had observed that while Norman appeared to be unconscious during her periods of "mad-laughter," she was conscious when she cried. Sandford reminded the jury that Behrend had said that on the evening of November 1 Norman had been crying.

At the center of Sandford's closing statement was an angry, disorganized outburst rather than the cool argument he had promised. Beginning with Eve, he asserted, it was women, not men, who were responsible for seduction: "The first seduction was in Paradise, where Adam was persuaded by the Woman to eat; that the Woman excused herself by saying the Serpent beguiled her, and she did eat; and that the woman had beguiled the man from that day to this." In the present day, he continued, "we have been recently told that there were 350 houses of ill fame in one ward of this city," citing statistics produced by the American Female Moral Reform Society, and "12,000 public women who lived by prostitution." If Amelia Norman was acquitted, he argued, those prostitutes would be empowered to "go out into the public streets and kill their seducers." He asked the jury: "I would ask you if you have not sons as well as daughters, and will you not protect them against the dirk of the assassin. Who among you would not rather that your daughter should loose [*sic*] her virtue than that your son should be stabbed in the streets by a prostitute."

Child responded to Sandford's argument in "Letter from New-York No. V." The city's prostitutes were "deeply injured women," she argued, whose destruction came when their warm hearts yielded their bodies to the "merely animal" impulses of men. The unnamed author of the piece on Norman's trial in the *Advocate of Moral Reform* agreed, pointing out that "thousands in our midst, vile as they are, have been once as deeply wronged as Amelia Norman."

With a degree of violence that must have surprised the readers of *The American Frugal Housewife* or *Flowers for Children*, Child suggested that if these women were to take their revenge "there would be a huge pile of dead citizens," and she didn't think they would spare the gentlemen of the courtroom: "I even thought it not impossible that some of the honorable court themselves might be among the missing."

She went further, proposing that Sandford's twelve thousand prostitutes were not less dangerous than the wives and daughters of respectable men:

> I protest against considering woman a chattel, or a plaything; and I ask men to consider well how fearfully this assumption is avenged in their own domestic life, by having mothers, wives, and daughters who *are* chattels and playthings. Here, and not elsewhere, lies the secret of Mr. Sandford's twelve thousand dangers. He asks "What if they were all armed, and abroad to redress their wrongs?" Alas they *are* armed; and the terrible wreck they make among human souls is more painful to the reflecting mind, than piles of dead bodies. Verily, they *have* their revenge, though "law and order" take no cognizance of the fact.

When "Letter from New-York No. V," which first appeared in the *Boston Courier*, was reprinted in the *National Anti-Slavery Standard* two weeks later, this inflammatory paragraph had been removed.

The two sides were finished. Tallmadge, from his high perch in the Court of Sessions, delivered his charge to the jury. Carefully, he went over the law the jurors were to apply to the arguments they had heard over the four days of the trial. The job of the jury, he reminded them, was to determine if Norman had attacked Ballard and if she had done so with intent. "Much had been said of mitigating circumstances in this case," he instructed, but it was for the court to consider these when deciding

punishment, not for the jury when deciding guilt or innocence according to the law. Tallmadge admitted that the evidence he had heard from
Joel Behrend and Dr. McCready demonstrated insanity, but all the jurors
needed to concern themselves with was whether or not Norman had been
able to tell the difference between right and wrong at the moment she
committed the assault. Tallmadge told the jury that to him it appeared
that premeditation and intent were at work, not momentary insanity:
Norman had brought a knife with her, and she afterward declared that
"she wished she had killed him." He closed by warning the jury "against
being actuated by sympathy for the prisoner or by the sympathies of the
public."

The jurors filed out of the courtroom, which began to hum with the
voices of the anxious crowd. "I sincerely hope," wrote Mike Walsh, "for
the honor of our city, that the present jury will acquit the unfortunate
girl without leaving their seats." Less than ten minutes later the jury was
back. Tallmadge begged the crowded room to stay calm, regardless of the
verdict. The clerk asked the jury if they had agreed upon their verdict, and
the foreman of the jury replied, "Yes, we have. We find Amelia Norman
the accused NOT GUILTY!" The room, trampling hard over Tallmadge's
plea, exploded with shouting, clapping, and stamping. The people standing outside the courtroom and hundreds of people standing outside in
the street contributed to the din. Lydia Maria Child recorded that "the
building shook with such a thunder of applause as I never before heard.
Some of the very officers appointed to keep order, involuntarily let their
tip-staffs fall on the floor, and clapped with the multitude. It was the surging of long repressed sympathies coming in like a roaring sea." Nearly
every man in the room got to his feet and shook hands with his neighbor
"in congratulation of the result."

Mike Walsh expressed his approval of the verdict for the working-class
readers of his *Subterranean*: "The jury were perfectly right in acquitting
her. What if it was contrary to the law and the evidence? They are the
judges of both, and the eternal laws of right and justice are above all
human laws." And he told them why, he believed, the jury, men like themselves, had decided against Ballard and in favor of Norman: "It was his
villainy in deceiving her—his meanness in abandoning her, and his cow-
ardice in appearing against her, which called forth a feeling of pity for her,
and of indignant contempt for him, in the breast of every chivalrous and

high-minded man in the community." George Wilkes also had something to say: "Amelia Norman," Wilkes wrote in his *Mysteries of the Tombs*, "who remained suffering and unnoticed by the public for months in her solitary cell, was suddenly delivered from her peril by the sympathy of that public, when their sympathy could be requited by the novelties of an interesting trial."

A crowd gathered around Graham, Morrill, and Carpentier, and they too were subjected to "a trial of handshaking as severe though not so protracted as that which so disturbed the equanimity of Lafayette when he was in New York" during the 1824–1825 tour during which crowds of cheering Americans turned out to see the Revolutionary War hero. John Morrill—not the sickly Sandford or the frail but steely Graham—was overcome, and had to lean on Graham for support. Amelia Norman fainted and had to be revived with water. When she returned to her cell she was surrounded by her lawyers, prison officials, and even some of the judges, who offered sympathy and congratulations. The next day, Lydia Maria Child, one part of her task complete, the next just beginning, took Amelia Norman home.

8

THE LAW OF SEDUCTION

The brand is on her cheek—stand back proud world
And let her perish like a down-trod leaf—
Aye, only mock her when she asks relief;
Down to perdition let her soul be hurled,
And in the eddying gulf of woe be whirled—
C.C.B., "Amelia Norman," *Liberator*, March 8, 1844

One day in February 1844 Lydia Maria Child ended a hurried letter to her husband: "I do love you, and thank you heartily for your kind letter. But I am obliged to write in great haste. Amelia has returned, and is *very* sick. I hope she will die." In 1844 death was the expected, the deserved fate of the fallen woman. "From all we learn," reported the *Christian Register* the same month, "her mind and health have received a blow which will probably ere a great while, place her beyond the need of kindness or of friends." The poem about Norman attributed to "C.C.B." suggests the same.

As the author of sentimental stories on the theme of the fallen woman and her fate, Child knew this trope better than anybody. Maybe that day it spilled over from fiction to fact when she was overwhelmed by Norman's illness, possibly one of the fits that her former employers had struggled with. In fact, Child was doing everything she could to help Norman live. The *Christian Register* approvingly reported that Child had taken Norman home to live with her "as an intimate of her family," but Child's sacrifice was even more than the *Register* realized, since Child's "family" was no one but the absent and exasperating David, and her home was only her rented rooms at the Hoppers'. Norman told Child "I don't know as it is worth while to try to make anything of me. I am nothing but a wreck," but Child observed that "her constitution is naturally good," and remarked that, as time went on, the more her "native energies and strong affections may be restored and purified, to aid and bless society." In "Letter from New-York No. V," Child noted, without explanation, another factor that contributed to Norman's sorrow: "It pains her to speak or think of her child. The fountain of maternal love has been poisoned at the source."

During the months that Norman lived with Child in the spring of 1844, and during the next few years as Child kept track of her, Child got to know her better than she had been able to when Norman was a prisoner at the Tombs. Norman had "strong deep feelings," something Child very much admired, and that the reporters at her trial had been able to glimpse even when her face was hidden by a veil. It was these, Child believed, that drove her to "the verge of madness by the baseness and cruelty with which she had been treated." She could manifest what Child described as "Indian implacability" when "*much* injured." But at normal times she was quiet, reserved, and "docile to the influence of those she loves." She was neither irritable nor petty, she had "good taste, judgment, and economy. She is quiet and lady-like in her manners, quick and capable with her needle, and a great favorite with children, of whom she is very fond. . . . She has a great deal of natural refinement, and uncommon capability." To Maria Lowell, wife of poet and diplomat James Russell Lowell, to whom Child recommended Norman for a job as a personal maid, Child wrote that "If treated with friendly interest, she would become strongly attached to you, though she would show it more in her *action* than words. If treated as *some* ladies treat those who serve them, she would be cold and proud, and perhaps somewhat indifferent." "A proper education would have made of her a noble woman," Child wrote regretfully.

Child published her "Letter from New-York No. V" in February, while Norman was living with her. The "Letter" is a jeremiad against the failure of law to protect women and the men who made the law. "May I be forgiven, if, at times, I hated law, so unequal in its operations, so crushing in its power," she wrote. The column was so passionately furious that when it was republished in the *National Anti-Slavery Standard* several weeks later, six of its bitterest paragraphs, along with Child's observation on Norman's shadowy baby, had been cut. When Child published a second edition of her collected columns, *Letters from New York*, she left this letter out.

Child focused much of her anger on Ballard's lawyer, Edward Sandford, and the statements he made at the trial. His competence as a lawyer was "a kind of ability from which my open-hearted nature shrinks, as it would from the cunning of the fox, and the subtlety of the serpent." She scoffed at Sandford's biblical arguments, in particular his claim that Eve was the first seducer, and that women had been tempting and persecuting men ever since. "This was putting the saddle on the wrong horse, with a vengeance!"

Throughout she dwelled repeatedly on her mistrust, even hatred of the law, which she found no more respectful of the rights of women and the poor than it was of the slaves in whose cause she had worked for years. The hours she spent at the Tombs during the trial "were very sad to me," she wrote. Seeing "poor ragged beggars summarily dismissed to the penitentiary, for petty larcenies," she concluded that "society is carrying on a great system of fraud and theft, and that these poor wretches merely lacked the knowledge and cunning necessary to keep theirs under legal protection." David Graham, Norman's principal lawyer, was a bright exception, Child felt, in the legal murk. She told how he returned his fee when "his heart was touched by" the wrongs Norman had suffered, and she praised his performance.

The solution Child proposed to strengthen women's position was the one pressed by the American Female Moral Reform Society—a law to criminalize seduction. "Seduction is going on by wholesale," Child argued. "In our cities almost every girl, in the humbler classes of life, walks among snares and pitfalls at every step, unconscious of their presence, until she finds herself fallen, and entangled in a frightful net-work, from which she sees no escape." Like David Graham, Child pointed out that a woman's virtue was a form of property that deserved legal protection:

"Life and property are protected," she argued, "but what protection is there for pure hearts, confiding souls, and youthful innocence?" Just as the jurors at Norman's trial had ignored their charge and acquitted her, "law will yield, like a rope of sand before the influence of humane sentiments, in cases of this kind, until the laws are better regulated." But, she admitted, "Let me not be understood as hoping much from penalties."

"Letter from New-York No. V" was the only piece of writing Child devoted wholly to Norman, but in the stories she published in magazines in this period she used fictionalized bits and pieces of Norman's experience, often mixing them with the commonly used trope of the madness and death of the fallen woman. In these stories beautiful, innocent young women are orphaned, suffer under indifferent stepmothers, are sent out to work, seduced, abandoned, lose their minds, and die. Child used these stories as vehicles for her causes, wedging in commentary on slavery and women's rights. Some were based on real cases Isaac Hopper had encountered in his prison reform work; she occasionally inserts Hopper himself into her fiction. In 1846 she published a collection of her stories, most of them previously published in magazines, titled *Fact and Fiction*, a hint to how Child wanted her readers to understand them—as fictions grown out of kernels of real events.

A few of Child's stories contain more pointed references to Norman. "An Affecting Tale of Truth" appeared in the *Mother's Assistant and Young Lady's Friend* in April 1844, with an editorial note explaining that the author was "the same lady who took such an interest in the fate of *Amelia Norman*." Its unnamed heroine, the country-born daughter of a poor widow, comes to the city and gets a job covering umbrellas. She catches the eye of Lord Henry Stuart, who is staying at the hotel opposite. She, "as ignorant of the dangers of a city, as the squirrels of her native fields," misunderstands his advances as the preliminaries to a marriage proposal, and in a weak moment steals some silk from her employer to make into a dress she can wear with him on a July 4 excursion. When Lord Stuart makes his sexual request more explicit, the girl, finally understanding, bursts into tears and pulls away. Her distress "stirred the deep fountains of his better nature," and he retreats. Then he forgets her—for him, her memory would be "as the recollection of last year's butterflies." On her side the feelings are much deeper, and so are the consequences. She is arrested for the theft, but, like Amelia Norman, "had sufficient presence of mind to assume a false name when arrested." In jail Isaac Hopper, in his role as prison visitor, finds her, as Dr. McCready found Amelia Norman, "lying on the floor of her cell, with her face buried in her hands, sobbing as if her heart would break." Thanks to Hopper's intercession, the girl is rehabilitated, unlike most of Child's fictional fallen women. Years later, after she has married a "highly respectable man," she returns to thank Hopper. The optimistic ending of the "Affecting Tale" may be Child's public expression of hope for Norman, despite what she wrote her husband in a desperate moment.

Another story, "Rosenglory," first published in the *Columbian Lady's and Gentleman's Magazine* in 1846, also contains explicit references to Norman. Susan Gray is orphaned and sent to work for a grocer's wife. Susan loses her job when her employer finds that her son, Robert, has grown close to Susan. Her next employer, an alderman, attempts to seduce her, and she steals a purse from him as she leaves his house, and is soon arrested. Released from jail, she can't find work. The magistrate who sent her to jail offers to help her, but only in exchange for sex. She wonders how "men should be magistrates, when they practise the same things for which they send women to Blackwell's Island," site of the city penitentiary. "She had never heard anything about 'woman's rights'; otherwise it might have occurred to her that it was because men made all the laws, and elected all the magistrates."

When she again encounters Robert, her first employer's son, he seduces her, then establishes her as his mistress. "Those who deem the poor girl unpardonable for consenting to this arrangement would learn mercy if they were placed under similar circumstances of poverty, scorn and utter loneliness," the author reminds her readers. When Robert casts her off to marry a rich woman, he tells her, as Henry Ballard told Amelia Norman, to "keep out of his way, and get my living as others in my situation did." She turns to prostitution, and when her brother, a sailor, returns home and finds her, she explains pathetically, "I was like a withered leaf, and the winds blew me about." Finally, "a haggard spectre," whose "great staring dark eyes look crazy," she dies in the "home for former prostitutes on Tenth Street," a reference to the Isaac T. Hopper Home, a halfway house for women released from prison, operated by Hopper's daughter, Abigail Hopper Gibbons.

Like Child, the press and its public remained interested in Norman after her trial. Some papers reported that Norman had been seen around the city behaving very unlike the sad and contrite woman Child described. Less than a week after the verdict, the *True Sun* claimed that she had been spotted promenading on Broadway, "looking well, and escorted by a fashionable young man." The *Spirit of the Times* reported slyly that "Miss Amelia Norman, the 'New York unfortunate' if the papers speak true left an adult Child behind her when she forsook her late patroness." And the *Aurora*, reporting that Norman had left Child "under circumstances at which her sympathizing advocates would blush," wondered mockingly, "Suppose, after all, it is ascertained that popular indignation has been thrown into the wrong side of the balance?"

The most detailed and lascivious of these sightings was not of the real Amelia Norman, but of a representation of her at a demimondaine costume party, possibly a brothel ball. The "little episodes" that took place there "would have been worthy of the pencil of Eugene Sue," reported the *Herald*, referring once again to the author of the *Mysteries of Paris*, who was known for his evocation of the Paris underworld; the costumes of some of the women were "bewitchingly free from prudery." Among the crowd of costumed partygoers was a "Miss K," who came dressed as Amelia Norman, and a "Mr. E." as Henry Ballard.

Child stepped forward to challenge these assertions of an Amelia Norman escaping from propriety. In a letter to the editor of the *True Sun*, Child countered that paper's accusation: "Amelia Norman came directly from the prison to my house, which she has never left for a single moment, except under my own protection. Her health is feeble, her mind bewildered, and her spirits exceedingly depressed." Child appealed to the "manliness of New-York editors" to stop publishing "malicious rumors, concerning this poor, heart-broken girl." She added: "I never saw stronger indications of a wish to return to the paths of virtue, and to atone, as far as possible, for past errors, by a life of modest seclusion and usefulness." The *New York Evening Post* backed her up, stating that there was no truth to the story that Norman had left Child to go out on the town, and scolded that "this continued persecution of a helpless and broken-hearted woman is shameful." The *New York American* was more ambivalent. After hailing Child for her generosity toward Norman, the *American* argued that "the best fortune, the greatest boon for her is, that she may be forgotten of men," while she "seeks to reconcile herself to offended Heaven." Given her sins, it was best to say no more about her: "Let us then hear no more of the name of Amelia Norman in the public journals; and especially let it not, from any misjudging sympathy, be pronounced with the reverence due alone to unstained female purity."

Disregarding this admonition, the curious dug further and discovered that the Norman family may not have been as respectable as Amelia's lawyers had represented them at her trial. Two weeks after Norman's acquittal, the *Baltimore Sun* learned about her brothers' troubles, reporting briefly and confusedly that at the Sussex County Court "three indictments were found against her brother for petit larceny." "We regret to learn that the family of Amelia Norman are not famous for their good character," opined the *Sun*. That spring the phrenologist J.R.L. reported in greater detail what the Norman boys had been up to with their neighbors' bees, chickens, and whiskey, their grandfather's adventures with his brother's horse, and their mother's "revengeful disposition." The phrenologist, however, sympathized with Amelia and believed that her violence was the fault of her heredity. Ballard, in his view, was a "licentious scoundrel," and her "attempt to assassinate the villain was almost justifiable." At the same time, her attempt "shows that she possessed at least some of the assaulting disposition of her brothers. The traits of character in this family are no doubt hereditary."

Child resisted what she called the "counter current" that set in soon after the trial, as the almost unbridgeable wall of sympathy for Norman began to crack. In her "Letter from New-York No. V" she wrote, "Uncontrollable pity has had its way, and now men begin to talk of law and order, dangerous precedents, &c." She urged the "kind-hearted jurymen" to resist this countercurrent and have no regrets about their verdict. "The moral influence of their decision will be good rather than evil. Society needs regenerating on the subject of woman's defenceless position, and this trial will do much toward it."

Despite the continued probing of the press and her own despondence, Norman did finally succeed, with Child's help, in getting back on her feet. As Norman recovered, Child began looking for work and a new home for her, as she had done for Caroline Henshaw, the mistress of John Colt, a little over a year earlier. By the end of April 1844, Child had succeeded in finding Norman a job as a housekeeper for a friend in a country town in her home state of Massachusetts. Only these employers, an "intelligent, worthy, and cultivated woman" and her husband, a "highly respectable gentleman," knew her name and history. Once again, Norman slipped out of her identity to start a new life. Child believed this step was necessary "for her own state of mind, to which I think a manifestation of public curiosity would be very injurious." Norman's success at this job confirmed Child's belief in the unfairness of the law. "When I look at this poor misguided girl," Child wrote a friend who had helped her search for a position for Norman, "now so useful, and improving daily in her views of things, and think what she *would* have been, had they sent her to Sing Sing, my feelings with regard to society's treatment of criminals grow stronger and stronger."

During the spring of 1844, while Norman recovered under Child's care, editorials multiplied in the press ruminating on what the whole episode had meant. The papers, like Child and the moral reformers, concluded that Norman's acquittal revealed that the meaning of seduction in law as it related to women had to change. For years the *Advocate of Moral Reform*, the American Female Moral Reform Society's paper, had been arguing that seduction ought not to be simply a trespass punishable with damages, as the existing tort provided, but that it should be made a crime punishable by law. They had linked their support of a law to criminalize seduction to Norman's case as soon as they learned about it in the fall of 1843. "*Let seduction be at once made a State prison offense*" demanded Bennett of the *Herald*; "make the seducer a felon, as he is, and let the law avenge the wrongs and sufferings of betrayed and ruined women." The *Christian Watchman* editorialized that the facts of Norman's case demonstrated that "our laws are wrong somewhere. . . . It is time that seduction be recognized by our laws as an infamous and penal offence." The *Berkshire Whig* cried "O cruelly insufficient Law!" adding, "When the Law makes Ballards to be stabbed and Amelia Normans to stab them, what right has the Law to complain?"

Now the moral reformers stepped up their campaign, publishing editorials and urging their readers to send petitions to the New York legislature. "We cannot but hope," they editorialized in a piece titled "Trial and Acquittal of Amelia Norman," "that the expression of public sentiment in the present instance will have some weight with the legislatures of the several states, whose votes on our petitions will be given again during the present session." A group of Society members published a letter in the *New York Tribune* to say that they hailed Norman's acquittal "with joy," since her case had drawn women to their cause, and urged readers to petition New York's legislature to pass a bill criminalizing seduction. "Will you permit us, Mr. Editor," they asked politely, "to inquire through your widely circulated Journal, if those whose sympathies have been so deeply enlisted in the recent trial will not have the goodness before their interest abates, to call at the Advocate Office, 36 Park Row, and sign the petition, soon to be sent to the Legislature, asking for a law to *protect virtue* and *punish or prevent* vice."

The surge of interest created by Norman's trial, what the *New York Herald* called "the extraordinary moral impulse of an excited community," helped boost the moral reformers' campaign. Petitions flooded into the legislature in Albany, and in February 1844 a bill against "licentiousness," encompassing both seduction and adultery, was introduced. This bill failed, as others like it had done before. "Those who lie in wait to destroy, prowl about unchecked," remarked the *Advocate*, bitterly disappointed. Then, four years later, on March 22, 1848, after a decade of petitioning by members and supporters of the American Female Moral Reform Society, a bill to criminalize seduction was passed by New York's legislature.

The "Act to Punish Seduction as a Crime" was a mixed triumph for the reformers. It stated that any man who "under promise of marriage" seduced and had "illicit connexion"—sex outside of marriage—with any unmarried woman "of previous chaste character" would be guilty of a misdemeanor and sentenced to serve five years in a state prison. The act disallowed the testimony of the woman who had been seduced, a demonstration of the all-male legislature's mistrust of a woman's word.

A few other states took steps in the 1840s to make seduction a crime, but many more addressed the question in a different way. They worked to revise their torts of seduction, removing loss of services to the father or master as a cause, and giving the seduced woman the right to sue on her own behalf. New York was among the states that took steps to revise its law to allow a seduced woman to sue on her own behalf. Participating in this effort, perhaps even central to it, was Norman's lawyer, David Graham.

In 1847 New York's legislature appointed Graham one of three members of the Commission on Practice and Pleadings. The commission was the outcome of a resolution passed by the state's constitutional convention of the previous year that resolved to create a code of law for New York and to simplify and modernize its legal procedures. The international codification movement, of which New York's effort was a part, was rooted in the idea that systems of law that had accreted over centuries had become too laden with jargon and arcane procedures to be responsive to the needs of the people. Charles Dickens's 1853 novel *Bleak House*, which centers on a never-ending legal case that entangles generation after generation of plaintiffs, can be understood as a cry of frustration by this populist author against the slow, costly, and byzantine procedures of British law. In the United States, law reform was associated with the anti-authoritarian and democratic spirit of the Jacksonian period.

Mike Walsh, Amelia Norman's former jail mate, and by 1847 a member of the New York legislature, supported law reform in New York, favoring the exclusion of what he called "all this beastly Latin jargon and old humbug mystification" that made law inaccessible to the poor and poorly educated. Walsh also supported the appointment to the commission of his and Norman's former lawyer, David Graham. Graham, according to Walsh, was "one of the best of men, as well as lawyers, that the city contains," and the performer of "many noble, God-like acts without seeking any reward beyond that afforded by the approval of his own conscience." Graham really did make a sacrifice when he agreed to serve on the commission, since the sales of his own successful books on the practice of law in New York would be hurt if the procedures they described were changed.

The leader of the codification movement in the United States was New York lawyer David Dudley Field (brother of Cyrus Field, who was behind the project to lay the first transatlantic cable). Field was also a member New York's Commission on Practice and Pleadings, and the code of civil procedure that he, Graham, and the third commissioner, Arphaxad Loomis, completed in 1849 came to be known as the Field Code. Included among the many pages of the Field Code is a brief section, 604, headed, simply, "Seduction." Its entire text reads: "An unmarried female may prosecute, as plaintiff, an action for her own seduction, and may recover therein such damages as shall be assessed in her favor." With this language the old idea that a woman's seduction could only be compensated on the basis of loss of services to her father or master was wiped out.

In the explanation they attached to Section 604, the commissioners recognized a woman's separate legal identity, arguing that, given the seriousness of seduction, which they described as an injury "of the gravest character," the law should provide a remedy, "not by means of a fiction," that of the loss of services to her father or master, "but open and direct, in favor of the person injured." They defined seduction, "by which is meant inducing her by persuasion, threats, or fraud, to consent to the sacrifice of her virtue." Even though she had consented, they argued, she was no less a victim of fraud than a man who had lost money on a property deal based on a false representation, or on stocks, or gambling, or on money "borrowed upon usury." He, too, had consented, but there were legal remedies for him, and none directly for the female victim of seduction.

The commissioners' understanding of a woman as a separate and equal adult, one with just as much right to compensation for fraud as a man, was limited by their belief that women were weaker beings in need of special protection. "The woman and her seducer do not stand upon equal grounds; she is the weaker party and the victim of his arts," they argued. To their explanation they appended a long quotation from the eighteenth-century British moral philosopher William Paley, who corroborated their identification of seduction with fraud, and provided a list of the dangers seduction posed to society, including the woman's loss of reputation and, with it, her marriage prospects; the possibility that a woman might destroy her baby out of shame; and the possibility that seduced women might turn to prostitution, since "after her first sacrifice," women were likely to enter "a life of public lewdness."

When, however, the commissioners equated a woman's seduction with the financial ruin that might befall a man who had been defrauded, they legitimized her loss on their own, male terms. These terms were painfully meaningful to so many in the aftermath of the long depression that followed the Panic of 1837, the same economic catastrophe that shook up the Meriam household and thrust the family's young servant, Amelia Norman, out into the world. With Section 604 of the Field Code, David Graham and his fellow commissioners argued that a woman who had been seduced had just as much right to fight her way back from ruin—sexual ruin—as a man who had been financially ruined by a bank crash or a fraudster.

What moved the commissioners to include what one legal historian calls a "revolution in women's standing to sue for seduction"? And what, exactly, was David Graham's role in its composition? By the first half of the nineteenth century the seduction tort was outdated. The family structure in which male household heads legally owned the labor of their daughters was disintegrating. The unmarried daughters of farming and working-class families increasingly worked for wages as domestic servants or in mills, often in cities far away from their homes and outside the protection of their fathers. At the same time, the lives of middle-class daughters, especially in cities, were being redefined by standards of gentility that excluded paid labor from their lives, and also by increasingly severe expectations of chastity. The nineteenth-century cult of the "fallen woman," the notion that a woman who had sex before or outside of marriage was irretrievably "ruined," gave a new color to the tort of seduction. The emotional catastrophe experienced by the woman began to seem more important than the financial loss potentially felt by her father or master. Because of these shifting social, emotional, and economic factors, antebellum American courts began to interpret as a "legal fiction" the idea that an unmarried woman's seduction represented a loss of services to her father and master and to see the seduction tort as a relic of values and circumstances that were rapidly disappearing. The commissioners' move to allow a woman to sue on her own behalf was a recognition of these changing circumstances.

Although there is no direct evidence, it seems likely that Graham had an influence in the commission's revision of the seduction tort. During Amelia Norman's trial he came into contact with the moral reformers who had worked for a decade to criminalize seduction and who made Norman's trial a weapon in that effort. He also got to know Lydia Maria Child, who supported the reformers' effort to criminalize seduction. In "Letter from New-York No. V," Child protested the antiquated and, to her, outrageous terms of the seduction tort. Surely Graham read this column about the trial he had just concluded, which also included praise for himself. In a passage that appeared in the version of "Letter from New-York No. V" that appeared in the *Courier* but was left out when it was reprinted in the *Standard*, Child wrote,

What is the redress for a broken heart, blighted reputation, the desertion of friends, the loss of respectable employment, the scorn and hissing of the world? Why, the woman must acknowledge herself to be the *servant* of somebody, who may claim *wages* for lost time! With indignation and scorn, I appeal to common sense, and common justice, against this miserable legal fiction—this impudent assumption that I am a chattel personal. It is a standing insult to woman kind; and had we not become the slaves we are deemed in law, we should rise *en masse*, in the majesty of moral power, and sweep that contemptible insult from the statute book.

Graham had also positively stated his agreement with Child and the moral reformers at Norman's trial in 1844. Echoing Child, who wrote that "life and property are protected, but what protection is there for pure hearts, confiding souls, and youthful innocence?" Graham spoke in his closing statement of the "lamentable want of law to protect female virtue, and the absence of all criminal enactments to punish the base and villainous seducer—while property and every other thing of value, were protected by laws." He deprecated the way Norman had taken the law into her own hands with a violent act, but, he argued, she had done it because there was no law to protect her virtue "other than in an action for damages." Graham's refusal to take a fee for Norman's defense, and his assertion to Lydia Maria Child that Norman's case "involved considerations higher and holier than the relations of lawyer and client," seem to show his commitment to the idea of reforming the law of seduction. Had Graham been inclined to forget about Amelia Norman's case and the problem of seduction, his memory would have been awakened by the journey of several bills to criminalize seduction through the New York legislature as he was at work on the commission. One was an 1847 bill that failed. Another was the bill that succeeded in 1848.

The Field Code became a model for many American states and territories, and it was influential in Great Britain and its colonies. Between 1851 and 1930 thirteen American states that adopted the Field Code, either in whole or in part, adopted with it some version of Section 604, granting women the right to sue for seduction on their own behalf. Most of these states also explicitly dropped loss of services as a cause of action. In doing so they pared away the old definition of a woman and her labor as the property of a man, instead recognizing a woman's separate, legally visible self. The irony of the Field Code is that while it originated in New York,

New York's legal community resisted it, and the state legislature passed it only in a "wounded" and "fragmentary" form. Among the sections of the Field Code that New York did not pass was Section 604. The result was that while New York criminalized seduction, its tort for seduction went untouched.

The criminal law and the tort experienced different fates. The moral reformers, who had worked so hard to criminalize seduction, turned their attention to new projects after their success in 1848. Exhausted by their work with wayward women, they turned to helping poor children. This refocusing of their petitioning and publicity efforts may have been one of the reasons that the criminal law languished, largely unused. Meanwhile, even in places where the tort was unrevised and women still had to rely on their fathers to bring suit, the tort flourished, probably because it offered women and their families monetary damages, which may have been more satisfying than watching a seducer wither in prison. By the 1930s, a time when a woman's sexual activity outside of marriage was no longer immediately associated with her ruin, the tort fell out of favor. It came to be associated with "gold diggers," women seeking to entrap wealthy men, and, starting in the 1930s, states began to abolish it, including New York in 1935.

As Graham and his fellow Commissioners of Practice and Pleadings were at work they must also have been aware of other developments in the expansion of legal rights for women in the state of New York. On April 7, 1848, less than a month after the state legislature passed the law criminalizing seduction, it passed a married women's property act. New York's married women's property act was first proposed a decade earlier, around the same time that the law to criminalize seduction was first brought before New York's legislature. The act allowed wives to keep the property they owned before marriage and any they separately acquired while they were married. The act helped to dismantle coverture, the legal phenomenon, inherited from British law, in which a woman lost her separate civil identity at marriage, and control of her property passed into the hands of her husband. In the middle of the nineteenth century almost every state (and Britain and Canada) passed a married women's property law or one like it. New York's is considered the first significant such law and a model for the laws that immediately followed it.

Among those who lobbied for the act was Elizabeth Cady Stanton, soon to become a leader of the women's rights movement in the United States; but the depression that followed the Panic of 1837 had as much to do with the act's passage as any sentiment in favor of equal rights for women. By allowing wives to hold their property separately, the law protected families' assets from husbands' creditors. Like the law criminalizing seduction, which was passed by the same group of legislators, it was no more than partially committed to improving women's condition. It, and the laws that later modified it, ultimately led to greater independence for women, but the fact that the 1848 law did not apply to a woman's earnings demonstrates how little it was intended to liberate wives from economic dependence on their husbands.

Graham and his colleagues on the commission may also have heard about a weekday gathering that took place at the Wesleyan Church in Seneca Falls, New York, on July 19 and 20, 1848. The Seneca Falls convention, dreamed up and realized by Stanton, Lucretia Mott, and a few others, has been regarded by historians as the event at which the organized movement for women's rights in the United States coalesced into being, and the starting point of the fight for women's suffrage.

Lydia Maria Child, ever ambivalent about participating in organized movements, did not attend. Stanton, thirteen years younger than Child, admired the older woman's long career in writing and reform and hoped she would at least contribute a letter of support to read at the convention. Child did not do even that. Despite her absence, Child's influence was felt at Seneca Falls. For the speech Stanton delivered at the convention, she plundered Child's 1835 *History of the Condition of Women* for references to women's oppression by men in a variety of times and cultures. Stanton's speech, and the Declaration of Sentiments and Resolutions passed by the convention, seconded views Child had been expressing for years, on the innate equality of men and women, on the obligation of men to be as "pure" as women, and on women's equal right to opportunities in education and work. Stanton, like Child, spoke with furious resentment of the violence, masquerading as protection, that men used to uphold their dominance and rob women of their rights. Men would call a woman an angel, Stanton declared at Seneca Falls, nourishing her vanity; to make her believe that her organization is so much finer than theirs, that she is not fitted to struggle with the tempests of public life, but needs their care and protection!! Care and protection—such as the wolf gives the lamb—such as the eagle the hare he carries to his eyrie!! Most cunningly he entraps her, and then takes from her all those rights which are dearer to him than life itself—rights which have been baptized in blood—and the maintenance of which is even now rocking to their foundations the kingdoms of the old World.

With the latter reference Stanton was evoking the democratic revolutions that erupted in European cities in 1848, explicitly linking her own nascent movement to them.

The Declaration of Sentiments Stanton presented to the women's rights convention at Seneca Falls in the summer of 1848 might have been a recitation of the circumstances of Amelia Norman's life. Modeled on the Declaration of Independence, but using "he" to mean "man," instead of King George III, its list of "abuses and usurpations" included "He has monopolized nearly all the means of profitable employment, and from those she is permitted to follow, she receives but a scanty remuneration," and "He has denied her the facilities for obtaining a thorough education—all colleges being closed against her," and "He has created a false public sentiment by giving to the world a different code of morals for men and women, by which moral delinquencies which exclude woman from society are not only tolerated but deemed of little account in man," and "He has endeavored in every way that he could, to destroy her confidence in her own powers, to lessen her self-respect, and to make her willing to lead a dependent and abject life."

What *had* the whole episode meant? Did the two legal movements bolstered by Amelia Norman's trial, one to criminalize seduction, the other to grant a woman the right to sue for seduction on her own behalf, contribute significantly to the movement for women's rights? Although both resulted in the passage of laws, those laws ultimately fizzled out, and by the twentieth century seduction had become an antiquated and long-forgotten concept. But even though these two efforts were ultimately dead ends, they were, along with the more successful married women's property act that germinated alongside them, part of the fitful churn of events that ultimately contributed to the emergence of American women from dependence to legal autonomy. They contributed to the quiet rumbling that preceded the stronger, louder, more focused movement for women's rights, including suffrage, that first found its collective voice at Seneca Falls. That voice was often furious. "Would to God you could know the burning indignation that fills woman's soul when she turns over the pages of your statute books, and sees there how like feudal barons you freemen hold your women," Elizabeth Cady Stanton declared in a speech to New York's legislature in 1854.

Amelia Norman may or may not have understood her place in the roil of history. Unable to write, as Child and Stanton did so powerfully, she left no letter, diary, or speech to say whether or not she thought her attack on Henry Ballard had any meaning beyond what it meant to her in that frenzied moment on the Astor House steps. Impoverished by her spare education and by the stingy work opportunities available to her, captive, with her child, to Henry Ballard's whim, Norman had expressed in violent action all the boiling feminist fury that Child and Stanton did in words.

EPILOGUE

Harlot's Fate

And wilt thou dare to hold in scorn
The creature thou hast made me now—
Who found'st me pure as day's first dawn
Upon the mountain's grassy brow,
But left me to a harlot's fate,
Fallen, despoiled, and desolate?

Thomas Ragg, "The Fallen One to Her First Seducer,"
Advocate of Moral Reform, May 1, 1844

The later years and final fates of many of the players in Amelia Norman's story are not hard to learn. Mike Walsh, the Democratic politician and journalist who had championed Norman, who shared her lawyer, and whose stay in the Tombs overlapped with hers, returned to his newspaper career, then served in the New York Assembly and the United States Congress. Later, his life descended into a sad mess of drink and dissipation. It ended in the early hours of St. Patrick's Day, 1859, at the bottom of a steep flight of stone steps beneath a milliner's shop on Eighth Avenue where he had either toppled or was pushed. "All are reminded," the *New York Ledger* lamented, "of his sympathy for the poor; of his hatred of oppression." A crowd of five thousand New Yorkers gathered to view his body in its coffin, laid out on the sidewalk in front of his house on West Twenty-First Street, then followed it on foot and in forty-one carriages to

Greenwood Cemetery in Brooklyn, honoring him for the years he spent championing their interests.

Amelia Norman's other celebrated jail mate, George Wilkes, had better luck than Walsh, his old friend and colleague. He capitalized on his experience in the Tombs, producing two publications. One was his prison memoir, *Mysteries of the Tombs*. The other was the story of another fellow inmate, David Babe, a pirate, which he planned, ghoulishly, to publish on the day of Babe's execution. Wilkes preserved a bit of the texture of feeling in the Tombs, when he recorded one of his interviews with Babe while both men were still in jail. "Were the proceedings of the trial irksome to you?" Wilkes asked. "No, interesting, but painful. I was amused sometimes though to see the reporters stare me in the face at the introduction of every new witness." "Did you express any emotion?" asked Wilkes. "I did, a little," replied the pirate.

In later years Wilkes took advantage of the opportunities available to men in the expanding republic and across the Atlantic. He promoted the transcontinental railroad, and settlement in Baja California. He escorted an American prizefighter to England to take part in a famous fight. On his return to New York after this fight he was honored at a banquet at the Astor House for the "manly, high toned course pursued by you in upholding the national honor on the field, upon the water and on the turf." In 1845 he cofounded the *National Police Gazette*, and in 1856 he bought into, and later took over, another sporting paper, the *Spirit of the Times*. Both papers benefited from the caution he learned after his early prosecutions for libel and obscenity and lasted much longer than the ephemeral *Sunday Flash*. He reported from the battlefields of the Civil War and, in 1871, from Paris, where he was a sympathetic witness to the workers' uprising known as the Paris Commune. In his last book he considered Shakespeare "from an American point of view," including the theory that Sir Francis Bacon was the real author of Shakespeare's work. During his last years he lived in London and Paris, until ill health forced him home.

Wilkes married twice, but by the end of his life had shed whatever family he had managed to accumulate. Less than two years before his death he adopted two young orphans, but soon became estranged from one. When he died in 1885 his adopted daughter, a little girl of twelve, was his sole heir. Fewer than twenty people attended his funeral, in contrast to the mob that followed Walsh to the cemetery. The press used Wilkes's late fall into obscurity as an opportunity to comment on the mutability of fortune: "His death caused no more sensation than that of an altogether unknown person," wondered the *New Hampshire Sentinel*. "Yet, twenty years ago, and for many years preceding that time, George Wilkes was one of the best known men in New York."

Frederick Tallmadge, the city recorder who had been the principal judge of the Court of Sessions and who had struggled in vain to persuade the jurors to ignore the context of Amelia Norman's crime, repeatedly aligned himself in the years following her trial with what the *New York Times* in his obituary described as the "prosperity and business interests of the Metropolis." He developed a reputation for defending these interests against the city's poor, immigrants, and workers. When in the spring of 1849 working-class rioters hurling paving stones besieged the Astor Place Opera House, Tallmadge, as recorder, stood in the street and read them the riot act. When his appeal failed, police and militia units fired on the crowd. The following day Mike Walsh addressed a large crowd at City Hall Park. A *Herald* reporter noted that in "the minds of many" present, the violent events of the previous evening involved "nothing short of a controversy and collision between those who have been styled the 'exclusives,' or 'upper ten,' and the great popular masses." "Three groans for Recorder Tallmadge," the crowd roared. Walsh ominously evoked the great class riots that had erupted the previous year in European cities—just as Elizabeth Cady Stanton had done at Seneca Falls the previous year—and he declared that Tallmadge was among those who "deserve hanging a thousand times." "Hang them up—hang them up," replied the crowd. The working-class anger that had fueled sympathy for Amelia Norman five years earlier was, if anything, hotter now.

A decade later, Tallmadge was again at the center of New York's political and class conflict. In an effort to control the unruly Democratic city, state legislators, mainly Republicans, formed a series of state commissions meant to take over powers that had belonged to city government. One of these was the Metropolitan Police Commission, which combined and took jurisdiction over New York (Manhattan, which then encompassed all of New York City), King's (Brooklyn), Richmond (Staten Island), and Westchester Counties, wresting control from local police departments and creating in their place the Metropolitan Police. Frederick Tallmadge became superintendent of the Metropolitan Police District of New York. Fernando Wood, the city's Democratic mayor, defiantly refused to dissolve the city's police department, and for a while the two departments, the Municipals and the Metropolitans, operated simultaneously.

The situation reached a climax in June 1857 when the Metropolitan Police, headed by Tallmadge, marched to City Hall to arrest the mayor. At City Hall they were met by the Municipal Police, headed by none other than chief George Washington Matsell, who earlier in his career had been the special justice who rushed to the Astor House on November 1, 1843, and then interviewed Amelia Norman for her indictment.

The rival police forces fought on the steps of City Hall until the Seventh Regiment, which had been on its way to a Bunker Hill celebration in Boston, turned around and intervened. "Bloodshed!—Collision between the Old and the New Police," shrieked the *National Police Gazette*, in advertisements for "a Fine engraving of this Terrible Encounter." In July 1857, the Court of Appeals ruled in favor of the Metropolitan Police, and Matsell stepped down. In 1858 he became the publisher of the *National Police Gazette*, the sensational crime paper previously published by George Wilkes. In 1859 he published his dictionary of the language of criminals. Matsell had long understood the storytelling potential in crime.

The abortionist Madame Restell, who had testified reluctantly at Norman's trial, also remained in the news in the decades that followed. Taking advantage of a public whose traditional acceptance of abortion had not yet eroded even as medical doctors, protecting their own profession, pressed the passage of one law after another against it, she worked and prospered. The protection from official persecution she enjoyed was most likely bought with bribes to the police, including Police Chief Matsell.

Restell's bribe-bought barrier against persecution by the police may have been what kept her out of jail most of the time, but it was dangerously vulnerable. In September 1847 she was arrested for performing an abortion on Maria Bodine, a servant in the household of a cotton mill owner in Orange County, New York. One of the lawyers Restell hired was David Graham Jr., whom she had seen perform at Amelia Norman's trial alongside John Morrill more than three years earlier. Despite his efforts, an ordeal of two years followed. After stays in the Tombs and the Eldridge

Street Jail, Restell was convicted and sent for a year to the penitentiary on Blackwell's Island.

Like Amelia Norman, Madame Restell learned that life in jail was more dangerous to body and reputation for a woman than it was for a man. At Blackwell's Island she had a comfortable cell, light work, and daily visits from her husband—all bought, most likely, with bribes—but the experience of vulnerability and confinement nonetheless shook her deeply. A police officer who worked on Blackwell's and knew Restell there reported that she "seemed to feel her imprisonment greatly," and that when she was finally released from the island in the fall of 1849 she declared she would never go back there again.

For almost thirty years Restell succeeded in staying out of jail—until she was cornered and finally captured by Anthony Comstock, founder and head of the New York Society for the Suppression of Vice. Comstock, born on a Connecticut farm in March 1844, the year of Amelia Norman's trial, convinced the federal government to pass a law "for the suppression of trade in and circulation of obscene literature and articles of immoral use" and to make him a special agent for its enforcement. The law, popularly known as the Comstock Law, outlawed possessing, selling, or circulating obscene literature and prohibited sending it through the US mail. It specifically targeted literature, instruments, and drugs meant to promote or practice contraception and abortion.

In January 1878, Anthony Comstock, pretending to represent a woman who wanted an abortion, went to see Restell at her luxurious, four-story brownstone mansion on Fifth Avenue and Fifty-Second Street. The following month he returned and, using the power delegated to him by the federal government, arrested Restell and seized what he could find of the evidence of her trade. Comstock took Restell before a judge, who committed her to the Tombs. Released on bail, Restell became distraught at the thought of spending any more time locked up.

On the night before the day of her trial, April 1, 1878, Restell went to bed. At around 2 a.m. she got up, went down to the kitchen, took down the bell that served as a burglar alarm, and found a carving knife. Then she went back upstairs, ran a bath in her elaborate bathroom, undressed, sat in the warm water, and, after one unsuccessful attempt, used the knife to cut her own throat. Like Amelia Norman, Restell made the decision to die rather than face her trial; unlike Norman, she succeeded. Anthony Comstock, who was to have testified against Restell at her trial, made a neat, cold summary of his accomplishment in his notes on her case, concluding, "a bloody ending to a bloody life."

Just as tragic, if not as colorful, were the too-early ends of David Graham and Edward Sandford. Graham's consumptive frailty was apparent even before Norman's trial, and his labor on the code commission a decade later appears to have fatally worn him down. A legal gossip reported this unfunny joke, part of an overheard conversation between two lawyers, one of whom, unnamed, was one of Graham's fellow commissioners, the other evidently one of the members of the bar who resisted the code:

> Advocate.—"Do you know how Mr. Graham is?"
> Codifier.—"He is very ill—completely broken down. The code has ruined the health of all of us who were engaged upon it, the labor was so intense."
> Advocate (dryly).—"I am not surprised, for it has made all the bar sick."

By 1851 Graham's illness had advanced into what fellow lawyer George Templeton Strong described as "some very painful, harassing disease that required repeated surgical aid and that has worn him into consumption." Strong believed that Graham's unhappy marriage contributed to the breakdown of his health. Matilda Graham, according to Strong, a "handsome, negligent, extravagant, heartless, harridan of a wife has aggravated the case sadly." In an effort to recover his health, Graham sailed for the warm shore of Nice, accompanied by his brother, John, and paid for by a subscription collected by his colleagues. He died there in June 1852, at age forty-four. "A sad end of a brilliant career," Strong commented.

Years later John Graham, also a prominent lawyer, remembered his brother when he connected Amelia Norman with the unwritten law in two highly publicized cases in which men shot and killed their wives' lovers. In 1859 John Graham was defending New York congressman Daniel Sickles for the murder of Francis Barton Key, the United States district attorney for Washington, DC (and son of Francis Scott Key, author of "The Star-Spangled Banner"). Key had been carrying on an affair with Teresa Sickles, Daniel Sickles's wife. When Sickles discovered the affair, he decoyed Key to the couple's place of assignation on Lafayette Square in Washington, just blocks from the White House. When Key appeared, Sickles shot and killed him. Reminding the jury of the great interest the public had taken in Norman's case fifteen years earlier, Graham likened Sickles's act to Norman's: both had acted in "obedience to the instincts of our natures." In 1870 John Graham again invoked Amelia Norman. This time he was defending Daniel McFarland, who had killed journalist Albert Richardson, the lover of his wife, Abby Sage McFarland. After once again relating Norman's story, Graham asked the jury "whether a man could be other than frenzied under the provocation." The outcome of Norman's trial had taught him that a woman's violence in defense of her own honor was as forgivable as a man's on her behalf. He noted that the women who heard his narrative of the Norman case at the McFarland trial listened "with indescribable interest."

Two years after David Graham's death, Edward Sandford, Graham's opposite at Amelia Norman's trial and Henry Ballard's friend, was also dead. Like Graham, he went to Europe to benefit his health, not from a dire illness such as Graham had, but just so he could "return to his labors with renewed vigor and hope." His wife and daughters were in Paris, where they were enjoying the "advantages of Parisian education and society," and he was on his way to join them there. Instead, his trip came to a tragic end off the coast of Newfoundland, when his ship, the *Arctic*, collided with another ship and quickly sank. Survivors were taken to Halifax, Nova Scotia, but Sandford, age forty-five, was not among them. The *New York Times* reported that "the City was filled with mourning for the loss of so many valuable lives, and all classes of the community felt for the calamities of others as though they had been their own. We do not remember an occasion when sympathy so universal and unaffected has been bestowed upon the sufferers by a terrible catastrophe." The *Times* singled out Edward Sandford as one of the lost citizens who would be most missed.

Lydia Maria Child continued to live at 20 East Third Street with Isaac and Hannah Hopper after Amelia Norman's trial. Her husband David, who had nominally taken her place as editor of the *National Anti-Slavery Standard*, gave it up in the spring and returned to Massachusetts. He dropped in and out of Child's life during the second half of the 1840s, continuing to move "from one failure to another with unbounded enthusiasm," as one friend of the family wryly put it. His name appears at the Hoppers' address in *Doggett's New York City Directory for 1846 and 1847*, probably for the sake of propriety. More unusually, his wife's does also. Privately published city directories like *Doggett's* listed the name, address, occupation, and color (for blacks only) of heads of household and business owners. Widows and women who operated businesses independently, such as nurses and boardinghouse keepers, were listed there, but married women almost never were. Lydia Maria Child, who continued to maintain her independence from David without absolutely breaking the tie, was an exception. Doggett lists her at 20 East Third Street, separately from her husband, as "Child, L. Maria, authoress."

In 1847 Child had a shock when John Hopper eloped with a younger woman, Rosalie DeWolf. Soon after the newly married couple moved into the house on East Third Street, Child left for a rented room on a farm in New Rochelle. She tried to put a good face on it, writing a friend that she "could never see my way clear about leaving my impulsive and ardent friend John without some companion who could make a home for him. Now he *has* such a companion, and I can at once study economy and their convenience by transferring my apartments to them." To another friend she was more candid, writing that "the news of their marriage came upon me like a thunder clap," and, sadly, "John used to think he could *never* get accustomed to living without 'little Zippy Damn,' and I thought I could not possibly get along without *him*."

In the years that followed, John Hopper shed the Quakerism he had always worn lightly, but his childhood training in reform stayed with him all his life. Days before the Civil War began a friend reported that he was "in great glee and rejoices in these rumors of war as much as if he had not been born a Quaker." When his poor eyesight—and probably also his age, as he was forty-six in 1861—prevented him from joining up, he contributed to the Union effort in every way he could. Taking advantage of his work—by this time he was an insurance agent—he bought life insurance for poor men who wanted to join the Union army. He also supported his sister, Abigail Hopper Gibbons, who spent most of the war nursing wounded soldiers at the front. "John is at work for the cause with all his might," reported the same friend.

Hopper died in 1864, so he did not live to see the end of the Civil War or the liberation of the slaves, his and his parents' great cause. He was forty-nine. "What power of love the man had! How it welled out of him, how it overflowed!" mourned Octavius Frothingham, the Unitarian preacher and friend who led his funeral service. The warm generosity Hopper demonstrated when he visited Amelia Norman in her cell in the Tombs, located a lawyer for her, and had her trial postponed after her suicide attempt, continued to the end. A few years before he died he adopted Robert Denyer, a crippled boy from one of the children's institutions on Randall's Island outside Manhattan in the East River. Denyer died in 1861, and Hopper was buried with him. A single headstone memorializes them both.

The Hoppers' son, William DeWolf Hopper, born in 1858, was only six when his father died, but John's effervescence and passion for the theater lived on in him. Using the name DeWolf Hopper, he grew up to become a well-known musical comedy performer. In 1913 DeWolf Hopper married, as the fifth of his six wives, a young actress called Elda Furry, later known as Hedda Hopper, the Hollywood gossip columnist. In 1933, on his seventy-fifth birthday, he reminisced about his career and mentioned his childhood: "And it may also surprise you to learn," he told a reporter from the *New York Times*, "that I was born on Third Street, just off the Bowery." The manufactured family story he repeated in his memoir was that his grandfather, Isaac Hopper, a "rabid abolitionist," so constrained his fun-loving father that before his marriage to Rosalie DeWolf he never saw a play. DeWolf would have been surprised to learn not only about his father's avid theatergoing, but about the ménage, featuring his father and Lydia Maria Child, in his grandparents' Third Street home long before he was born. He died in 1935 after a long career in the theater and a short flirtation with film.

After the defection of John Hopper and her flight to New Rochelle, Child returned to the Hoppers in New York. In 1850 she reunited with her husband, and the two of them returned to Massachusetts, settling first on a rented farm in West Newton outside Boston. Child continued to help young women, whom she thought of as her "adopted daughters." Some of these women, like Amelia Norman, were troubled and in need of rescue; others were talented authors or artists in whom she saw aspects of herself.

The most celebrated of these young women was the author, abolitionist, and runaway slave Harriet Jacobs. Born in North Carolina around

1815, Jacobs fled her master in 1835, then, incredibly, hid in her grand-mother's attic for seven years, when she finally found a way to escape to New York. In New York in the 1850s, at the urging of Amy Post, an abolitionist friend, she wrote the story of her adventurous escape. In 1860 Jacobs approached Child for help when the Boston publisher Thayer and Eldridge agreed to publish the book, but only if Child would write the preface. Child saw Jacobs's book as an opportunity to contribute to the abolitionist cause, and she did more than just write a preface. She edited the manuscript, negotiated the contract, corrected the proofs, and once the book was published she wheedled her friends into buying copies. The book, *Incidents in the Life of a Slave Girl*, was published in 1861 on the eve of the Civil War under a pseudonym, Linda Brent.

Child signed Jacobs's contract with the publisher under her own name, then ensured Jacobs's ownership of her book by having her sign a docu-ment for the publisher naming Jacobs as the author. She wrote Jacobs that "under the circumstances *your* name could not be used, you know." Jacobs evidently agreed that it was necessary to submerge her identity, not because she was in danger of recapture—her New York employer had purchased her freedom and that of her two children before the book came out—but because of the book's sexual frankness. Jacobs had been sexually vulnerable as a slave, and like all slaves, legal marriage had been denied to her; she was embarrassed about publicly owning her sexual history. As with Amelia Norman, Child believed it was best for a compromised woman to shed her name with her past and move on.

Despite Child's well-meant but heavy-handed erasure of Jacobs's iden-tity as the author of her memoir, the two women became friends. Jacobs wrote that when she and Child met they "soon found the way to each oth-er's heart," and she came to feel that Child was a "whole-souled woman." Child continued to support Jacobs's work as a writer, helping her publish pieces in the *Liberator* and the *Standard*. At the same time, Child's role in the book meant that Jacobs's authorship, now proven by the discovery of Child's letters to her, was long doubted.

Before and during the Civil War, Child recommitted herself to the cause of the slaves and, after emancipation finally came, to the welfare of the freedmen. Child and her husband attended antislavery meetings, some-times facing the wrath of pro-slavery mobs. Her abolitionist colleague Wendell Phillips remembered her courage in facing one of these, her "resolute rebuke, spoken in the street, to the leader of one of the Sunday mobs of 1861,—so stern, brief, and pungent that it left him dumb" (one would like to know what she said). She wrote articles and pamphlets in favor of emancipation, and edited *The Freedmen's Book*, published in 1865, a collection of biographical essays by herself and other authors, including Harriet Jacobs ("the names of the colored authors are marked with an asterisk"), constituting a "true record of what colored men have accomplished under great disadvantages." Meant to inspire former slaves in their new lives, it was sold at cost, and Child donated the proceeds to the Freedman's Aid Association.

Most dramatically, and most in keeping with her history as a nurturer of the wounded, was Child's offer to go to Virginia to nurse the radical abolitionist John Brown. After taking hostages and attacking the federal arsenal at Harpers Ferry in a failed attempt to liberate local slaves, Brown had been wounded, captured, and jailed. Like many northerners, Child was galvanized by Brown's failed blow against slavery. On October 27, 1859, the day after Brown's raid, Child wrote him. As in the case of Amelia Norman, Child was attracted by a dramatic gesture and, at the same time, she claimed, repelled by its violence. "Believing in peace principles," she wrote Brown, "I cannot sympathize with the method you chose to advance the cause of freedom." But, she told Brown, she honored his intentions and his courage. "In brief, I love and bless you. . . . I long to nurse you, to speak to you sisterly words of sympathy and consolation." Child packed her trunk and prepared to go, but then stayed at home when Brown's wife arrived in Virginia to nurse him. Brown redirected Child's concern by asking her to help raise money for his family instead.

During the John Brown affair Child entered into a correspondence with Governor Henry Wise of Virginia, and with Margaretta Mason, a defender of slavery and the wife of Virginia senator James M. Mason, who had drafted the Fugitive Slave Act of 1850. The American Anti-Slavery Society published this correspondence as a pamphlet in 1860. It sold three hundred thousand copies, an "immense circulation," according to John Greenleaf Whittier. Along with Brown's conviction and execution on December 2, 1859, Child's pamphlet helped heat the political atmosphere in which Abraham Lincoln was elected president, the Southern states began to secede from the Union, and the United States went to war against itself in April 1861.

In contrast to Child's passionate rededication to abolition and the welfare of former slaves, her commitment to the organized women's rights movement that emerged out of the Seneca Falls convention that she failed to attend in 1848 was ambivalent, although her belief in the equality of men and women was not. She believed there were differences between men and women, that there was "sex in souls," but she also believed that until the doors of opportunity opened for women there was no way to tell what women were capable of. "It is in vain to speculate about the *nature* of woman, so long as her nature is every way repressed by false customs, which men perpetuate for their own convenience, and then quarrel with the consequences," she wrote fellow author and activist Theodore Tilton in 1866. The same year she wrote Elizabeth Cady Stanton to say, "I sympathize entirely with your views concerning woman's true position in society, and I cordially wish you God speed." Her support included an endorsement of women's right to vote. "How absurd it seems," she wrote a friend, "that any tipsy, ignorant fool, with a *hat* on, can vote, while *such* a woman [Stanton] is disfranchised. Oh dear! what a labor it is, to get this world right side up!"

Despite Child's endorsement of Stanton's views, she did not join the National Woman Suffrage Association, organized by Stanton and Susan B. Anthony in 1869. To another friend she complained, "They seem to have no discretion; no restraining grace; several things made me distrustful of their judgment, and I was afraid to venture, though my sympathies went with the *principles* they were seeking to advance." But: "Though tired of battling, I cannot keep my hands off 'the woman question.' It is decidedly the most important question that has been before the world." To Stanton, Child wrote,: "I am old, and, having fought through a somewhat long campaign of reform, I feel little energy for enlisting in a new war." She never really gave up, though. The following year, showing some of her old fire, Child closed a letter of support to a woman's suffrage organization in Iowa: "Yours for the unshackled exercise of every faculty by every human being."

In their old age Child and her husband David experienced a renewal of their marriage. Living in Wayland, Massachusetts, in a house inherited from her father, they were remote from the world, "entirely dependent upon each other for intellectual companionship." Child continued to write—magazine pieces, a novel, a biography of Isaac T. Hopper, who died in 1852, a study of religion, and a pamphlet advocating the cause of the Indians, as well as her antislavery pieces. After David died in 1874 at the age of eighty, she lovingly compiled a memoir of their life together, composed of extracts from their letters and diaries and knit together with her commentary. She breezed over her years in New York as a time when "pecuniary necessities compelled us to labor far apart from each other. I throw a veil over all these sad memories." She included his touching appreciations of her, and her recollection of him as "the most loving husband God ever bestowed upon woman. In his old age he was as affectionate and devoted as he was when he was the lover of my youth; nay, he manifested even more tenderness." Despite their mutual love, his fecklessness continued to the end, with the result that he left her nothing. But she was used to that. She wrote her sister-in-law: "My good, darling David was the kindest, best soul alive; but the fact is, he never had any business-faculty. It was a marvel to everybody, who knew him, that a man so intelligent, so learned, so capable, so energetic, and so industrious, was *always* in pecuniary difficulty." It was she who had supported them both on her earnings.

After David's death, Child escaped from the lonely house in Wayland for part of the year and began spending her winters in Boston. She continued to write and publish, including a eulogy for her old friend William Lloyd Garrison, who died in 1879. The following year, at age seventy-eight, she died of a heart attack in Wayland. Another old abolitionist friend, Wendell Phillips, remembered how she had been "ready to die for a principle and starve for an idea; nor think to claim any merit for it! . . . A dear lovable woman. . . . We feel we have lost one who would have stood by us in trouble, a shield. She was the kind of woman one would choose to represent woman's entrance into broader life."

There were no eulogies, newspaper tributes, or crowds of mourners to mark the death of Henry Ballard, when it came. He left New York on Saturday, January 20, the day after the verdict, possibly frightened by the violent threats of his assailant's supporters. He may also have been alarmed by suggestions in the press that he would be prosecuted for the abortions he had been party to. He took a boat for Bridgeport, Connecticut, and by

Sunday he was in New Haven, where he kept to himself but excited suspicion when he signed a hotel register with his own name. Early Monday morning he left for Hartford, probably on his way to Boston.

The importing business Henry ran with his brother Francis in New York continued after Amelia Norman's trial, but it seems that Francis, now living in Brooklyn, ran it while Henry stayed in Boston. By 1850 Henry Ballard had a business address on Washington Street in Boston, where the Ballard family businesses were, although he seems to have worked for one of these businesses rather than owning one himself. That year, at the age of thirty-seven, he died of erysipelas, an infectious disease. C.C.B., the poet who imagined that Amelia Norman would "perish like a down-trod leaf," believed that Ballard's future would be one in which "every sail of prosperous life unfurled." The poet failed to take into account the murderous democracy of infection, which did not care at all who was the seducer and who was the seduced.

What happened to Amelia Norman? In October 1845 the press belatedly located her in the job Child had found for her a year and a half earlier, despite the secrecy she was trying to maintain. They reported that she was "now in a country town in Massachusetts, acting in the capacity of housekeeper in the family of a gentleman of high respectability," helping to care for his wife who was "afflicted with a long illness." They noted that Norman was behaving well: "acting with great propriety," and "much respected in her situation." They must not have found out exactly where she was, or what name she used, because if they had learned these things they certainly would have told. This flurry of attention may have alarmed Norman and Child, since by December 1845 Child was once again casting around for a new job for Norman.

Child had heard that her friend Maria White Lowell and her husband, poet James Russell Lowell, were planning to go to Europe in the spring and hoped they would be willing to take Norman along as a waiting maid. Child told Lowell that Norman was having "certain difficulties" with her health and that her doctors recommended a voyage. "I am therefore desirous to have her go to Europe as a waiting-maid, for one or two years, preparatory to learning a trade, for a dependence in her declining years." As it turned out, Child's information about the Lowells' plans was wrong. Maria Lowell, who gave birth to her first child just days after Child wrote this letter, did not go to Europe that spring, and there is no evidence that the Lowells ever hired Amelia Norman. Child's letters contain no trace of any further effort to place Norman.

In 1851 Peter Norman made his will (his motivation was probably not the onset of debility; in his mid-seventies Peter was still a working farmer, and his two youngest children had still to be born). He remembered his errant daughter, but the will does not reveal if he was in touch with her or knew where she was; if anything, it suggests he had lost track of her. He listed his three married daughters, Phebe, Jane, and Harriet, together with their husbands, but he listed Amelia with her maiden name, as he did his youngest daughters, Rebecca and Mary, both of whom were still unmarried. If he knew the name she used he did not mention it—an important oversight, since without it, the executor of his estate would have had trouble finding her. There was no confusion about the location of Peter's other errant child, Oliver. Convicted for assault and battery in 1847, he was serving a five-year term in the New Jersey State Penitentiary. Peter signed his will with a mark indicating that, like his daughter, he could not write.

Peter Norman died in 1863 at age eight-four. By then he owned his farm, worth approximately $1,500, a bond and mortgage owed him by a neighbor, worth $554, and $95 worth of farm and household possessions. These included two cows and two hogs, six bushels of buckwheat, "corn ears in the crib," a plow and a grindstone, and an "old waggon" worth one dollar. After providing for his second wife, Ellen, he chose not to distinguish his two black sheep from the rest of his children, specifying that the remainder of his estate should be divided equally among all of them, "share and share alike."

Amelia Norman may have disappeared into private life under a new name, but her moment in public continued to live in print. In 1845 Margaret Fuller mentioned Norman in her influential book, *Woman in the Nineteenth Century*. Specifically, she commended her friend Child for her "straight-forward nobleness, undeterred by custom or cavil from duty towards an injured sister," and for her success in "arresting the attention of many who had before shrugged their shoulders, and let sin pass as necessarily a part of the company of men. They begin to ask whether virtue is not possible, perhaps necessary, to man as well as to woman." She predicted, "This is a crisis. The results of this case will be important."

Others were less high-minded. In 1846 the *American Phrenological Journal* used Norman's "fiendish daring" on the Astor House steps as an example of "what enraged woman will dare and do." Three years later the novelist George Thompson used Amelia Norman to make a similar point when he included her as a character in *The Countess; or Memoirs of Women of Leisure. Being a Series of Intrigues with the Bloods, and a Faithful Delineation of the Private Frailties of Our First Men.* Thompson's conceit was that a criminal secret society of women originating in ancient Rome had resurrected itself in nineteenth-century New York as the "Daughters of Venus—Empire City Division." Thompson's narrator insinuates himself into a midnight meeting of the society, held in a room titillatingly decorated with pornographic artworks, in a building "in full view of the Park, and in close proximity to the famed Astor House." To heighten his readers' excitement Thompson made the society's eight members real women, among them Madame Restell and Amelia Norman.

Thompson was a practitioner of the city-mystery genre initiated by Eugène Sue, whose *Mysteries of Paris* enthralled legions of readers during Amelia Norman's trial. Like Sue, Thompson was a champion of the poor and oppressed. He also styled himself a supporter of the rights of women: "Is that respect given her which her intrinsic value demands—her mind consulted, or the dictates of her reason followed beyond the threshold of the social circle? We think not," he wrote in *The Countess.* Thompson's feminism, however, was filtered through his sensational and pornographic style. He painted the Daughters of Venus as both sexually voracious and terrifyingly vengeful, responsible for "murders, robberies, and, in fact, all the most heinous offences in the statute book," the perpetrators of "deeds, daring in the extreme." These deeds, Thompson argued, "will prove to any reader, who has a shadow of susceptibility in his mind, that woman's pride and jealousy are omnipotent, and can only be appeased by being gratified."

Another courtroom character of the 1840s who was remembered in fiction was Singleton Mercer. George Lippard, another city-mystery author, adapted Mercer's story in *The Quaker City: or, The Monks of Monk Hall.* The novel began appearing serially in the fall of 1844 and was subsequently adapted into a play and a book. When the play was scheduled to open in the Chestnut Street Theater in Philadelphia in the fall of 1844, Mercer, taking offense at his portrayal, attacked the theater's billposter and tried to start a riot by buying up tickets for his friends. Fearing violence, the mayor ordered the play withdrawn. Mercer further annoyed the theater manager when he asked for a refund for the tickets.

Norman's story is still remembered by historians, legal and literary scholars, and other authors, in studies of abortion, prostitution, seduction in law and literature, the "unwritten law," female murderers, and in studies and biographies of Lydia Maria Child. Sometimes she appears fleetingly in a footnote; at other times portions of her story are considered at greater length. Not infrequently facts, chronology, and context are slightly distorted—understandable confusions, since the story was originally reported in so many voices, each eagerly forwarding its own point of view.

In 1878 Lydia Maria Child, seventy-six years old, widowed, and living in her last home in Wayland, Massachusetts, suggested, without naming her, that Amelia Norman had come to a bad end. In three cases, Child wrote her friend Sarah Shaw, she, Child, had "tried the experiment of taking a cast-a-way into my own room for several months. While they were

Figure E.1. In 1913 the Astor House was torn down to make way for the subway. Library of Congress, Prints and Photographs Division, George Grantham Bain Collection.

with me, all went well; but every case proved a failure after they went out into the world to earn their living." She did not name Norman or the other two, but the reference seems clear. "Oh Sarah," the old reformer confessed, "my heart is very weary striving to solve this strange problem of human life." Child may have been right. Or maybe Norman had removed herself out of reach of Child's strangling empathy. Or maybe she died in 1855, as one shaky genealogical source suggests. I wanted to know what happened to her, as maybe, by now, you do too, but no amount of trolling through newspapers and genealogical sources could find her. The afternoon I spent walking through the cemetery at the First Presbyterian Church in Sparta was no more successful. I think that after her moment on the stage, Amelia Norman wanted to go where she could not be found. Let's leave her there.

ACKNOWLEDGMENTS

My biggest debt is to the New-York Historical Society, which in 2006 awarded me a Bernard and Irene Schwartz Postdoctoral Fellowship to begin research for this book. I am also grateful for the fellowship I received in 2008 from the Gilder-Lehrman Institute of American History. Both of these fellowships granted me the precious gifts of time and encouragement at the outset of this project.

This book could not have been written without the resources of the New-York Historical Society, New York Public Library, New York Municipal Archives, Library of Congress, New Jersey State Archives, Sussex County (New Jersey) Historical Society, Baker Library Special Collections at Harvard University Business School, Cornell University Division of Rare and Manuscript Collections, and New York University Library. Digitization of books, newspapers, and archives has transformed historical research in recent years. I could not, for example, have discovered how far Amelia Norman's story spread in the press without digital databases of historical newspapers revealing articles in far-flung papers I would never have thought to look in. I also would not have been able to read so many old, rare, and obscure books at home, in my slippers. All of this is possible because of the work of libraries, over many years, collecting, cataloging, preserving, and, lately, digitizing their collections. Libraries are bastions of our diverse, shared civilizations, and treasure houses of memory and creative expression, without which our cultural lives would be fatally impoverished. Rather than making libraries obsolete, digitization only demonstrates how essential they remain.

I am grateful for the willingness of audiences at the Berkshire Conference of Women Historians, the New-York Historical Society, the New School for Social Research, and the Women's History Discussion Group at the Library of Congress to hear me talk about Amelia Norman, and for their comments.

Thank you to the friends and colleagues who read and commented on drafts of this book or provided other forms of help and encouragement, including Arlene Balkansky, Carol Berkin, Joan Jacobs Brumberg, Chris Carduff, Nathan Dorn, Peter Eisenstadt, Cassandra Good, Gerald Markowitz, John Matteson, Edward Redmond, Stephanie Stillo, Daniele Turello, Daun Van Ee, Victoria Van Hyning, and Kathy Woodrell. Thank you to the readers assigned by Cornell University Press to review this book, Sarah Crosby and Lori Ginzberg, and the anonymous third reader. Thank you to editor Michael McGandy at Cornell University Press for believing in it. I would also like to thank my parents for awakening my interest in the past, long ago.

APPENDIX

Lydia Maria Child's "Letter from New-York No. V"

Lydia Maria Child's most sustained discussion of Amelia Norman appears in one of her "Letters from New-York" as "Letter from New-York No. V." It was published on February 6, 1844, in the *Boston Courier*, then reprinted in the *National Anti-Slavery Standard* on February 22. The *Standard*'s version was notably different from the one that was published in the *Courier*: six angry paragraphs had been cut. Also missing were two poignant sentences about Norman's mysterious baby. Other newspapers reprinted or excerpted "Letter from New-York No. V," but Child's association with the *Standard*, even though she was no longer its editor in 1844, suggests that she made the cuts there herself.

Child became the editor of the *Standard*, the New York–based weekly paper of the American Anti-Slavery Society, in May 1841. She originated her column, Letters from New-York, there that August. She resigned from the *Standard* in May 1843 and by the end of that year moved the Letters column to the *Boston Courier* at the invitation of its editor, Joseph T. Buckingham.

When Child left the *Standard*, her husband, David Lee Child, who had been her assistant editor (probably no more than nominally, since he did not regularly live in New York during this period), took over in her place. But even though she published her "farewell" in May 1843, her name persisted on the masthead until late July, covering for her husband until he arrived in the city in August. The whereabouts of David Child during the fall and winter of 1843 and 1844 are not fully documented, but it appears that after a stint in New York he left the city in January and was still out of town in February. His name was on the *Standard*'s masthead as editor on February 22, 1844, when his wife's "Letter from New-York No. V" appeared in the paper. He might have made the changes, or approved changes that she made. Or she might have been covering for him, as she had before, and made the changes herself.

If Child made the cuts herself, she probably did so as part of her effort to rehabilitate her reputation after the battering it took in the aftermath of the publication in 1833 of *An Appeal in Favor of That Class of Americans Called Africans*, and the redirection of her energies to abolition over the following decade. In January 1843, as she was preparing to leave the *Standard*, she wrote her friend Francis Shaw: "If God spares my life in the coming year, I intend to start afresh in the race, and rebuild my literary reputation." To another friend, the Boston lawyer and abolitionist Ellis Gray Loring, she wrote that spring: "I am exceedingly anxious to get well-established in business connexions here, and make publishers and printers *desirous* to be in connection with me."

As part of this effort to restart her literary career, Child prepared a collection of "Letters from New-York." As she worked on the first edition, which was published just as she exited the *Standard*, in August 1843, she selected carefully, hoping to appeal to as wide an audience as possible. By December 1843, just four months after it was published, the book was sold out (it was just at this time that Joseph Buckingham, editor of the *Courier*, recognizing the column's popularity, asked Child to publish it in his paper). Her strategy of moderation had evidently worked. By February 1844, the same month that both versions of Letter No. V were published, Child had the second edition of her book ready for the publishers. Still showing caution, she excluded "Letter from New-York No. V" from the book.

As Child cut "Letter from New-York No. V" for the *Standard* (if that is what she did) and edited the second edition of *Letters from New York*, Amelia Norman was living with her in the Hoppers' house on Grand Street. Did conversations with her unhappy houseguest influence her as she made these decisions? Child recorded no such conversation, so it is impossible to know.

And Norman's baby? The two, brief sentences Child included in the *Courier* and then cut from the *Standard* read as follows: "It pains her to speak or think of her child. The fountain of maternal love has been poisoned at the source." These words are Child's impression of how Norman felt about her child, but contain no substantive information about the baby's whereabouts or welfare. The child's fate remains a mystery.

The text below is the version of "Letter from New-York No. V" that was published in the *Boston Courier* on February 6, 1844. The cuts made in the letter as it was reprinted in the *National Anti-Slavery Standard* on February 22, 1844, are shown in bold. There are also smaller editorial changes—corrections, removals, and additions of words, hyphens, and punctuation—which I have noted in bold and brackets to make them easier to see. Most of these are trivial, but a few are more substantive. Collectively, they suggest that somebody, probably Child herself, worked over the column carefully before it was reprinted in the *Standard*.

[For the *Courier*]

Letter From New-York
No. V

Unusual excitement has prevailed in this city for a fortnight past, concerning the trial of Amelia Norman for an assault on Henry S. Ballard, with intent to kill. That the prosecutor is a Bostonian by birth, is a fact I would gladly suppress, for the credit of my native city, and for the sake of his worthy and highly respectable parents.

There was a host of witnesses, many of them of the highest respectability, ready to prove that this was a case of deliberate seduction and base desertion. That the poor girl had been subjected to wrongs and insults[,] enough to drive her mad. At the period of her arrest, she was living at the house of a respectable and kind-hearted German, by the name of Behren [*sic*]. He supposed her to be a widow, and hired her to iron shirts for his clothing store [**clothing-store**]; an employment which she would not have been likely to seek, if she had been the abandoned creature Ballard chooses to represent her. The German testified that for several days previous to her arrest, he and his family considered her insane; that she acted in the wildest way, and was evidently quite unconscious what she was doing; that at times, her anguish seemed intolerable, and vented itself in sobs and tears; then she would laugh, by the half hour together, with a mad laughter. Whether she was an accountable being at the moment she committed the desperate deed, and how far she was in a state to be capable of deliberate intent, passes the wisdom of mortals to decide. She herself says: "God alone can judge me, for he alone knows to what a dreadful state of agony and desperation I was driven."

In prison, her despair was most painful to witness. The physician, as he passed and repassed her cell, in the course of his professional duties, often saw her for hours together, lying on the stone floor, sobbing and groaning in mortal agony. I shall never forget her pale and haggard looks, and the utter hopelessness of her tones, when I first saw her in that tomb-like apartment. May I be forgiven, if, at times, I hated law, so unequal in its operation, so crushing in its power. The kind-hearted physician made the most touching representations concerning the state of her health, and his continual fear of suicide. The bail demanded for her temporary release[,] was $5[,]000. Efforts were made to reduce this sum; but Ballard's counsel, aware that her situation excited commiseration, spared no pains to prevent it. Exertions were made to obtain affidavits that she still continued to say she would kill her seducer, if ever she could get at him. But the sympathies of all who approached her were excited in her favor, and the worst thing they could report of her was, that in one of her bitter moods, she said, "she sometimes thought turn about was fair play." Two thirds of the community, nurtured and trained as they are in the law of violence, needed to summon all *their* respect for law and order, to keep from openly expressing sympathy with this opinion. Let them ask themselves what they would have said and done, if they had been situated like her, [;] with all those terrible wrongs eating into her heart and brain, like fire. May this consideration lead no one to excuse or palliate the dreadful crime of murder, but may it teach them, to reflect well on the false structure of society.

William Thom, the Beggar Poet of England, says, with impetuous eloquence:

> "Here let me speak out—and be heard, too, while I tell it—that the world does not at all times know how unsafely it sits: when Despair has loosed honor's last hold upon the heart—when transcendent wretchedness lays weeping Reason in the dust—when every unsympathizing on-looker [on looker] is deemed an enemy—who THEN can limit the consequences? For my own part, I confess that, ever since that dreadful night, I can never hear of an extraordinary criminal, without the wish to pierce through the mere judicial views of his career, under which, I am persuaded, there would often be found to exist an unseen impulse—a chain with one end fixed in nature's holiest ground, that drew him on to his destiny."

The trial was to have commenced on Monday, the 15th. On the preceding Saturday afternoon, the prisoner's counsel announced the necessity of withdrawing his services, in order to attend to another important case, which came on the same day. The idea of transferring her case to a stranger, without time to examine into its merits, proved the drop too much for a spirit that had so long been under the pressure of extreme despondency. The unfortunate girl made preparations for suicide, by braiding a rope from her bed-clothes [bedclothes]. In twenty minutes more, she would have passed beyond the power of human tribunals; but the keeper chanced at that moment to enter her gallery, to summon another prisoner, and discovered her preparations.

Ballard's counsel was extremely desirous to push the case through on Monday. He seemed to calculate that it would be an easy matter to thrust aside this "vile prostitute," as he termed her, and by adroit management of legal technicalities, screen his client from public exposure. But, thank God, human sympathies are warm and active, even amid the malaria of cities. The young friend to whom I dedicated my volume of New-York Letters, whose kindness of heart is only equalled by his energy of purpose, gained the ear of the judges, and earnestly entreated for postponement. He took upon himself the expenses of the trial, trusting Providence for aid. A noble-souled, warm-hearted stranger, a Mr. Kearny, formerly of Boston, [a Mr. Carney, of Boston] though a man of limited means, offered fifty dollars, and went with him to procure the services of David

Graham, Esq. [esq.], one of the ablest lawyers in our criminal courts. The sum was of course much smaller than his usual fee, but he was influenced by higher motives than pecuniary recompense. When he entered upon the case, he was surprised at the amount of respectable testimony in favor of the girl's character, previous to her acquaintance with Ballard. His heart was touched by the story of her wrongs, confirmed as it was by a multitude of witnesses. On the second day of the trial, he wrote me a noble letter, returning the money, for the prisoner's benefit, declaring that this trial involved considerations higher and holier than the relation of lawyer and client. The blessing of God be with him! During four weary days, he exerted himself with watchful vigilance and untiring zeal. His appeal in behalf of outraged womanhood, was a noble burst of heartfelt eloquence, which I shall forever remember with gratitude and admiration.

The case was likewise conducted with great ability on the part of Mr. Sandford, counsel for the prosecution, and a personal friend of Ballard's; but it was a kind of ability from which my open-hearted nature shrinks, as it would from the cunning of the fox, and the subtlety of the serpent. He could not have managed the case as he did, if he had ever had sister or daughter thus betrayed. This consideration abated the indignation which sometimes kindled in my soul, at witnessing so much power exerted against a poor human being, already so crushed and desolate. Moreover, I pitied him for obvious ill-health, for having the management of so bad a cause, and for the almost total absence [want] of sympathy to sustain him in his trying position.

In opening the case, he assured the jury that Amelia Norman was a woman of the town, before Ballard became acquainted with her; that she had decoyed him to her lodgings, and had followed him up with a series of annoying persecutions[,] to obtain money, according to the custom of prostitutes with their poor victims. That on one occasion, she had even gone to his store with an infamous companion, and beat him with their parasols. He did not, however, mention that this companion was another victim of his treacherous client. Having thus blackened the character of the unfortunate prisoner, he contended that no evidence concerning her character or Ballard's should be admitted; that the testimony must be strictly confined to the evening when the stabbing took place. The judge sustained him; and for two days, there was a perpetual fighting with witnesses, to keep the truth out of court. Sandford contended that the jury were to decide solely upon the fact whether the woman assaulted Ballard with intent to kill; and that they had nothing to do with the prior or subsequent history of either of the parties. Graham, on the other hand, urged that it was necessary to prove the wrongs she had suffered, and her consequent state of mind and health, in order to decide upon her intent. There was keen sparring between the lawyers, and the witnesses were sometimes bewildered which to answer. This suppression of evidence, after defaming the character of the girl in such wholesale terms, doubtless produced its effect on the mind of the jury, and somewhat influenced their verdict.

But though Mr. Sandford sprung every way, to stop up any crevice through which the impertinent light might enter, enough did get before the jury, to satisfy them that Amelia Norman had been a virtuous, discreet, amiable and quiet girl, before her acquaintance with Ballard; and that the history of her wrougs [**wrongs**] was no fiction of romance.

The counsel for the prisoner, on his part, described her seducer's character and conduct in terms that must have been any thing [**anything**] but soothing or agreeable to his ear. Mr. Sandford reminded the jury that one lawyer's word was just as much to be believed as another; that it was their duty to be guided only by the evidence. Mr. Graham retorted, "But where is *your* evidence? There stand *our* thirty witnesses, ready to prove every word we have stated, and a good deal more, if the court will only allow them to be heard." And then he distinctly named the witnesses, their occupations, places of residence, &c., with what they *would* testify, if opportunity were given.

It was an adroit game; as exciting to watch, as a skilful game of chess. I never before felt so much intellectual respect, and so much moral aversion, to [**for**] the legal profession.

Mr. Sandford's Biblical arguments evinced much less acuteness than his legal distinctions. While portraying the horrors of murder, he urged the usual plea, that the Divine abhorrence of it was evinced by the requisition of "blood for blood," and he sustained this position, by the mark which God set upon Cain. He apparently forgot that the mark was set upon Cain in order than men should *not* slay him. Unfortunately for the advocates of capital punishment, this is the only case on record, where the direct agency of God was interposed in a case of murder.

Mr. Sandford likewise found the first seducer in the Bible, in the person of our mother Eve, and said the serpent had been busy with the sex ever since. He drew a lively picture of poor innocent men tempted, betrayed, and persecuted by women. This was putting the saddle on the wrong horse, with a vengeance! And he himself afterward implied as much; for he reminded the jury that there were twelve thousand prostitutes in New York [New-York], supported by money that came from our citizens; and added, that *all these prostitutes had the same wrongs to revenge upon some body [somebody]*. He asked the jury whether it would be worse to have the virtue of their daughters ruined, or their young and generous sons brought home stabbed by the hands of prostitutes? [**no question mark in the** *Standard*] If this precedent were established, he feared that strangers visiting New York [New-York] would stumble over the dead bodies of citizens, at the very thresholds of their own doors.

I had no doubt that if all deeply injured women were to undertake to redress their wrongs in this bad way, there would be a huge pile of dead citizens. [I even thought it not impossible that some of the honorable court themselves might be among the missing.] [**brackets switched to parentheses in the** *Standard*] I was aware that ribs all around the room felt unsafe in view of the picture the pleader had drawn. It unquestionably was an argument that came home to men's business and bosoms. Yet I felt no very active pity for their terrors. I indignantly asked what had been done to the twelve thousand men, who made these poor creatures prostitutes? I remembered that strangers visiting our city continually stumbled upon something worse than dead bodies, viz: degraded, ruined souls, in the forms of those twelve thousand prostitutes; and I asked, What do "law and order" do for *them?* Mr. Sandford declared that women could take care of themselves as well as men. Perhaps so; but his twelve thousand facts show that men [**women**] do *not* take care of themselves; and he urged that "generous youth[s]" were continually led astray by this band of prostitutes, though, of course, the temptation must be merely animal, unmingled with the seductive influence of the affections, which so often leads woman to ruin, through the agency of her best impulses.

He said that betrayed women had redress at the civil law. I never hear that assertion without burning indignation. *What* **is the redress for a broken heart, blighted reputation, the desertion of friends, the loss of respectable employment, the scorn and hissing of the world? Why, the woman must acknowledge herself the** *servant* **of somebody, who may claim** *wages* **for her lost time! With indignation and scorn, I appeal to common sense,**

and common justice, against this miserable legal fiction—this impudent assumption that I am a chattel personal. It is a standing insult to woman-kind; and had we not become the slaves we are deemed in law, we should rise *en masse*, in the majesty of moral power, and sweep that contemptible insult from the statute-book.

Let me not be understood as hoping much from penalties. *They* will be cheering to me only as indications of public opinion in the process of regeneration. By attraction, and not by repulsion, must a better state of things be induced. In the mean time, I protest against considering woman a chattel, or a plaything; and I ask men [to] consider well how fearfully this assumption is avenged in their own domestic life, by having mothers, wives, and daughters, who *are* chattels and playthings. Here, and not elsewhere, lies the secret of Mr. Sandford's twelve thousand dangers. He asks "What if they were all armed, and abroad to redress their wrongs?" Alas they *are* armed; and the terrible wreck they make among human souls is more painful to the reflecting mind, than piles of dead bodies. Verily, they *have* their revenge, though "law and order" take no cogni-zance of the fact.

But to return to the trial:[;] Mr. Graham dwelt strongly on the point that unless the jury deemed there was sufficient evidence of deliberate intent, to constitute murder in case the man had died, they were bound to acquit. The jury were doubters [**doubtless**] in a state to go through any legal loophole, that might be opened. The frantic state of the prisoner's mind, so clearly shown in the evidence, seemed to them too nearly akin to insanity to be easily distinguished. The inequality of the laws roused their sense of justice, and probably made them feel that a verdict of guilty would be like tying down the stones and letting the mad dogs loose. They felt little anxiety to protect Ballard, by sending his victim to Sing Sing, that he might feel safe to prowl about after other daughters and sisters of honest families. The popular indignation, which was with difficulty sup-pressed by a strong constabulary force, showed plainly enough that the public would like to say to them—

> "I beseech you,
> Wrest once the law to your authority;
> To do a great right do a little wrong;
> And cure this cruel devil of his will."

I believe they strove to resist this magnetic influence, and to return such a verdict as they honestly believed the testimony in the case rendered lawful. When the foreman pronounced the words "Not Guilty!" the building shook with such a thunder of applause as I never before heard. Some of the very officers appointed to keep order [,] involuntarily let their tip-staffs fall on the floor, and clapped with the multitude. It was the surging of long-repressed sympathies coming in like a roaring sea.

There is now, as usual in such cases, a counter current setting in. Uncontrollable pity has had its way, and now men begin to talk of law and order, dangerous predecedents, &c. Let the kind-hearted jurymen indulge no regrets. The moral influence of their decision will be good rather than evil. Society needs regenerating on the subject of women's defenceless position, and this trial will do much toward it. Should any of the jurors survive this unfortunate girl, I trust that her purified spirit will hover round their dying bed, in robes of light, and at heaven's gate whisper to the recording angel, "Here is one of those who said to me, Go thy way, and sin no more."

I am by no means deaf to the plea for the preservation of law and order. My compassion for the prisoner's wrongs has never for a moment blinded me to the guilt of revenge. But legislators may rest assured that law will yield, like a rope of sand, [comma removed] before the influence of humane sentiments, in cases of this kind, until the laws are better regulated. Seduction is going on by wholesale, with a systematic arrangement, and a number and variety of agents, which would astonish those who have never looked beneath the hypocritical surface of things. In our cities, almost every girl, in the humbler classes of life, walks among snares and pitfalls [pitfalls] at every step, unconscious of their presence, until she finds herslf [herself] fallen, and entangled in a frightful net-work, from which she sees no escape. Life and property are protected, but what protection is there for pure hearts, confiding souls, and youthful innocence?

Another difficulty arises in these cases. Our institutions, and our opinions, are incongruous, mismated, sometimes antagonistical; and therefore men become tangled in their own contradictions. The law of violence has been grafted on the gospel of peace, under the imposing name of church and state. It is considered noble for nations to revenge wrongs by bloodshed, even when those wrongs amount to nothing more than obstructions to trade. Men fight duels, for real or imagined insults, and so large a class

of the community palliate the deed, that it is extremely difficult to enforce any penalty for the broken law.

When Mercer killed Heberton for seducing his sister, the community sustained him almost by acclamation; and this was a legitimate result of the universal teaching, which endorses retaliation and violence under the name of the law of honor. If revenge is ever to be excused, what circumstances can be imagined so extenuating, as those which exist in the case of a virtuous girl seduced, deserted, and insulted? Man cannot inflict on *man* any injury, any provocation, to be compared with hers. Considerations like these have led some of the New-York editors to excuse the course taken by Amelia Norman, even if she were at the time in possession of a sane mind. "She had no brother to avenge her wrongs," say they, "and who can wonder that she took redress into her own hands?" I abhor this conclusion, because I abhor the premises. *All* revenge is crime, all violence is of the devil. But if society approves of it in return for lesser evils, they cannot avoid confusion and entanglement, while trying to prevent it in return for aggravated wrongs.

During the two first days of the trial, Ballard was brought into court, by subpoena from the prisoner's counsel, and they took mischievous satisfaction in calling him forward when the court opened. But forward he would *not* come. He hid behind stove-pipes [**stove pipes**], and skulked in corners. This was, perhaps, a prudent measure, for the populace were in that excited state[,] that it might have been unsafe for him to have been generally recognized. As he passed out of court, the citizens around the door would call out, "Don't come too near us! It is as much as we can do to keep our canes and umbrellas off your shoulders." The expressions were rude, but the sentiment which dictated them was noble. I hope I have not spoken too harshly of this individual. I certainly wish him nothing worse than he has brought upon himself. What can be more pitiful than the old age of a seducer, going unmourned to his grave, with the remembered curses of his victims? What more painful than the consciousness of such a return to all a mother's love, and a mother's prayers? What penalty more severe than the loss of those pure domestic affections, which he has so wantonly desecrated? What punishment equal to the recollections of his dying bed? God pity him! For him, too, there is a return path to his [**our**] Father's mansion; would that he might be persuaded to enter it.

The conduct of the prisoner, during the trial, was marked by a beautiful propriety. Sad and subdued, she made no artificial appeals to sympathy, and showed no disposition to consider herself a heroine of romance. When the verdict was given, she became very faint and dizzy, and for some time after seemed stunned and bewildered. Her health is much shattered by physical suffering and mental excitement; but her constitution is naturally good, and under the influence of care and kindness[,] the process of renovation goes rapidly on. She is evidently a girl of strong feelings, but quiet, reserved, and docile to the influence of those she loves. A proper education would have made of her a noble woman. I sometimes fear that, like poor Fleur de Marie, she will never be able to wash from her mind the "stern inexorable P[p]ast." **It pains her to speak or think of her child. The fountain of maternal love has been poisoned at the source.** I shall never forget the mournful smile with which she said, "I don't know as it is worth while to try to make anything of me. I am nothing but a wreck." "Nay, Amelia," replied I, "noble vessels may be built from the timbers of a wreck."

The more I see of her, the more my hope is strengthened, that her native energies and strong affections may be restored and purified, to aid and bless society, instead of being returned a danger and a curse, as she probably would have been had she been sent to Sing Sing. As for a pardon, in case an unfavorable verdict had been rendered, I had little hope that it would have been obtained, though Mr. Sandford held out that idea to the jury. The strenuous effort to make her appear a great deal worse than she ever was, assuredly did not proceed entirely from a regard to public order. Ballard had friends likely to exert a strong influence with the ruling powers; and their active opposition to her being released for awhile on bail, showed that it would be no fault of theirs, if she were not safely locked up in prison for a long time.

The public sympathy manifested in this case[,] has cheered my hopes, and increased my respect for human nature. When the poor girl returned to her cell, after her acquittal, some of the judges, several of the jury, her lawyers, and the officers of the prison, all gathered round her to express congratulation and sympathy. There was something beautiful in the compassionate respect with which they treated this erring sister, because she was unfortunate and wretched. I trust that no changes of politics will ever dismiss Dr. Macready [*sic*], the physician of the Tombs, or Mr. Fallon, the keeper. I shall always bless them; not merely for their kindness to this poor girl, but for the tenderness of heart, which leads them to treat all the prisoners under their care with as much gentleness as possible. May the foul moral atmosphere of the place never stifle their kind impulses.

The hours I spent in that hateful building, awaiting the opening of this case, were very sad to me. It was exceedingly painful to see poor ragged beggars summarily dismissed to the penitentiary, for petty larcenies; having the strong conviction, ever present in my mind, that all society is carrying on a great system of fraud and theft, and that these poor wretches merely lacked the knowledge and cunning necessary to keep theirs under legal protection.

The Egyptian architecture, with its monotonous recurrence of the straight line and the square, its heavy pillars, its cavernous dome of massive rings, its general expression of overpowering strength, is well suited to a building for such a purpose. But the graceful palm leaves, intertwined with lotus blossoms, spoke soothingly to me of the occasional triumph of the moral sentiments over legal technicalities, and of beautiful bursts of eloquence from the heart. Moreover, I remembered that time had wrought such changes in opinion, that thousands of convents had been converted into manufactories and primary schools; and I joyfully prophesied the day when regenerated society would have no more need of prisons. The Tombs, with its style of architecture too subterranean for picture galleries or concert rooms, may then be reserved for fossil remains and mineralogical cabinets.

L.M.C.

ABBREVIATIONS

CC   *The Collected Correspondence of Lydia Maria Child, 1817–1880*. Edited by Patricia G. Holland, Milton Meltzer, and Francine Krasno, associate editor. Millwood, NY: Kraus Microform, 1980.

LMC   Lydia Maria Child

LNY   "Letter from New-York." These letters are numbered: e.g., "Letter from New-York No. V" is "LNY5."

SL   *Lydia Maria Child, Selected Letters, 1817–1880*. Edited by Milton Meltzer and Patricia G. Holland. Amherst: University of Massachusetts Press, 1982.

NOTES

Prologue

1   *On November 1, 1843*: *New York Weekly Express*, November 3, 1843; *New York Morning Express*, November 2, 1843; [James Gordon Bennett], "The Case of Amelia Norman and Ballard—the Crime of Seduction," *New York Herald*, January 19, 1844; *Herald*, January 17, 1844. The portrait appeared in the *Herald* on January 18. Since nearly every article about Norman's trial was titled "Trial of Amelia Norman," or "General Sessions," I will cite these by paper title and date only, unless there is a reason to distinguish one of them. In the nineteenth century neither articles nor editorials were signed, but as the paper's editor, Bennett wrote the editorials—and his tone is unmistakable.

2   *"go and get her living"*: *New York Post*, *New York Sun*, *New York Tribune*, January 17, 1844, and George Wilkes, *Mysteries of the Tombs: A Journal of Thirty Days Imprisonment in the New York City Prison for Libel* (New York, 1844), 42. The newspapers give different dates for this exchange: The *Sun* puts it at October 8, the *Post* on the night of November 1.

2   *"the vengeance of a woman"*: *New York Herald*, November 2, 1843.

2   *The trial of Amelia Norman attracted*: *New York Herald*, January 17, 1844; *New York Tribune*, January 18, 20, 1844; *New York Tribune*, January 20, 1844; *Charleston (SC) Southern Patriot*, January 24, 1844. Courtroom capacity: Richard G. Carrott, *The Egyptian Revival: Its Sources, Monuments, and Meaning, 1808–1858* (Berkeley: University of California Press, 1978), 167.

2   *"so great was the public interest"*: Opening Speech of John Graham, Esq., to the Jury on the Part of the Defence, on the Trial of Daniel E. Sickles in the Criminal Court of the District of Columbia, Judge Thomas H. Crawford, Presiding, April 9th and 11th, 1859 (New York: T. R. Dawley, [1859]), 71. John Graham was the brother of David Graham Jr., one of Norman's lawyers.

3   *After her trial*: The connection between David Graham and the modification of New York's seduction tort was first made by Andrea L. Hibbard and John T. Parry in their article "Law, Seduction, and the Sentimental Heroine: The Case of Amelia Norman," *American Literature* 78 (June 2006): 325–355. Before this book, Hibbard and Parry's article was the only work devoted to Norman since the time of her trial.

3   *Two very different voices*: Patricia Cline Cohen, Timothy J. Gilfoyle, and Helen Lefkowitz Horowitz, *The Flash Press: Sporting Male Weeklies in 1840s New York* (Chicago: University of Chicago Press, 2008), 1, 40–46; Donna Dennis, *Licentious Gotham: Erotic Publishing and Its Prosecution in Nineteenth-Century New York* (Cambridge, MA: Harvard University Press, 2009), 52–58, 80–82, 88–89; Helen Lefkowitz Horowitz, *Rereading Sex: Battles over Sexual Knowledge and Suppression in Nineteenth-Century America* (New York: Knopf, 2002), 179–191; Alexander Saxton, "George Wilkes: The Transformation of a Radical Ideology," *American Quarterly* 33 (Autumn 1981): 437–458. Wilkes recorded his observations of Amelia Norman in his prison memoir, *Mysteries of the Tombs*, 42, 64. On the transforming economy and its effect on workingmen in this era see Sean Wilentz, *Chants Democratic: New York City and the Rise of the American Working Class, 1788–1850* (New York: Oxford University Press, 1988), on Walsh, 327–335. On working-class masculinity in nineteenth-century New York, in addition to Wilentz, see Joshua R. Greenberg, *Advocating the Man: Masculinity, Organized Labor, and the Household in New York, 1800–1840* (New York: Columbia University Press, 2008). On manhood and masculinity in the nineteenth-century United States, Michael S. Kimmel, *Manhood in America: A Cultural History* (New York: Oxford University Press, 2006), and E. Anthony Rotundo, *American Manhood: Transformations in Masculinity from the Revolution to the Modern Era* (New York: Basic Books, 1993).

4   *In her "Letter from New-York"*: Lydia Maria Child, "Letter from New-York No. V," February 6, 1844, *Boston Courier*, and February 22, 1844, *National Anti-Slavery Standard*. I will hereafter refer to Lydia Maria Child as LMC and the "Letters from New-York" as LNY; this one will be LNY5.

4   Fact and Fiction: Lydia Maria Child: *Fact and Fiction* (New York: C. S. Francis, 1846).

4   *Novelists, including Edgar Allan Poe*: Amy Gilman Srebnick, *The Mysterious Death of Mary Rogers: Sex and Culture in Nineteenth-Century New York* (New York: Oxford University Press, 1995); Daniel Stashower, *The Beautiful Cigar Girl: Mary Rogers, Edgar Allan Poe, and the Invention of Murder* (New York: Dutton, 2006). For the interconnections between public interest in trials and crime and the development of the detective novel in the 1840s see Daniel A. Cohen, *Pillars of Salt, Monuments of Grace: New England Crime Literature and the Origins of Popular Culture, 1674–1860* (New York: Oxford University Press, 1993); Karen Halttunen, *Murder Most Foul: The Killer in the American Gothic Imagination* (Cambridge, MA: Harvard University Press, 1998); David S. Reynolds, *Beneath the American Renaissance: The Subversive Imagination in the Age of Emerson and Melville* (New York: Knopf, 1988). See also Simon Schama, *Dead Certainties (Unwarranted Speculations)* (New York: Knopf, 1991).

5   *George Wilkes read and admired*: Wilkes, who read *Mysteries of Paris* in jail, wrote of
     Sue: "The descriptions of the author are masterly, and the effects of imprisonment are
     depicted with an almost omnipotent pencil." *Mysteries of the Tombs*, 33.

5   *The penny press*: James L. Crouthamel, "The Newspaper Revolution in New York,
     1830–1860," *New York History* 45 (April 1964): 91–113.

5   *"beautiful female corpse"*: Patricia Cline Cohen, *The Murder of Helen Jewett: The
     Life and Death of a Prostitute in Nineteenth-Century New York* (New York: Vintage
     Books, 1998), 16.

5   *circulation jumped*: James L. Crouthamel, *Bennett's New York Herald and the Rise of
     the Popular Press* (Syracuse, NY: Syracuse University Press, 1989), 30. For Bennett and
     the *Herald* see also Oliver Carlson, *The Man Who Made News: James Gordon Bennett*
     (New York: Duell, Sloane, and Pearce, 1942); Crouthamel, "James Gordon Bennett,
     the *New York Herald*, and the Development of Newspaper Sensationalism," *New York
     History* 54 (July 1973): 294–316; Crouthamel, "The Newspaper Revolution in New
     York, 1830–1860," *New York History* 45 (April 1964): 91–113. For Jewett: Cohen,
     Murder of Helen Jewett. George Wilkes also cashed in on interest in Jewett, although
     more than a decade later: George Wilkes, *The Lives of Helen Jewett and Richard P.
     Robinson* (New York, 1849).

6   *Bennett initially sympathized*: Cohen, *Murder of Helen Jewett*, 302, 364; "The At-
     tempt at Murder in Broadway," *New York Herald*, November 3, 1843; "The Case
     of Amelia Norman and Ballard—the Crime of Seduction," *New York Herald*, Janu-
     ary 19, 1844.

6   *When she was asked to sign*: "The People vs. Amelia Norman, November 23, 1843"
     (indictment and witness interviews), District Attorney Indictment Records, New York
     County, MN 5221, Roll 221, Municipal Archives, Department of Records and Infor-
     mation Services, New York, NY. On sign literacy: Linda K. Kerber, *Women of the Re-
     public: Intellect and Ideology in Revolutionary America* (Chapel Hill: University of
     North Carolina Press, 1980), 164.

7   *Amelia Norman's story*: This book owes a lot to a series of wonderful recent and
     not-so-recent biographies of unknown women, and to the overlapping tradition of
     "microhistory," which focuses on the lives of ordinary people to draw bigger con-
     clusions about their worlds. For example: Robert Darnton, *The Great Cat Massacre
     and Other Episodes in French Cultural History* (New York: Basic Books, 1984); Nat-
     alie Zemon Davis, *The Return of Martin Guerre* (Cambridge, MA: Harvard Univer-
     sity Press, 1983); John Demos, *The Unredeemed Captive: A Family Story from Early
     America* (New York: Knopf, 1994); Carlo Ginzberg, *The Cheese and the Worms: The
     Cosmos of a Sixteenth-Century Miller* (Baltimore: Johns Hopkins University Press,
     1980); Jill Lepore, *Book of Ages: The Life and Opinions of Jane Franklin* (New York:
     Knopf, 2013); Jean Strouse, *Alice James* (Boston: Houghton Mifflin, 1980); Laurel
     Thatcher Ulrich, *A Midwife's Tale: The Life of Martha Ballard, Based on Her Diary,
     1785–1812* (New York: Knopf, 1990). Patricia Cline Cohen's *The Murder of Helen
     Jewett: The Life and Death of a Prostitute in Nineteenth-Century New York* (New
     York: Vintage Books, 1999) brilliantly describes the world that Amelia Norman also
     inhabited.

8   *"This is a crisis"*: Margaret Fuller, *Woman in the Nineteenth Century*, ed. Made-
     leine B. Stern (Columbia: University of South Carolina Press, 1980), 134–135. Lydia
     Maria Child and Elizabeth Cady Stanton voiced the same sentiment. In 1843, before
     she met Norman, Child wrote, "Would it not be an improvement for men also to be

scrupulously pure in manners, conversation and life? . . . Whatsoever can be named as loveliest, best, and most graceful in woman, would likewise be good and graceful in man" (LNY34, February 16 and 23, 1843, in *A Lydia Maria Child Reader*, ed. Carolyn L. Karcher (Durham, NC: Duke University Press, 1997), 359. Stanton, at the first women's rights conference at Seneca Falls, New York, in 1848, said, "I would not have woman be less pure, but I would have man more so. I would have the same code of morals for both": see "Address Delivered at Seneca Falls," July 19, 1848, in *The Elizabeth Cady Stanton–Susan B. Anthony Reader*, ed. Ellen Carol DuBois (Boston: Northeastern University Press, 1981), 30.

1. I Am Murdered

9   *On the evening of October 31*: Joel Behrend's observations of events on October 31 and November 1, 1843, are from his testimony at Amelia Norman's trial, "Case of Amelia Norman," *New York Tribune*, and "Trial of Amelia Norman for Assault and Battery with Intent to Kill Henry S. Ballard," (both) *New York Herald*, January 19, 1844. Joel Behrend was born in Germany and naturalized in the United States in 1842: *Index to Petitions for Naturalization Filed in New York City, 1792–1989*, November 7, 1842, Common Pleas Court, New York County, vol. 32, Record Number 57, accessed December 16, 2010, www.ancestry.com.

10   *"she rubbed the cotton"*: The metal plates of daguerreotypes, one of the earliest types of photograph, were polished before they were sensitized in preparation for receiving an image. Robert Taft, *Photography and the American Scene: A Social History, 1839–1889* (New York: Dover, 1964), 3–8. See also "Daguerreotypes," Library of Congress, http://memory.loc.gov/ammem/daghtml/daghome.html. In his testimony at Norman's trial, Behrend describes a little servant boy in the household taking pictures of Norman: *New York Herald*, January 19, 1844. These images, if they existed, are lost.

10   *That same evening*: When they were interviewed at Norman's indictment, Henry and Francis Ballard both gave their address as 15 Warren Street: "The People vs. Amelia Norman, November 23, 1843," District Attorney Indictment Records, New York County, MN 5221, Roll 221, Municipal Archives, Department of Records and Information Services, New York, NY. Overcoat: *New York Herald*, January 17, 1844. Weather: "The Democracie in the Park," *New York Herald*, November 2, 1843.

11   *Bustling along*: For the advance of Broadway and its bustle see Gloria Deák, *Picturing New York: The City from Its Beginnings to the Present* (New York: Columbia University Press, 2000), 163–184; [John Disturnell], *Guide to the City of New York; Containing an Alphabetical Listing of Streets &c.* (New York: J. Disturnell, 1836), 4; [Asa Green], *A Glance at New York* (New York: A. Green, 1837), 3–5; Anne Royall, *Sketches of History, Life, and Manners in the United States, by a Traveller* (New Haven, CT: Printed for the author, 1826), 241–268.

11   *"No stint of omnibuses"*: Charles Dickens, *American Notes for General Circulation* (1842; London: Penguin Books, 1985), 128–130.

12   *"Poverty, wretchedness"*: Dickens, *American Notes*, 136. The tour of the underworld in which the author stepped outside of the narrative to offer himself as a guide to the reader was a common literary device in nineteenth-century novels and city guidebooks. See "The Virgilian Invitation," in Eric Homberger, *Scenes from the Life of a City: Corruption and Conscience in Old New York* (New Haven, CT: Yale University Press, 1994), 30–37.

12   *"Fashionable, aristocratic Broadway!"*: George G. Foster, *New York by Gas-Light and Other Urban Sketches by George G. Foster*, ed. Stuart M. Blumin (Berkeley: University of California Press, 1990), 70.

12   *Visible seepage*: Comparisons between the dark and light sides of nineteenth-century cities were a frequently used literary device. "Lights and shadows," "darkness and daylight," and "mysteries and miseries" appeared in the titles of novels and city guidebooks in this period. For example: Ned Buntline [E. Z. C. Judson], *The Mysteries and Miseries of New York: A Story of Real Life* (New York: Bedford, 1847); Helen Campbell, *Darkness and Daylight; or, Lights and Shadows of New York Life* (Hartford, CT: Hartford Publishing Co., 1895); James D. McCabe Jr., *Lights and Shadows of New York Life; or, The Sights and Sensations of the Great City* (Philadelphia: National, 1872; reprint, New York: Farrar, Straus and Giroux, 1970). Lydia Maria Child mocked these "vituperative alliterations, such as magnificence and mud, finery and filth, diamonds and dirt, bullion and brass-tape, &c. &c.," LMC, LNY1, August 19, 1841, in *Letters from New-York*, ed. Bruce Mills (Athens: University of Georgia Press, 1998), 9.

12   *brothels masquerading*: On prostitution see Patricia Cline Cohen, *Murder of Helen Jewett* (New York: Vintage Books, 1998); Timothy J. Gilfoyle, *City of Eros: New York City, Prostitution, and the Commercialization of Sex, 1790–1920* (New York: W. W. Norton, 1992); Marilynn Wood Hill, *Their Sisters' Keepers: Prostitution in New York City, 1830–1870* (Berkeley: University of California Press, 1993).

13   *Dickens, no admirer*: Dickens, *American Notes*, 130.

13   *The speculator*: On urban deceptions see Karen Halttunen, *Confidence Men and Painted Women: A Study of Middle-Class Culture in America, 1830–1870* (New Haven, CT: Yale University Press, 1982).

13   *At four o'clock*: "The Democrats in the Park" and "The Great Meeting of the Locofocos in the Park Yesterday," *New York Herald*, November 2, 1843; "The Election Tomorrow," *New York Herald*, November 6, 1843; Robert Ernst, "The One and Only Mike Walsh," *New-York Historical Society Quarterly* 36 (January 1952): 47–48. On the transformation of the Democratic Party in the Jacksonian era see Daniel Walker Howe, *What God Hath Wrought: The Transformation of America, 1815–1848* (New York: Oxford University Press, 2007); Arthur Schlesinger Jr., *The Age of Jackson* (Boston: Little, Brown, 1945); Sean Wilentz, *Chants Democratic: New York City and the Rise of the American Working Class, 1788–1850* (New York: Oxford University Press, 1984).

13   *The meeting, whose estimated size*: According to the *New York Herald* it was twelve thousand: "The Great Meeting of the Locofocos in the Park Yesterday," November 2, 1843. The *New York Morning Express*, the same day, gave the number as five thousand.

13   *"dense mass of human beings"*: "The Great Meeting of the Locofocos," *New York Herald*, November 2, 1843.

14   *But it was the workingmen*: Richard McCormick, "Suffrage Classes and Party Alignments: A Study in Voter Behavior," *Mississippi Valley Historical Review* 46 (December 1959): 404; Kirk H. Porter, *A History of Suffrage in the United States* (Chicago: University of Chicago Press, 1918), 55–68; Alexander Keyssar, *The Right to Vote: The Contested History of Democracy in the United States* (New York: Basic Books, 2000), 24. The New York constitutional convention of 1821, which dropped property requirements for white men, paradoxically, after much debate, allowed black men to vote only if they owned property worth $250. Porter, *History of Suffrage*, 67–68.

14   *Using language*: "The Great Meeting of the Locofocos in the Park Yesterday," *New York Herald*, November 2, 1843. By this time the mayor was Robert H. Morris (Moses King, *King's Handbook of New York City* [Boston: Moses King, 1892], 234), not Elijah Purdy, who interacted twice with Amelia Norman, first as acting mayor in the summer of 1843, and then as one of the judges who presided at her trial.

14   *"immense mass," the "magnificent mob"*: "The Democracts in the Park," *New York Herald*, November 2, 1843.

15   *Ascending the platform*: "The Great Meeting of the Locofocos in the Park Yesterday," *New York Herald*, November 2, 1843.

15   *The following day*: "The Great Meeting of the Locofocos in the Park Yesterday," and "Horrible Attempt at Murder in Broadway," *New York Herald*, November 2, 1844. [Mike Walsh], "Trial of Amelia Norman," *Subterranean*, January 20, 1844, 222; "Acquittal of Amelia Norman," *Subterranean*, January 27, 1844, 228–229.

15   *When Ballard reached the intersection*: Several years later novelist Ned Buntline imagined a similar meeting at the same intersection, where a group of "fashionable young *gentlemen* of the 'first families'" accost a young prostitute, characterized by Buntline as "a lily among nettles, or a dove among vultures." Ned Buntline [E. Z. C. Judson], *The Mysteries and Miseries of New York: A Story of Real Life* (New York: Bedford, 1847), 10–11.

15   *"pretended to have something to say"*: Testimony of Henry Ballard, "The People vs. Amelia Norman, November 23, 1843."

15   *The Astor House*: Henry Ballard lived at the Astor House between 1838 and 1842: *Longworth's American Almanac, New-York Register, and City Directory* (New York: Thomas Longworth, 1837–1841). In his testimony William Crummie, the Astor House driver, said, "I have often seen Mr. Ballard there [the Astor House], for a year past" when he was living nearby on Warren Street: *New York Sun*, January 17, 1844. The *Berkshire County Whig* (Pittsfield, MA), February 1, 1844, reported that "Mr. Ballard is a Cedar street merchant, now about 30 years of age, unmarried, and boards at the Astor House."

15   *Where the stone steps*: "The Old Astor House: History Made in Hotel Threatened by Subway," *New York Sun*, May 3, 1913. The Astor House was demolished in 1913.

15   *English traveler*: Isabella Lucy Bird Bishop, *The Englishwoman in America* (London: John Murray, 1856), quoted in Bayrd Still, *Mirror for Gotham: New York as Seen by Contemporaries from Dutch Days to the Present* (New York: Fordham University Press, 1994), 155–156.

16   *When Ballard and Norman reached the Astor House steps*: Testimonies of William Crummie, Samuel Floyd, and John K. Liston, in *New York Express*, January 17, 1844; *New York Herald*, January 17, 1844; *New York Post*, January 18, 1844. On November 1, 1843, the sun set at 4:59 p.m.: *New-York City Directory for 1843 & 1844* (New York: John Doggett Jr., 1843), 6–7. For the phase of the moon on that date see "Phases of the Moon," https://www.timeanddate.com/moon/phases/.

16   *Crummie then saw Norman*: Testimony of William Crummie, *New York Express*, January 17, 1844; *New York Herald*, January 17, 1844. Samuel Floyd mentioned the veil: see *New York Sun*, January 17, 1844.

16   *"That woman"*: Closing statement of Norman's lawyer, John Morrill, *New York Herald*, January 20, 1844.

16   *Witnessing a conversation*: Statement of Samuel Floyd at Norman's indictment, "People vs. Amelia Norman, November 23, 1843." For Floyd's occupation as a commission

merchant: *New York Herald*, January 17, 1844. He lived at 171 South Street: *New-York City Directory for 1844 & 1845* (New York: John Doggett Jr., 1844).

16   *"I am stabbed"*: "Horrible Attempt at Murder in Broadway," *New York Herald*, November 2, 1843. For the "light surtout," or overcoat, that Ballard wore see Samuel Floyd's testimony, *New York Herald*, January 17, 1844. For the profusion of the blood see testimony of Dr. Alexander T. Watson, *New York Express*, January 17, 1844. At Norman's trial in January, witnesses would remember somewhat differently what the two protagonists had said. William Crummie thought Ballard cried "Oh, I'm stabbed": *New York Herald*, January 17, 1844. Samuel Floyd thought he heard Ballard say "She has stabbed me," or "I'm stabbed": *Herald*, January 17, 1844, and at his statement for Norman's indictment, "People vs. Amelia Norman, November 23, 1843."

16   *"ran up and catched her"*: Testimony of William Crummie, *New York Herald*, January 17, 1844.

16   *As he held her*: Testimony of William Crummie, *New York Sun*, January 17, 1844.

17   *"did not seem to be angry"*: Testimony of William Crummie, *New York Sun*, January 17, 1844.

17   '*"Do not hold me"*': Testimony of Samuel Floyd, *New York Herald*, January 17, 1844.

17   *"very pale and languid"*: Testimony of John K. Liston, *New York Herald*, January 19, 1844.

17   *"there were loud exclamations"*: Testimony of John K. Liston, *New York Post*, January 18, 1844, and *New York Herald*, January 19, 1844.

17   *"a little excitement"*: Testimony of William Crummie, *New York Sun*, January 17, 1844.

17   *"sorry she had not killed him"*: Testimony of William Crummie, *New York Herald*, January 17, 1844.

17   *all he could do with her*: Testimony of William Crummie, *New York Express*, January 17, 1844. Crummie said "That was all I could do with her." I've changed the pronoun.

17   *"what sized knife"*: *New York Express*, November 3, 1843. At the time of the crime, and later at the trial, Norman's remark was reported variably by the *New York Herald*: "I can't kill the d—d Yankee, any how," *Herald*, November 2, 1843; "sorry she had not killed the damned Yankee," *Herald*, January 17, 1844.

2. Jersey Maid and Damn Yankee

18   *Amelia Norman was born*: At her indictment in November 1843, Norman gave her age as twenty-five: "The People vs. Amelia Norman, November 23, 1843," District Attorney Indictment Records, New York County, MN 5221, Roll 221, Municipal Archives, Department of Records and Information Services, New York, NY. A Norman family genealogy gives no birth date, but places her after a sister, Harriet Norman Osborne, who was born around 1812, according to the United States Census for 1850, where her age is listed as thirty-eight, and a brother, John, who was born around 1820, according to "John Norman," Ancestry, Library, accessed September 2, 2015, http://trees.ancestrylibrary.com/tree/38887313/person/19399082007. William E. Mecabe, *A History of the Norman Family of Northern New Jersey* (Watertown, CT: W. H. Mecabe, 1958), 9. Mecabe gives Norman's name as "Amena" and cites her father's will as the source. Peter Norman's will: March 31, 1853, filed April 15, 1863, Surrogate Court, Sussex County, New Jersey, 3248S, New Jersey State Archives, Trenton. Of Amelia, Mecabe writes (45) that "nothing more is

known than that she is mentioned in her father's will in 1855," evidence of her early departure from the family, and possibly their shame about her notoriety. Oliver is listed in Mecabe, *Norman Family*, 9, 47, but, as with Amelia, Mecabe claims nothing is known about him. In 1850 the United States Census (http://www.ancestrylibrary.com) found Oliver Norman in the New Jersey State Penitentiary in Nottingham, Mercer County, and gave his age as twenty-five, so he was born around 1825. Mecabe, *Norman Family*, 41, gives Charles's birth date as 1809.

18   *On November 3, 1843*: Oliver Norman et al., Petty Larceny, November, 1843, Sussex County Indictments, Court of Common Pleas, box 18, folder 63, New Jersey State Archives, Trenton. In 1842–1843 New York City cartmen earned 31.25 cents for each load of bricks they hauled: David T. Valentine, *Manual of the Corporation of the City of New-York for the Year 1842–1843* (New York: Thomas Snowden, 1842), 61. In 1845 Horace Greeley, editor of the *New York Tribune*, estimated that New York City laborers earned about one dollar per day: quoted in Edward K. Spann, *The New Metropolis: New York City, 1840–1857* (New York: Columbia University Press, 1981), 71.

18   *Less than two weeks later*: Oliver Norman et al., Sussex County Indictments.

19   *Charles, a blacksmith*: Mecabe, *Norman Family*, 41.

20   *Oliver's story*: Oliver's criminal career is documented in Sussex County Court of Common Pleas, Indictments, boxes 4 (1843), 18 (1844), 19 (1847, 1853), 21 (1867), New Jersey State Archives, Trenton. The 1850 United States Census shows him in the New Jersey Penitentiary, Nottingham Township, Mercer County. For contemporary commentary on the Norman family's criminal heritage see "The Parentage of Amelia Norman, with Other Hereditary Facts," *American Phrenological Journal* 6 (June 1844): 157.

20   *Charles, Amelia, and Oliver*: The documentation for Rebecca Chamberlin's history with the two Norman brothers, Amelia's father Peter (1778–1863), and her uncle Oliver (b. 1763) is murky and hard to verify. Mecabe (*Norman Family*, 2) notes that Oliver operated a forge on Norman Pond but claims that he did not marry. An entry for Oliver Norman in Ancestry.com finds that he was born in Orange County, New York, in 1763, married Rebecca Chamberlin (1785–1825) in 1801, was in Muskingum County, Ohio, in 1805, and died there in 1826: http://trees.ancestrylibrary.com/tree/57402899/person/48424322901, accessed September 2, 2015. The story that Oliver moved from New Jersey to Ohio while his wife remained behind and married his brother Peter appears in a March 29, 1998, posting by Helen Nichols Battleson on RootsWeb, Cornish-L Archives, http://archive.rootsweb.ancestry.com/th/read/CORNISH/1998-03/0891215301, accessed September 1, 2015 (now subsumed into Ancestry.com). Entries for Rebecca Chamberlain (Chamberlin is sometimes spelled Chamberlain in the sources) and Oliver Norman in FamilySearch shows Rebecca partnered (if not legally married) to Oliver Norman in about 1801, and then to Peter Norman, in around 1804. Rebecca Chamberlain: https://www.familysearch.org/tree/person/details/LW3R-N9K; Oliver Norman, https://www.familysearch.org/tree/person/details/K2N1-HFZ, both accessed September 3, 2019. James Snell notes Peter Norman's purchase of Oliver Norman's forge, and Peter's marriage with Rebecca Chamberlin, in *History of Sussex and Warren Counties, New Jersey* (Philadelphia: Evarts and Peck, 1881), 406. No marriages for Peter or Oliver Norman or Rebecca Chamberlin appear in Howard E. Case, *Sussex County, New Jersey, Marriages* (Bowie, MD: Heritage Books, 1992), indicating that these may have been informal or common-law marriages. Peter and Rebecca Norman's children are recorded in Mecabe, *Norman Family*, 9.

20   *Lydia Maria Child*: Child, LNY1, August 19, 1841, in *Letters from New-York*, ed. Bruce Mills (Athens: University of Georgia Press, 1998), 9; *Advocate of Moral Reform*, April 15, 1840, 62; George G. Foster, *New York by Gas-Light and Other Urban Sketches by George G. Foster*, ed. Stuart M. Blumin (Berkeley: University of California Press, 1990), 233–234.

21   *After a short sojourn*: Mecabe, *Norman Family*, introduction (unpaginated) and 1. Mecabe gives no maiden name for Rachel Norman, and genealogical sources give only unlikely and conflicting information. For late eighteenth-century British emigrants to America see Bernard Bailyn, *Voyagers to The West: A Passage in the Peopling of America on the Eve of the Revolution* (New York: Knopf, 1986); for republican ideas in England see Bernard Bailyn, *The Ideological Origins of the American Revolution* (Cambridge, MA: Harvard University Press, 1967).

22   *"almost barefooted"*: John Hathorn to George Clinton, December 17, 1777, *Public Papers of George Clinton, First Governor of New York, 1777–1795*, vol. 1 (New York and Albany, 1899–1914), 292. John Norman's military service is documented in Mecabe, *Norman Family*, introduction (unpaginated); Russel Headley, ed., *The History of Orange County, New York*, vol. 1 (Middletown, NY: Van Deusen and Elms, 1908), 428; and on a list titled "Warwick Soldiers of the Revolutionary War," comp. Genevieve VanDuzer, http://www.albertwisnerlibrary.org/Factsandhistory/History/Revolutionarywar.htm, accessed June 29, 2019.

22   *Seven of*: Mecabe, *Norman Family*, 1.

22   *Sometime during the Revolution*: Since Peter Norman was born in New Jersey in 1778, I am deducing that the Normans moved from Warwick to Sparta during the American Revolution (1775–1783). For Peter's place of birth, US Census for 1860. For Sparta in the period when John and Rachel Norman brought their family there see Theodore F. Chambers, *Proceedings of the Centennial Anniversary of the Presbyterian Church at Sparta, New Jersey, November 23, 1886, Together with a History of the Village* (New York: Williams Printing Co., 1887); Abraham Van Doren Honeyman, ed., *Northwestern New Jersey: A History of Somerset, Morris, Hunterdon, Warren, and Sussex Counties* (New York: Lewis Historical, 1927); Snell, *History of Sussex and Warren*. "Drowned lands": Snell, *History of Sussex and Warren*, 332. For settlers' pragmatic, often destructive views of nature see Alan Taylor, "'Wasty Ways': Stories of American Settlement," *Environmental History* 3 (July 1998): 291–310.

22   *These early settlers*: For the Normans' Cornish origins see Mecabe, *Norman Family*, 1. For ethnic and religious diversity in New Jersey and in Sussex County see Chambers, *Proceedings*, 85–86; Honeyman, vol. 1, *Northwestern New Jersey*, 34; Richard P. McCormick, *New Jersey: From Colony to State, 1609–1789* (Newark: New Jersey Historical Commission, 1981), 82; John Pomfret, *Colonial New Jersey: A History* (New York: Scribner's, 1973), 199; Caper Schaeffer, *Memoirs and Reminiscences, Together with Sketches of the Early History of Sussex County, New Jersey* (Hackensack, NJ: Privately printed, 1907), 66, 75. For African Americans in New Jersey see Graham Russell Hodges, *Root and Branch: African Americans in New York and East Jersey, 1613–1863* (Chapel Hill: University of North Carolina Press, 1999).

23   *The stony, hilly landscape*: Thomas F. Gordon, *Gazetteer of the State of New Jersey* (Trenton, NJ: Daniel Fenton, 1834), 241; Honeyman, *Northwestern New Jersey*, 1:494; McCormick, *New Jersey*, 83; Pomfret, *Colonial New Jersey*, 87–88; Schaeffer, *Memoirs and Reminiscences*, 32–33, 42, 64, 66, 71–73.

23   *"seemingly flooded"*: Schaeffer, *Memoirs and Reminiscences*, 64.

23   "if the parties escaped": Honeyman, Northwestern New Jersey, 1:126; Schaeffer, Memoirs and Reminiscences, 65, 80–81. For background on this form of fighting see Elliott J. Gorn, "'Gouge and Bite, Pull Hair and Scratch': The Social Significance of Fighting in the Southern Backcountry," American Historical Review 90 (supplement), (February 1985): 18–43.

23   John Chamberlin, the maternal grandfather: J.R.L., "The Parentage of Amelia Norman, with Other Hereditary Facts," American Phrenological Journal 6 (June 1844): 157.

24   John Chamberlin does appear: John Chamberlin, Indictments, Sussex County Court of Common Pleas, Indictments, 1754–1936, box 8, folders 26 and 32 (1809); "Petition of John Chamberlin to the Governor, November 1, 1814, Item 650 A.M. Papers, Department of the Secretary of State, New Jersey State Archives, Trenton.

24   "a great majority of the people": George Washington to Richard Henry Lee, April 24[–26], 1777, Founders Online, National Archives, http://founders.archives.gov/documents/Washington/03-09-02-0241, accessed September 6, 2015. The 1784 remark is quoted in Charles Boyer, Early Forges and Furnaces in New Jersey (Philadelphia: University of Pennsylvania Press, 1931), 9.

24   The area around Sparta: John Bezís-Selfa, "A Tale of Two Ironworks: Slavery, Free Labor, Work, and Resistance in the Early Republic," William and Mary Quarterly 56 (October 1999): 677–700; Charles Boyer, Early Forges and Furnaces in New Jersey (Philadelphia: University of Pennsylvania Press, 1931), esp. "Sparta Forges," 200–201; Thomas Doerflinger, "Rural Capitalism in Iron County: Staffing a Forest Factory, 1808–1815," William and Mary Quarterly 59 (January 2002): 3–38. In 1826 mineralogist and mine owner Samuel Fowler, who lived near Sparta, described the area as "a section of country rich and interesting in minerals" and speculated that there was enough iron and zinc there to supply "all America." Samuel Fowler to Professor Barzelius, London, June 25, 1826, quoted in Snell, History of Sussex and Warren, 337. Traveler and author Anne Royall similarly commented that the iron ore in New Jersey "is said to be sufficient to supply the United States": Sketches of History, Life, and Manners in the United States (New Haven, CT: Printed for the author, 1826), 238. Iron mines and forges around Sparta are visible on the map of Sparta in G. M. Hopkins Jr., Map of Sussex Co. New Jersey (Philadelphia: Carlos Allen, 1860).

25   The mines and furnaces: For northwestern New Jersey farmers as ironworkers see Doerflinger, "Rural Capitalism," 35–36; for the Normans as ironworkers, Mecabe, Norman Family: John, introduction (unpaginated) and 1; Oliver, 2; William, 5; Peter, 9; Charles, 41; Peter Jr., 48. For Vulcan's Head see Mecabe, 40. Since Cornwall is a mining region, it is possible John Norman brought his metalworking skills with him, and may even have been attracted first to Orange County and then to Sussex because both were rich in iron ore. The Sterling Iron Works was founded in 1751 in Warwick, Orange County, New York, where John Norman lived before he left for Sparta. J. Leander Bishop, History of American Manufactures from 1608–1860 (Philadelphia: E. Young, 1861), 528. For labor in the iron industry, including the use of slaves, see John Bezís-Selfa, "Slavery and the Disciplining of Free Labor in the Colonial Mid-Atlantic Iron Industry," Pennsylvania History: A Journal of Mid-Atlantic Studies 64 (Summer 1997): 270–286, and Theodore W. Kury, "Labor and the Charcoal Iron Industry: The New Jersey–New York Experience," Material Culture 25 (Fall 1993): 19–33.

25   The iron industry: John Bezís-Selfa, "A Tale of Two Ironworks: Slavery, Free Labor, Work, and Resistance in the Early Republic," William and Mary Quarterly 56 (October 1999): 678, 680, 681, 687, 689, 696; Boyer, Early Forges, 1, 6, 7, 15–18, 200;

Doerflinger, "Rural Capitalism," 8, 11, 12; Pomfret, *Colonial New Jersey*, 201; Snell, *History of Sussex and Warren*, 414.

25 *Extreme heat*: For a forge washed away when a dam broke, killing a man, see Chambers, *Proceedings*, 95. "Sodom": Honeyman, *Northwestern New Jersey*, 1:495; Chambers, *Proceedings*, 66. E. P. Thompson used the example of the "law book" of the Crowley ironworks in England, dating from 1700, to make a point about the control of labor in this early industry: "Time, Work-Discipline, and Industrial Capitalism," in *Customs in Common: Studies in Traditional Popular Culture* (New York: New Press, 1993), 383–385.

25 *"tight coterie"*: Pomfret, *Colonial New Jersey*, 201.

25 *Because the large landowners*: Snell, *History of Sussex and Warren*, 163.

25 *the great family was the Ogdens*: "A Touch of Sparta, New Jersey: A Short History as Reported in the Sussex Magazine in 1950," *Old Sussex Almanack* 105 (Winter 2009): [9] (unpaginated); Boyer, *Early Forges and Furnaces*, 200; Chambers, *Proceedings*, 10–12, 69–71; Snell, *History of Sussex and Warren*, 177–179, 414; William Ogden Wheeler, *The Ogden Family in America, Elizabethtown Branch and Their English Ancestry*, ed. Lawrence Van Alstyne and Charles Burr Ogden (Philadelphia: J. B. Lippincott, 1907); entries on Aaron and Elias Ogden in Maxine N. Lurie and Marc Mappen, eds., *Encyclopedia of New Jersey* (New Brunswick, NJ: Rutgers University Press, 2004). Death notice for Robert Ogden Sr., *New-Jersey Journal and Political Intelligencer* (Elizabethtown), January 3, 1787; obituary for Robert Ogden Jr., *Centinal of Freedom* (Newark, NJ), February 21, 1826. Aaron Ogden is best known for his role in *Gibbons vs. Ogden*, the 1824 Supreme Court case that broke the New York steamboat monopoly established by Robert Fulton and Robert Livingston: see Edwin G. Burrows and Mike Wallace, *Gotham: A History of New York City to 1898* (New York: Oxford University Press, 1999), 432–433. The marriage of Euphemia Morris and Samuel Ogden: William Howard Adams, *Gouverneur Morris: An Independent Life* (New Haven, CT: Yale University Press, 2003), 143, 234. For the relationship between the Ogdens and the Burrs see Nancy Isenberg, *Fallen Founder: The Life of Aaron Burr* (New York: Viking, 2007), 5–6. Inscriptions for Ogden family tombstones are published in Mary Elinor Eppler, *Behold and See, As You Pass By: Epitaphs in the Old Cemetery, 1787–1924, of the First Presbyterian Church of Sparta* (Sparta, NJ: Mary Elinor Eppler, 1976).

26 *The Normans appear*: Chambers, *Proceedings*, 86; Snell, *History of Sussex and Warren*, 406.

26 *The Norman family attended*: Mecabe, *Norman Family*, 9. Ellen and Peter Norman buried their twelve-year-old son, Mahlon, who drowned in 1853, in the cemetery belonging to the Sparta Presbyterian Church: "Sussex County Gravestones, Sparta Presbyterian Church Yard (Old Part), copied by Rev. Warren Patten Coon and John Wesley Rude, *Genealogical Magazine of New Jersey* 5 (January 1930): 73.

26 *During the years*: Bounties for wolf and wildcat scalps: Chambers, *Proceedings*, 98; retreat of animals: Schaeffer, *Memoirs*, 80–82.

26 *"a very pleasant village"*: Thomas F. Gordon, *Gazetteer of the State of New Jersey* (Trenton, 1834; reprint, Baltimore: Clearfield, 2001), 241.

26 *The natural waterways*: For movements of goods, mail, and people on New Jersey roads see "Touch of Sparta" (unpaginated); Chambers, *Proceedings*, 14, 95–97; Honeyman, *Northwestern New Jersey*, 1:130–131; Snell, *History of Sussex and Warren*, 222. In 1811 there were six post offices in Sussex County, but none in Sparta village. By 1837 there were twenty-five post offices in the county, and by this time there was one in Sparta. Snell, *History of Sussex and Warren*, 164.

27   *They also brought newspapers*: For the press in Sussex County see Snell, *History of Sussex and Warren*, 216–227.

27   *During Amelia Norman's childhood*: An academy, or private school, was founded in Sparta in 1812, and the Sparta village school described by Gordon (*Gazetteer of the State of New Jersey*, 241) in 1834 may have been the same as one that opened there in 1816. In 1815, three years before Amelia was born, a boarding school for "young ladies" opened in Morristown, and in 1845, a decade after she left New Jersey, a "Young Ladies' Seminary" opened in Sparta. Chambers, *Proceedings*, 100; Snell, *History of Sussex and Warren*, 169, 171, 408, 409. A boarding school for young ladies in Morristown was advertised in the *Palladium of Liberty*, May 10, 1815.

27   *This proliferation of schools*: Linda Kerber, *Women of the Republic: Intellect and Ideology in Revolutionary America* (Chapel Hill: University of North Carolina Press, 1980); Lucia McMahon, "'Of the Utmost Importance to Our County': Women, Education, and Society, 1780–1920," *Journal of the Early Republic* 29 (Fall 2009): 475–506; Joel Schwartz, "The Struggle for Public Education in New Jersey before the Civil War," in *Jacksonian New Jersey*, ed. Paul A. Stellhorn (Trenton: New Jersey Historical Commission, 1979), 103–104.

27   *"it is solely by the knowledge"*: "Public Meeting," *New Brunswick (NJ) Fredonian*, June 13, 1827. The meeting was in Montgomery Township, Somerset County.

27   *"Nothing tends more to the Improvement"*: Advertisement for Mrs. Neill's boarding school for young ladies in Williamsburg, Virginia, *Virginia Gazette* (Williamsburg), January 3, 1777. For a brief period, ending before Amelia Norman was born, the New Jersey constitution did allow women to vote, until the right was taken away in 1808. See Judith Apter Klinghoffer and Lois Elkis, "'The Petticoat Electors': Women's Suffrage in New Jersey, 1776–1807," *Journal of the Early Republic* 12 (Summer 1992): 159–193.

27   *The Awakening*: Jon Butler, *Awash in a Sea of Faith: Christianizing the American People* (Cambridge, MA: Harvard University Press, 1990). For the arrival of revivalism in Sparta see Chambers, *Proceedings*, 43–45.

27   *"The exercises of the day"*: Quoted in Chambers, *Proceedings*, 44. For Robert Ogden Jr. as an elder in the Sparta Presbyterian Church see Chambers, *Proceedings*, 11. Robert Ogden Jr.'s obituary notes that he was "a true and firm believer in the Christian religion": *Centinal of Freedom* (Newark, NJ), February 21, 1826.

28   *One minister*: Livingston Willard, letter to unnamed recipient (probably Theodore F. Chambers), December 15, 1886, quoted in Chambers, *Proceedings*, 45.

28   *"distilled death"*: Extract from the report of Mr. McKee, agent of the State Temperance Society, "now in Sussex County," *Newark (NJ) Daily Advertiser*, December 29, 1835.

28   *This act did not compel children*: Schwartz, "Struggle for Public Education," 106–110. The statistics on literacy in Sussex County are from "Extract" (from the report of the Nassau Hall Bible Society literacy survey), *New Brunswick (NJ) Fredonian*, February 27, 1828.

28   *reading without writing*: Tamara Plakins Thornton, *Handwriting in America: A Cultural History* (New Haven, CT: Yale University Press, 1996), 4–7.

29   *In October 1834*: In the testimony she gave at Norman's trial, Eliza Meriam said she brought Norman to New York "9 years ago last October," thus in October 1834, when she was "between 15 and 16 years old." *New York Tribune*, January 19, 1844.

29   *The household was crowded with children*: Mecabe, *Norman Family*, 9. The US Census for 1830 and 1840 shows that in those years there were five people under the age of twenty living in Peter Norman's home.

29 *There is not enough evidence*: William W. Sanger, *The History of Prostitution: Its Extent, Causes, and Effects throughout the World* (1858; New York: American Medical Press, 1895), 499–500, 454. Rebecca Norman's birth in approximately 1828 is recorded in Mecabe, *Norman Family*, 9, 49.

30 *Amelia could not have known*: Mecabe gives no birth dates for Phebe, Jane, and Harriet, although he does give birth order, in *Norman Family*, 9 and 42 (Phebe), 43 (Jane), 44 (Harriet). I am extrapolating their birth dates from what they reported to the census taker in 1850. All three are listed, with their husbands, in Peter Norman's will at the New Jersey State Archives, Trenton. The US Census for 1850 shows Henry Bird, then thirty-two, living in Sparta with an older couple with a different last name, a sign that he may have been a laborer or boarder in their household. For Bird's death and burial in the Sussex County Welfare Home Cemetery, Branchville, New Jersey, https://www.findagrave.com/cemetery/1996976/sussex-county-welfare-home-cemetery, accessed July 2, 2019.

30 *"sterling integrity"*: Snell, *History of Sussex and Warren*, 416.

30 *"She hath done"*: Eppler, *Behold and See*, 50.

30 *Eliza's nephew*: Harry Harmon Cory, *The Cory Family, a Genealogy* (Minneapolis: Argus, 1941); Snell, *History of Sussex and Warren*, 406, 408, 409, 410, 416. Eliza Meriam identified herself as the husband of Francis Meriam when she gave testimony at Amelia Norman's trial: *New York Herald*, January 19, 1844.

30 *Francis Meriam*: A Merriam family had a shoe manufacturing business in Newton, New Jersey, starting in the 1870s, so it is possible that there were already Meriams or Merriams in Sussex County when Francis Meriam went there in the 1820s, although I have seen no record of them from that period. My thanks to the volunteers at the Sussex County Historical Society for this information.

31 *By 1827*: Richard Bushman and Claudia Bushman, "The Early History of Cleanliness in America," *Journal of American History* 74 (March 1988): 1225, 1233. *Longworth's American Almanac* (New York: T. Longworth, 1820–1844), a city directory published annually, listed Eben as a manufacturer of "fancy soap," or toilet soap. By 1825, the Meriams were listed as soap boilers. By 1836 Eben was described in *Longworth's* as manufacturing "soda soap."

31 *By the early 1840s*: On the Meriams: Charles Henry Pope, *Merriam Genealogy in England and America* (Boston: Pope, 1906), 103, 167. Eben's and Francis's home and business addresses in New York are in *Longworth's American Almanac*. "Eben Meriam, 1848–1854," Miscellaneous Manuscript File, New-York Historical Society, provides more information. Obituaries for Eben Meriam: *Brooklyn Eagle* and *New York Times*, March 21, 1864. There is a mention of Eben Meriam in Sven Beckert, *The Monied Metropolis: New York City and the Consolidation of the American Bourgeoisie, 1850–1896* (Cambridge: Cambridge University Press, 2001), 82. Eben Meriam published meteorological columns in *Scientific American* and other publications from the mid-1840s until 1863, a year before his death. They included "Statistics of Lightning; Odor of Lightning," *Niles National Register*, October 4, 1845; "Earthquakes, Lightning, Snow and Rain," *Scientific American*, April 24, 1847; "Frequency of Earthquakes," *New York Daily Times*, June 11, 1853; "The Heated Term," *New York Times*, August 7, 1863, and many others.

31 *Great spark*: "Meriam's Address to the Great Meteor," *Vanity Fair*, August 4, 1860. The poem is unsigned, but its author was identified by Charles I. Glicksburg as Fitz-James O'Brien: see "Charles Godfrey Leland and 'Vanity Fair,'" *Pennsylvania Magazine of History and Biography*, 1938, 320–321.

31   *In October 1834*: Francis and Eliza Meriam's children, their names and birth dates, are listed in Pope, *Merriam Genealogy*, 167.

32   *When she decided*: On the growth of cities in the nineteenth century largely as a result of migration into cities see Adna Ferrin Weber, *The Growth of Cities in the Nineteenth Century: A Study in Statistics* (1899; New York: Greenwood, 1969). Weber noted that women, more than men, migrated to cities, drawn there by work as domestic servants: 276, 278, 284. For the Mid-Atlantic region as the principal source of internal migrants, 1800–1860, with men dominating western migration, see Peter D. McClelland and Richard Zeckhauser, *Demographic Dimensions of the New Republic: American Interregional Migration, Vital Statistics, and Manumissions, 1800–1860* (Cambridge: Cambridge University Press, 1982), 5–8. For female domestic service in cities, and domestic service as the largest employer, see Christine Stansell, *City of Women: Sex and Class in New York, 1789–1860* (Urbana: University of Illinois Press, 1987), 155–168, and Faye Dudden, *Serving Women: Household Service in Nineteenth-Century America* (Middletown, CT: Wesleyan University Press, 1983). For the Irish women who took over the domestic service market from native-born women in the 1840s see Hasia Diner, *Erin's Daughters in America: Irish Immigrant Women in the Nineteenth Century* (Baltimore: Johns Hopkins University Press, 1983). Diner, like Weber, notes that women were in the forefront of immigration to cities, drawn by the protected, if poorly paid occupation of domestic service. On the development of the middle class in antebellum American cities see Stuart M. Blumin, *The Emergence of the Middle Class: Social Experience in the American City, 1760–1900* (Cambridge: Cambridge University Press, 1989), and Karen Halttunen, *Confidence Men and Painted Women: A Study of Middle-Class Culture in America, 1830–1870* (New Haven, CT: Yale University Press, 1982).

32   *So it was*: There is no record of their journey, but this is the route they would have taken in 1834. Hurd's tavern/temperance hotel: Chambers, *Proceedings*, 47, 91, 97; stage routes between New York and Sparta: Snell, *History of Sussex and Warren*, 164, 222. For the ferry to New York from Newark see advertisements: "Newark Bridge Dock and Morris Canal Line" and "Newark, New-York & Morris Canal Line," in *Sussex County Register*, September 28, 1835.

32   *His maternal grandmother's first name*: Henry Ballard's Puritan ancestor was William Ballard (1603–1639). His grandmother was Wait Comstock Greene. For this and other genealogical information about the Ballards see Charles Frederick Farlow, *Ballard Genealogy* (Boston: Charles H. Pope, 1911). For the so-called hortatory naming practices used by Puritans see Gloria L. Main, "Naming Children in Early New England," *Journal of Interdisciplinary History* 27 (Summer 1996): 17, and Daniel Scott Smith, "Child-Naming Practices, Kinship Ties, and Change in Family Attitudes in Hingham, Massachusetts, 1641 to 1880," *Journal of Social History* 18 (Summer 1985): 544.

32   *"worthy and highly respectable"*: Lydia Maria Child, "Uncollected Letter from New-York," in *A Lydia Maria Child Reader*, ed. Carolyn C. Karcher (Durham, NC: Duke University Press, 1997), 365. The "Uncollected Letter" is "Letter from New-York No. V." For the marriage of Hannah Greene and John Ballard Jr., Henry's parents, see *Columbian Centinel* (Boston), July 17, 1811.

32   *Like Norman's Pond*: The Ballard family businesses were J. and J. Ballard, Ballard and Prince, and Sweetser and Abbott. The city directories also list John Ballard as a merchant with a "counting room." Whereabouts of Ballard family homes and businesses are listed in *Stimpson's Boston Directory* (Boston: Charles Stimpson Jr., 1830–1846).

Genealogical information: Farlow, *Ballard Genealogy*. Ballard Place: "All the Streets in Boston," at http://bostonhistory.typepad.com, accessed summer 2007.

33   *In 1835*: Henry Ballard's movements in Boston are traceable in *Stimpson's Boston Directory* (Boston: Charles Stimpson Jr.), published annually in the 1830s.

33   *When the Astors built*: For the Tremont House and Isaiah Rogers see Donald Martin Reynolds, *Architecture of New York City* (New York: Macmillan, 1984), 97–98. For Dwight Boyden see "Astor House," Hotel Files, New-York Historical Society, and "Astor's Hotel," the *Albion*, June 4, 1836.

33   *When Henry Ballard was twenty years old*: Sarah Ballard's history is from her testimony and from the statements of Norman's lawyers at Amelia Norman's trial. Reported in the *New York Post*, January 17, 1844; *New York Sun*, January 17, 1844; *New York Herald*, January 19, 1844; *New York Tribune*, January 19, 1844.

34   *In 1837 Henry Ballard left*: Ballard last appears in *Stimpson's Boston Directory* in 1836 and first appears in a New York City directory in 1837: *Longworth's American Almanac, New-York Register and City Directory, 1837–1838* (New York: Thomas Longworth, 1837).

34   *He resettled Sarah*: J. S. Carpentier, one of Norman's lawyers, stated at her trial that Ballard brought Sarah Ballard with him to New York: *New York Sun*, January 17, 1844.

34   *As New York became*: Thomas Kessner, *Capital City: New York City and the Men behind America's Rise to Economic Dominance, 1860–1900* (New York: Simon & Schuster, 2003), 28–30. For a few examples of jokes about Yankee trickiness published in newspapers during a representative year, 1840, when Ballard was in New York, see "Yankeeism," *New York Evening Post*, August 27, 1840; "Yankee vs. Wolvereen," *Log Cabin* (New York), May 30, 1840; "Yankee Pedlar," *New York Mercury*, July 9, 1840.

34   *"are either natives"*: Cooper, quoted in Bayrd Still, *Mirror for Gotham: New York as Seen by Contemporaries from Dutch Days to the Present* (New York: Fordham University Press, 1994), 105.

35   *"the flames of the great conflagration"*: *Newark (NJ) Daily Advertiser*, December 23, 1835, reprinted from the *Newton (NJ) Register*.

35   *The sculptor*: Lydia Maria Child wrote about the sculptor, Ball Hughes, weeping over the ruined statue of Hamilton, in LNY4, September 9, 1841, in *Letters from New-York*, ed. Mills, 20.

35   *"thousands upon thousands"*: "Dreadful Calamity," *Commercial Advertiser*, December 17, 1835; "Destructive Conflagration!," *Commercial Advertiser*, December 17, 1835; "The Late Fire, Further Particulars," *New York Post*, December 18, 1835; Burrows and Wallace, *Gotham*, 596–601.

36   *Just one year later*: A *Summary Historical, Geographical, and Statistical View of the City of New York* (New York: J. H. Colton, 1836), 19, 20.

37   *The cheeky optimism*: *Boston Traveler*, September 4, 1835.

37   *The Panic of 1837*: Daniel Walker Howe, *What Hath God Wrought: The Transformation of America, 1815–1848* (New York: Oxford University Press, 2007); Samuel Rezneck, "The Social History of an American Depression, 1837–1843," *American Historical Review* 40 (July 1935): 662–687; Alasdair Roberts, *America's First Great Depression: Economic Crisis and Political Disorder after the Panic of 1837* (Ithaca, NY: Cornell University Press, 2012); Charles Sellers, *The Market Revolution: Jacksonian America, 1815–1846* (New York: Oxford University Press, 1991). Diarist Philip

Hone noted the start of the bank collapses in New York on March 17, 1843: *The Diary of Philip Hone*, ed. Allan Nevins, vol. 1 (New York: Dodd, Mead, 1927), 248.

37   *They translated what they saw*: "The Most Dangerous Year," *Commercial Advertiser*, February 14, 1837; "A Mob," *New York American*, February 17, 1837; Hone, *Diary*, 1:241, 243.

37   *James Gordon Bennett*: "Great Public Meeting—Twenty Thousand Assembled—the Revolution Begun," *New York Herald*, February 14, 1837; "Riots—Rent—Food—Fuel," *New York Herald*, February 16, 1837.

37   *Bennett, whose sentiments*: for Bennett's pro-working-class, antiestablishment views see James L. Crouthamel, *Bennett's New York Herald and the Rise of the Popular Press* (Syracuse, NY: Syracuse University Press, 1989), 92–95.

39   *The Astor House, which opened*: Astor House menu, farewell dinner, 1913, "Astor House," Hotel Files, New-York Historical Society; James D. McCabe Jr., *Lights and Shadows of New York Life; or, The Sights and Sensations of the Great City* (Philadelphia: National, 1872; reprint, New York: Farrar, Straus and Giroux, 1970), 304–306.

39   *When Ballard moved in*: Alexander Mackay, *The Western World; or Travels in the United States in 1846–7*, cited in I. N. P. Stokes, *Iconography of Manhattan Island, 1498–1909* (New York: R. H. Dodd, 1915–1928), 3:657; Charles Dickens, *American Notes for General Circulation* (London: Penguin Books, 1985), 136.

40   *The novelist Henry James*: Henry James, *A Small Boy and Others* (London: Macmillan, 1913), 8.

40   *It challenged City Hall*: For the construction of City Hall see Elliot Willensky and Norval White, *AIA Guide to New York City*, 3rd ed. (New York: Harcourt, Brace, Jovanovich, 1988), 61.

40   *The Astor House offered*: From 1836, when it was built, through 1853, when it was eclipsed by the St. Nicholas Hotel, the Astor House was considered New York's principal hotel and an important attraction, much commented on at the time and afterward. See "The Astor House, in New York," *American Magazine of Useful and Entertaining Knowledge*, February 1, 1836, 260; "Astor's Hotel," *Albion, a Journal of News, Politics and Literature*, June 4, 1836, 183; Richard Bushman and Claudia Bushman (who note that the Astor House was one of only a few "elegant hotels" in the United States that had baths and showers), "The Early History of Cleanliness in America," *Journal of American History* 74 (March 1988): 1225; Gloria Deák, *Picturing New York: The City from Its Beginnings to the Present* (New York: Columbia University Press, 2000), 280; McCabe, *Lights and Shadows*, 304–306; Reynolds, *Architecture of New York City*, 97–98; Still, *Mirror for Gotham*, 81, 86, 90, 126 (on the Astor's eclipse by the St. Nicholas Hotel), 155–156; Stokes, *Iconography of Manhattan Island*, 3:527, 656, 657, 976; "Astor House," Hotel Files, New-York Historical Society. Plumbing: Reynolds, *Architecture of New York City*, 98; hot and cold baths, "theaters, balls," *New York New Mirror*, August 19, 1843, 311. The Astor House closed in 1875: see "The Astor House, Origin and History of the World-Famous Hotel," *New York Times*, January 31, 1875.

40   *All of this made the great hotel attractive*: "The Astor House, Origin and History of the World-Famous Hotel," *New York Times*, January 31, 1875. In 1913, when the Astor House was threatened with destruction, the *Sun* nostalgically, perhaps apocryphally, recalled that Edgar Allan Poe "went there frequently for refreshment and news": "The Old Astor House: History Made in Hotel Threatened by Subway," *New York Sun*, May 3, 1913.

41   *"trussed fowl"*: [Asa Greene], *A Glance at New York* (New York: A. Greene, 1837), 32.

41   *"Dollars and cents"*: Henry Cooke, "Notes of a Loiterer in New York," *Bentley's Miscellany* 16 (1844), 598.

41   *Lydia Maria Child*: LMC, LNY34, in Karcher, *Reader*, 363–364.

41   *A preacher*: "Meeting of Female Moral Reformers," *New York Herald*, May 9, 1839.

3. Go and Get Your Living

43   *During the years Norman lived on Leonard Street*: For construction of the Tombs between 1835 and 1838 see Richard G. Carrott, *The Egyptian Revival: Its Sources, Monuments, and Meaning, 1808–1858* (Berkeley: University of California Press, 1978), 6.

44   *"theatres and places of amusements"*: *New York Herald*, January 20, 1844.

44   *"free, light-hearted woman"*: *New York Tribune*, January 19, 1844; *New York Herald*, January 19, 1844.

44   *Amelia left the Meriams*: The whereabouts of Francis and Eliza Meriam for this period and their new occupation as boardinghouse keepers can be traced in *Longworth's American Almanac, New York Register and City Directory* (New York: T. Longworth, 1834–1841) and in the US Census, 1840, New York, Ward 2, 1840, roll 299, p. 73. In her testimony at the trial Eliza Meriam gave her address as 54 Beekman Street. Isabella Hurley described the Meriams' home at the time Amelia Norman lived with them as at the corner of Benson and Leonard Street: *New York Herald*, January 19, 1844. For Pearl Street as the location of auction houses see Thomas Kessner, *Capital City: New York City and the Men behind America's Rise to Economic Dominance, 1860–1900* (New York: Simon & Schuster, 2003), 6. Eben Meriam's last Manhattan addresses, at 178 and 180 ("soda soap factory") Chapel Street appear in *Longworth's, 1839–1840* directory, published in 1839.

44   *Throughout this time*: In the testimony Eliza Meriam gave at Norman's trial she said "I was intimate with her all this time": *New York Tribune*, January 19, 1844, or, "she has been intimate in my family since," *New York Herald*, January 19, 1844.

46   *This time*: For Norman's stays with the Ealers and Callenders see Eliza Merriam's testimony: *New York Herald*, *New York Tribune*, January 19, 1844. These two papers, both reporting on Meriam's testimony at Norman's trial, conflict about the amount of time Norman stayed with the Ealers. An article in the *Advocate of Moral Reform* confirms that she was in the "employ" of the Callenders: see "Police Office—the Stabbing Case near the Astor House," *Advocate of Moral Reform*, November 15, 1843, 173. For the political career of Samuel Sparks, a Whig, see the *New-Yorker*, "The New York Charter Election," April 14, 1838; *New-Yorker*, "City Election," April 6, 1839. City directories show that he was a grocer, who lived on William Street at the corner of Duane.

46   *"She was subject to fits"*: Testimony of Eliza Meriam, *New York Herald* and *New York Tribune*, January 19, 1844.

46   *Amelia's fits*: Testimony of William Callender, *New York Herald* and *New York Tribune*, January 19, 1844.

46   *At her trial*: Testimony of William Callender, *New York Herald* and *New York Tribune*, January 19, 1844.

47   *What followed*: Opening statement of lawyer J. S. Carpentier, *New York Herald* and *New York Post*, January 17, 1844. The culture of commercial amusements in New York is described by George G. Foster in his journalistic exposé *New York by Gas-Light*, first published in 1850. The plots of popular seduction novels, such as Samuel Richardson's *Clarissa* and Susanna Haswell Rowson's *Charlotte Temple* (both originally published

in England in the eighteenth century and then reprinted in the United States, where they were widely read) were echoed, as warnings, in the stories of ruined country girls in the pages of the American Female Moral Reform Society's *Advocate of Moral Reform*. Samuel Richardson, *Clarissa, or, The History of a Young Lady* (1748); Susanna Haswell Rowson, *Charlotte Temple* (London: William Lane, 1791; reprinted, Philadelphia: Mathew Carey, 1794). On seduction novels see Cathy N. Davidson, *Revolution and the Word: The Rise of the Novel in America* (New York: Oxford University Press, 1986); Linda Kerber, *Women of the Republic: Intellect and Ideology in Revolutionary America* (Chapel Hill: University of North Carolina Press, 1980); and Susan Staves, "British Seduced Maidens," *Eighteenth-Century Studies* 14 (Winter 1980–1981): 109–134. That Norman's story sounds like the plot of a seduction novel may mean that she and her lawyers heightened the similarity for effect. But it may also demonstrate the way fact and fiction borrowed from each other. For an example of the blending of fact and fiction in another genre, the foundling note, see Julie Miller, *Abandoned: Foundlings in Nineteenth-Century New York City* (New York: NYU Press, 2008), 27–30; on this theme more broadly: Natalie Zemon Davis, *Fiction in the Archives: Pardon Tales and Their Tellers in Sixteenth-Century France* (Stanford, CA: Stanford University Press, 1987).

47   *She went to stay with Mary Moore*: Testimony of Mary Moore, *New York Herald* and *New York Tribune*, January 19, 1844. The *Tribune*'s account of Moore's testimony quotes her saying that "she said she had expected to be married"; the passage I quote is from the *Herald*. While "boxes of pills" could be prescribed for any ailment, they were among the treatments used to induce abortion, as abortionist Madame Restell explained at Amelia's trial: *New York Herald*, *New York Sun*, and *New York Tribune*, January 19, 1844. For another reference to "boxes of pills" prescribed by Restell for abortion see *Wonderful Trial of Caroline Lohman, alias Restell. . . (Reported in Full for the National Police Gazette)*, 3rd ed. [1847], 6.

48   *"She came to my house"*: Testimony of Isabella Hurley, *New York Herald* and *New York Tribune*, January 19, 1844.

48   *"could not find the place"*: Testimony of Isabella Hurley, *New York Herald* and *New York Tribune*, January 19, 1844.

48   *"doomed"*: Edgar Allan Poe, *Doings of Gotham*, ed. Jacob Spannuth (Pottsville, PA: Jacob Spannuth, 1929), Letter 1, May 14, 1844, 25–26. For Poe's residence on a farm see Dwight Thomas and David K. Jackson, *The Poe Log: A Documentary Life of Edgar Allan Poe, 1809–1849* (Boston: G. K. Hall, 1987), 463. As late as 1836 the built-up part of the city had only reached Fourteenth Street: see *Guide to the City of New York, Containing an Alphabetical Listing of Streets, &c.* (New York: J. Disturnell, 1836), map, iii. Edwin G. Burrows and Mike Wallace note that in the 1830s Fourteenth Street was the "northern frontier": Burrows and Wallace, *Gotham: A History of New York City to 1898* (New York: Oxford University Press, 1999), 715. The northernmost square in a list of "Squares and Places" in the 1844–1845 edition of David Valentine's *Manual* is Madison Square, whose northern boundary is Twenty-Sixth Street. Valentine, *Manual of the Corporation of the City of New-York for the Years 1844–5* (New York: J. F. Trow, 1844), 227. For the markers at intersections, placed according to the grid plan designed in 1811, see Burrows and Wallace, *Gotham*, 422.

48   *"one mass of mud"*: LMC to Anna Loring, February 6, 1845, *SL*, 217.

49   *"never saw her at my house again"*: Testimony of Isabella Hurley, *New York Herald* and *New York Tribune*, January 19, 1844.

49   *"was not such as it should be"*: opening statement of lawyer J. S. Carpentier at Norman's trial, *New York Herald*, January 17, 1844. Carpentier outlines Norman's movements between summer 1841 and fall 1842, reported with variations in the *Herald*, *Post*, and *Sun*, January 17, 1844.

49   *While Amelia was at Stewart's Hotel*: These events were described by lawyer J. S. Carpentier in his opening statement at the trial: *New York Herald*, *New York Post*, and *New York Sun*, January 17, 1844.

49   *That this child*: At the trial in January 1844, lawyer J. S. Carpentier said that Norman had supported the child for thirteen months before her arrest, meaning that he or she (the baby's name and gender were never reported) would have been born in about September 1842: *New York Herald*, January 17, 1842. The *New York Evening Post*, January 17, 1844, reports that the child is "now" eighteen months old, putting its birth in August 1842. On early indifference to the welfare of children see Steven Mintz, *Huck's Raft: A History of American Childhood* (Cambridge, MA: Harvard University Press, 2004), 17; on the "child-saving" movement, which represented the gradual awakening of concern about the welfare of poor children, 154–184.

50   *Henry Ballard tried*: opening statement of lawyer J. S. Carpentier, *New York Herald*, *New York Post*, and *New York Sun*, January 17, 1844.

50   *Seduction was the term*: One legal historian has equated nineteenth-century seduction with modern "date rape": Brian Donovan, "Gender Inequality and Criminal Seduction: Prosecuting Sexual Coercion in the Early-20th Century," *Law and Social Inquiry* 30 (Winter 2005): 63. Another interprets it as sexual fraud: Jane E. Larson, "'Women Understand So Little, They Call My Good Nature "Deceit"': A Feminist Rethinking of Seduction," *Columbia Law Review* 93 (March 1993): 379–380. It was based on the idea, which developed in the first half of the nineteenth century, that since women lacked sexual passion, they could not be equal participants in seduction; they could only have been coerced. For this background see Nancy Cott, "Passionlessness: An Interpretation of Victorian Sexual Ideology, 1790–1850," *Signs* 4 (1978): 219–236, and Barbara Welter, "The Cult of True Womanhood, 1820–1860," *American Quarterly* 18 (1966): 151–174.

50   *The seduction tort*: For the tort of seduction see Patricia Cline Cohen, *The Murder of Helen Jewett* (New York: Vintage Books, 1998), 209–210; Michael Grossberg, *Governing the Hearth: Law and the Family in Nineteenth-Century America* (Chapel Hill: University of North Carolina Press, 1985), 45–49; Andrea L. Hibbard and John T. Parry, "Law, Seduction, and the Sentimental Heroine: The Case of Amelia Norman," *American Literature* 78 (June 2006): 325–355; Marilynn Wood Hill, *Their Sisters' Keepers: Prostitution in New York City, 1830–1870* (Berkeley: University of California Press, 1993), 140–144; Larson, "'Women Understand So Little'"; "Law Reform in New York—Report," *Western Law Journal* (April 1850); M. B. W. Sinclair, "Seduction and the Myth of the Ideal Woman," *Law and Inequality* 5 (1987–1988): 33–102; Staves, "British Seduced Maidens"; Lea VanderVelde, "The Legal Ways of Seduction," *Stanford Law Review* 48 (April 1996): 817–901. For the definition of a tort see "Tort," Legal Information Institute, Cornell Law School, https://www.law.cornell.edu/wex/tort, accessed March 10, 2019.

50   *The tort was rooted*: On the household head in colonial America: John Demos, *A Little Commonwealth: Family Life in Plymouth Colony* (New York: Oxford University Press, 1970). On the erosion of the power of the household head in the nineteenth century: Carole Shammas, *A History of Household Government in America* (Charlottesville: University of Virginia Press, 2002). For the definition of the child as the

servant of the father: Philippe Ariès, *Centuries of Childhood: A Social History of Family Life*, trans. Robert Baldick (New York: Vintage Books, 1962), 396–398; Larson, " 'Women Understand So Little,' " 382; and Sinclair, "Seduction and the Myth of the Ideal Woman," 35. For the power of fathers in ancient Rome to dispose of their children as they wished see John Boswell, *The Kindness of Strangers: The Abandonment of Children in Western Europe from Late Antiquity to the Renaissance* (New York: Vintage Books, 1988).

50   *His suit*: VanderVelde finds that few American masters of servants—she is not clear if she means bound servants or wage workers—brought seduction cases. She finds just one example from New York in 1833. American fathers, however, did bring these suits. VanderVelde, "Legal Ways of Seduction," 876 and 876n281.

51   *"obtain rooms"*: opening statement of lawyer J. S. Carpentier, *New York Herald*, *New York Post*, and *New York Sun*, January 17, 1844.

51   *Then, instead*: Opening statement of J. S. Carpentier, *New York Herald*, *New York Post*, and *New York Sun*, January 17, 1844; *Brooklyn Eagle* (copied from the *Plebeian*), January 17, 1844, and *Baltimore Sun*, January 19, 1844.

51   *That may be how*: On categories of prostitutes in nineteenth-century New York see Cohen, *Murder of Helen Jewett*; Timothy J. Gilfoyle, *City of Eros: New York City, Prostitution, and the Commercialization of Sex, 1790–1920* (New York: W. W. Norton, 1992); Hill, *Their Sisters' Keepers*; Christine Stansell, *City of Women: Sex and Class in New York, 1789–1860* (Urbana: University of Illinois Press, 1987).

51   *"vicious course of life"*: J. S. Carpentier's opening statement, *New York Sun*, January 17, 1844; "Police Office—the Stabbing Case near the Astor House," *Advocate of Moral Reform*, November 15, 1843, 173.

51   *He was joined on Warren Street*: Henry and Francis Ballard are listed as merchants at 64 Cedar Street in *The New-York City Directory for 1844 & 1845* (New York: John Doggett Jr., 1844). Doggett doesn't list their Warren Street address, but both brothers gave it when they were interviewed for Norman's indictment.

51   *Francis Ballard's trajectory*: Francis Ballard's career in Boston is traceable in *Stimpson's Boston Directory* (Boston: Charles Stimpson Jr., 1840–1842); information about his age is in Charles Frederick Farlow, *Ballard Genealogy* (Boston: Charles H. Pope, 1911), 50.

52   *Asa Greene*: [Asa Greene], *A Glance at New York* (New York: A. Greene, 1837), 19–20.

52   *Antebellum New York was home*: For the culture of "sporting men" and the related phenomenon of the "flash press" see Gilfoyle, *City of Eros*, 92–116, and Patricia Cline Cohen, Timothy Gilfoyle, and Helen Lefkowitz Horowitz, *The Flash Press: Sporting Male Weeklies in 1840s New York* (Chicago: University of Chicago Press, 2008); Helen Lefkowitz Horowitz, *Rereading Sex: Battles over Sexual Knowledge and Suppression in Nineteenth-Century America* (New York: Knopf, 2002). And George G. Foster, "The Model Artist Exhibitions," in *New York by Gas-Light and Other Urban Sketches by George G. Foster*, ed. Stuart M. Blumin (Berkeley: University of California Press, 1990), 77–83.

52   *another abortion*: The number and chronology of Norman's abortions are hard to determine because of the overly subtle way that her lawyers and the press referred to them. In his opening statement J. S. Carpentier referred to what appears to be one abortion and one live birth. But an article that appeared in the *New York Sun* on August 15, 1843 ("Alleged Seduction") implies that Norman's attack on Ballard at his

store that month came soon after a second abortion: "a second resort was had to a rival of Madame R[estell]," the result of a "second intimacy" with Ballard.

52   *On Tuesday, August 8*: Francis Ballard described Amelia Norman's visit to Warren Street in the interview he gave for Norman's indictment.

53   *"destroyer"*: *New York Herald*, January 22, 1844. The *Advocate of Moral Reform* also used the term "destroyer" and similar phrases to describe men who "ruined" women. For example, "The practiced spoiler," March 1, 1844; "the murderer of virtue," March 15, 1844; "Those who lie in wait to destroy," July 15, 1844. The *New York Tribune*, January 16, 1844, described such men as "human wolves."

53   *When they arrived*: The parasol incident is described in *Advocate of Moral Reform*, November 15, 1843; *New York Sun*, August 15, 1843; *Boston Daily Atlas*, August 17, 1843; *New York Tribune*, November 3, 1843. Also in the statement of J. S. Carpentier at Norman's trial, *New York Sun*, January 17, 1844; testimony of Sarah Ballard, *New York Herald* and *New York Tribune*, January 19, 1844; and statement of lawyer David Graham at the trial, *New York Tribune*, January 20, 1844.

53   *After this incident*: Ballard's complaint: Police Office Watch Returns Docket Book, August 11, 1843, vol. 5, p. 48, Municipal Archives, Department of Records and Information Services, New York, NY. The complaint labels Norman a "prostitute," with no mention of vagrancy, but Norman's lawyer David Graham stated in court that Ballard swore that Norman was "a vagrant and a prostitute": *New York Tribune*, January 20, 1844. On vagrancy and disorderly conduct as a means to arrest prostitutes see Cohen, *Murder of Helen Jewett*, 73–76, and Wood, *Their Sisters' Keepers*, 116–117. For Emma Richardson's arrest see *New York Morning Express*, August 5, 1843.

53   *The following day*: *New York Morning Express*, August 14, 15, 1843; *New York Sun*, August 15, 16, 1843; *Advocate of Moral Reform*, February 1, 1844. Norman's release from jail on August 13 is recorded in Police Office Watch Returns Docket Book, 48. Women did occasionally test the law by attempting, like Norman, to sue for seduction themselves: see VanderVelde, "Legal Ways of Seduction," 869 and 869n256 for references to cases in 1806, 1807, and 1844.

54   *Had Norman followed the script*: The attitudes of working-class women toward sexual morality and prostitution may have been less strict than those of middle-class women. For this view see Stansell, *City of Women*, 175–180. I suspect, however, that the prevalence of the notion of the "fallen" or "ruined" woman in popular fiction meant that working-class women were not indifferent to it. One of the earliest and most influential novels depicting the fate of the fallen woman was *Charlotte Temple* by Susanna Haswell Rowson. First published in Britain in 1791, it was republished in Philadelphia by Mathew Carey in 1794, where it became "America's first best-selling novel." It remained popular through the nineteenth century: Susanna Haswell Rowson, *Charlotte Temple*, ed. Cathy N. Davidson (New York: Oxford University Press, 1986), [x]. Another sympathetic fictional fallen woman was Fleur de Marie, heroine of Eugène Sue's *Mysteries of Paris*, which appeared in New York at the same time as Norman's crime and trial.

54   *To separate herself*: Joel Behrend's testimony: *New York Herald* and *New York Tribune*, January 19, 1844. Baby farmers: Miller, *Abandoned*, 20.

55   *"Go and get her living"*: *New York Evening Post*, *New York Sun*, *New York Tribune*, January 17, 1844. The *Sun* quotes Carpentier, one of Norman's lawyers, as stating that Ballard made this taunt on October 8. The *Post* places the taunt on the night of November 1.

4. An Awful Place

56   *The city jail*: For the fate of the Collect Pond see Tyler Anbinder, *Five Points: The Nineteenth-Century New York City Neighborhood That Invented Tap Dance, Stole Elections, and Became the World's Most Notorious Slum* (New York: Penguin, 2001), 14–15, and Gerard T. Koeppel, *Water for Gotham: A History* (Princeton, NJ: Princeton University Press, 2000), 52, 56–57, 60–61. For the construction of the Tombs between 1836 and 1838, and its subsequent history and mythology, see Richard G. Carrott, *The Egyptian Revival: Its Sources, Monuments, and Meaning, 1808–1858* (Berkeley: University of California Press, 1978), 6, 146–192; Henry Cooke, "A Loiterer in New York," *Bentley's Miscellany* 16 (1844), 600–601; Charles Dickens, *American Notes* for *General Circulation* (1842; London: Penguin Books, 1985), 131–133, 139–140; Timothy J. Gilfoyle, " 'America's Greatest Criminal Barracks,' the Tombs and the Experience of Criminal Justice in New York City, 1838–1897," *Journal of Urban History* 29 (July 2003): 525–554; James D. McCabe, Jr., *Lights and Shadows of New York Life; or, The Sights and Sensations of the Great City* (Philadelphia: National, 1872; reprint, New York: Farrar, Straus, and Giroux, 1970), 232–243; Charles Sutton, *The New York Tombs: Its Secrets and Its Mysteries* (New York: United States Publishing Co., 1874); George Wilkes, *Mysteries of the Tombs: A Journal of Thirty Days Imprisonment in the New York City Prison for Libel* (New York, 1844); American Female Guardian Society and Home for the Friendless, *Wrecks and Rescues* (New York: American Female Guardian Society, 1859), 120, 196–203.

57   *The building was meant to awe*: Ned Buntline [E. Z. C. Judson], *The Mysteries and Miseries of New York: A Story of Real Life* (New York: Bedford, 1847), 74; Cooke, "Loiterer in New York," 601; Dickens, *American Notes*, 131; Wilkes, *Mysteries of the Tombs*, 9–10.

58   *Some of this Dickensian rhetoric*: For the urban travelogue see Stuart M. Blumin, "George G. Foster and the Emerging Metropolis," in *New York by Gas-Light and Other Urban Sketches by George G. Foster*, ed. Blumin (Berkeley: University of California Press, 1990), and Eric Homberger, *Scenes from the Life of a City: Corruption and Conscience in Old New York* (New Haven, CT: Yale University Press, 1994), 10–85.

58   *The Tombs complex*: David T. Valentine, *Manual of the Corporation of the City of New York, for the Years 1842 & 3* (New York: Thomas Snowden, 1842), 52; Carrott, *Egyptian Revival*, 167; Wilkes, *Mysteries of the Tombs*, 11, 13.

58   *"in one of the cages"*: *New York Express*, November 3, 1843.

58   *The jail*: Carrott, *Egyptian Revival*, 167. On the gibbet: Cooke, "Loiterer in New York," 601; Dickens, *American Notes*, 133; LMC, LNY31, November 19, 1842, in Lydia Maria Child, *Letters from New-York*, ed. Bruce Mills (Athens: University of Georgia Press, 1998), 137–143.

59   *These innovations*: On the Tombs as a model of reform see Carrott, *Egyptian Revival*, 146–192; as an example of the separate system, 150–151, 154. For prison reform see Dorothea Dix, *Remarks on Prisons and Prison Discipline in the United States* (1845; Montclair, NJ: Patterson Smith, 1984), 7, 13, 16, 22, 70–86; David Rothman, *The Discovery of the Asylum: Social Order and Disorder in the New Republic* (Boston: Little Brown, 1971), 79–83.

59   *"the defects"*: Dix, *Remarks on Prisons*, 25. On social turmoil in nineteenth-century cities and middle-class response to it see Stuart Blumin, *Emergence of the Middle Class: Social Experience in the American City, 1760–1900* (Cambridge: Cambridge

University Press, 1989), and Karen Halttunen, *Confidence Men and Painted Women: A Study of Middle-Class Culture in America, 1830–1870* (New Haven, CT: Yale University Press, 1982). On Dix as a reformer see David Gollaher, *A Voice for the Mad: The Life of Dorothea Dix* (New York: Free Press, 1995).

59   *Since the Tombs*: Carrott, *Egyptian Revival*, 180n16. The separate plan was not fully carried out at the Tombs. Dorothea Dix noted that the design of the Tombs prevented separation: *Remarks on Prisons*, 16.

59   *"that most corrupting city-prison"*: Dix, *Remarks on Prisons*, 16–17; for more on the failure of the Tombs, 105–106.

59   *"the range of the whole Hotel"*: Wilkes, *Mysteries*, 25.

60   *Wilkes, born in New York's Sixth Ward*: Clarence B. Bagley, "George Wilkes," *Washington Historical Quarterly* 5 (January 1914): 3–11 (Bagley reprints the obituary for Wilkes in *Spirit of the Times*, September 26, 1885; "Burial of George Wilkes," *New York Herald*, September 27, 1885; "Dropped Out, the Mutability of Life as Illustrated by the Career of Mr. George Wilkes," *New Hampshire Sentinel*, October 21, 1885; Patricia Cline Cohen, Timothy J. Gilfoyle, and Helen Lefkowitz Horowitz, *The Flash Press: Sporting Male Weeklies in 1840s New York* (Chicago: University of Chicago Press, 2008); "George Wilkes" (obituary), *New York Herald*, September 25, 1885; Alexander Saxton, "George Wilkes: The Transformation of a Radical Ideology," *American Quarterly* 33 (Autumn 1981): 437–458. On expanding opportunities for working-class authors: Paul Erickson, "New Books, New Men: City-Mysteries Fiction, Authorship, and the Literary Market," *Early American Studies* 1 (Spring 2003): 273–312.

61   *In 1843*: Wilkes's trial and sentence: *New York Herald*, November 22, 1843; Cohen, Gilfoyle, and Horowitz, *Flash Press*, 40–46; Donna Dennis, *Licentious Gotham: Erotic Publishing and Its Prosecution in Nineteenth-Century New York* (Cambridge, MA: Harvard University Press, 2009), 52–58, 80–82, 88–89; Helen Lefkowitz Horowitz, *Rereading Sex: Battles over Sexual Knowledge and Suppression in Nineteenth-Century America* (New York: Knopf, 2002), 179–193.

61   *When Wilkes arrived*: *New York Herald*, November 22, 1843.

61   *Walsh, like Wilkes*: Robert Ernst, "The One and Only Mike Walsh," *New-York Historical Society Quarterly* 36 (January 1952): 51–52.

61   *Walsh, who lost the race*: *Subterranean*, August 11, 1843; "Trial of Michael Walsh for Libel," *New York Atlas*, October 15, 1843; *New York Post*, November 10, 1843; "Sentence of Mike Walsh," *New York Herald*, November 11, 1843; "Mike Walsh's Fate," *Baltimore Saturday Visiter*, November 18, 1843; "My Return," *Subterranean*, January 13, 1844; "The Tombs," *Subterranean*, January 20, 1844; "My Discharge," *Subterranean*, January 27, 1844; Ernst, "One and Only," 51–53. Walsh's editorials on Norman in the *Subterranean*: "Trial of Amelia Norman," January 20, 1844; "Acquittal of Amelia Norman," January 27, 1844.

61   *"unfortunate but high-minded girl"*: [Mike Walsh], "Acquittal of Amelia Norman," *Subterranean*. On economic and industrial change in this period and its effect on "manliness" and artisanal identity see Elliot Gorn, " 'Good-Bye Boys, I Die a True American': Homicide, Nativism, and Working-Class Culture in Antebellum New York City," *Journal of American History* 74 (September 1987): 338–410, and Sean Wilentz, *Chants Democratic: New York City and the Rise of the American Working Class, 1788–1850* (New York: Oxford University Press, 1984).

61   *"dastardly, base, mercenary"*: [Mike Walsh], *Subterranean*: "Acquittal of Amelia Norman," "Trial of Amelia Norman."

61   *"warm blooded"*: *Subterranean*, "Acquittal of Amelia Norman." For frontier violence translated to the urban scene see Gorn, "Good-Bye Boys."

62   *"full grown babe"*: "The Election Tomorrow," *New York Herald*, November 6, 1843.

62   *"scratch"*: [Mike Walsh], "Trial of Amelia Norman," *Subterranean*.

62   *"called forth a feeling of pity"*: [Mike Walsh], "Acquittal of Amelia Norman," *Subterranean*.

62   *sang, chatted*: Wilkes, *Mysteries*, 12, 22, 34–35, 57, 62.

62   *"limp and drooping"*: Dickens, *American Notes*, 131.

64   *"refuse and off-scourings"*: Wilkes, *Mysteries*, 42. On the gradual elimination of imprisonment for debt in New York in the nineteenth century see Peter J. Coleman, *Debtors and Creditors in America: Insolvency, Imprisonment for Debt, and Bankruptcy, 1607–1900* (Madison: State Historical Society of Wisconsin, 1974), 118–119.

64   *"peep anxiously"*: Dickens, *American Notes*, 132.

64   *As was the practice*: For the women's cells in the former debtors' prison at the Tombs see American Female Guardian Society, *Wrecks and Rescues*, 202; Carrott, *Egyptian Revival*, 152, 172–173, and plate 111; Wilkes, *Mysteries of the Tombs*, 42. For the plan to keep the debtor's prison separate see Carrott, *Egyptian Revival*, 154. For the use of inmate labor at city institutions see Julie Miller, *Abandoned: Foundlings in Nineteenth-Century New York City* (New York: NYU Press, 2008), 77–78, 169–171. For Wilkes's observations of female inmates and their work at the Tombs see his *Mysteries of the Tombs*, 42.

64   *"criminals of better caste"*: Wilkes, *Mysteries of the Tombs*, 42.

64   *continually ribald and indecent*: Wilkes, 33.

64   *"from her mistress to give to her poor relations"*: Wilkes, 59. On Long Island Farms see Miller, *Abandoned*.

64   *"Alas poor woman!"*: Wilkes, *Mysteries*, 38.

64   *"a little world"*: Wilkes, 52.

64   *Sue's popular novel*: Sue's *Mysteries of Paris* initiated a new genre of urban writing, the "mysteries" novel. Not detective stories, and not always strictly fiction, "mysteries" novels were tours of the urban underworld that were both realistic and heightened with sensation. Wilkes was only one of many American authors who copied Sue: in 1844 thirteen books with "mystery" in their titles were published in the United States; by the time of the Civil War there were sixty-four more. See Ronald J. Zboray and Mary Saracino Zboray, "The Mysteries of New England: Eugène Sue's American 'Imitators,' 1844," *Nineteenth-Century Contexts* 22 (2000): 457. Sue's book attracted much attention in the nineteenth century from critics including Edgar Allan Poe: "The Mysteries of Paris: A Novel, by Eugene Sue," *Graham's Lady's and Gentleman's Magazine*, February 1844, 93–95 (unsigned, attributed to Poe in Dwight Thomas and David K. Jackson, *The Poe Log: A Documentary Life of Edgar Allan Poe, 1809–1849* [Boston: G. K. Hall, 1987], 449), and "Marginalia, CX," in *The Works of the Late Edgar Allan Poe*, vol. 3, *Literati* (New York: Blakeman and Mason, 1859), 533. James Gordon Bennett commented on it: "Cheap Literature—the Mighty Revolution in Literature, Morals, Piety, Religion, Philosophy, and Fudgery," *New York Herald*, November 17, 1843. Karl Marx and Friedrich Engels commented on it in *The Holy Family, or, Critique of Critical Criticism* (1845). Supporters of Amelia Norman who commented on Sue's book include the *Advocate of Moral Reform*, "'Mysteries of Paris' and Other Trash," January 15, 1844, and Lydia Maria Child: LMC, LNY111, January 1, 1844, in *Collected Correspondence* (microfiche), ed. Patricia G. Holland and Milton Meltzer, Francine Krasno,

associate ed. (New York: Kraus Microform, 1980), 18/531. The modern critical literature on Sue's *Mysteries* and the genre he originated is voluminous. See, for example, James Smith Allen, *Popular French Romanticism: Authors, Readers, and Books in the Nineteenth Century* (Syracuse, NY: Syracuse University Press, 1981); Carol Armbruster, "Translating the *Mysteries of Paris* for the American Market: The Harpers vs the New World," *Revue Française d'Études Américaines* 1, no. 138 (2014): 25–39; Michael Denning, *Mechanic Accents: Dime Novels and Working-Class Culture in America* (London: Verso, 1987), 103–105; Edward R. Tannenbaum, "The Beginnings of Bleeding-Heart Liberalism: Eugène Sue's *Les Mystères de Paris*," *Comparative Studies in Society and History* 23 (July 1981): 491–507.

65   *"In this connection"*: Margaret Fuller, *Woman in the Nineteenth Century*, ed. Madeleine B. Stern and Joel Myerson (Columbia: University of South Carolina Press, 1980), 135.

65   *"I sometimes fear"*: LMC, LNY5, in *A Lydia Maria Child Reader*, ed. Carolyn L. Karcher (Durham, NC: Duke University Press, 1997), 372.

65   *Sue's novel was originally published*: Zboray and Zboray, "Mysteries of New England," 457. A notice in the *New York Herald* (January 24, 1844) states that "most of our readers will recollect that the romance is in nine volumes."

65   *"Nearly all of France"*: Gautier is quoted in Allen, *Popular French Romanticism*, 168.

65   *even to the Russian Pale of Settlement*: Robert M. Seltzer, "Going Home: The Personal Basis of Simon Dubnow's Ideology," *AJS Review* 1 (1976): 285n5.

65   *When it arrived in the United States*: *Subterranean*, November 11, 1843. The competing translations were Eugène Sue, *The Mysteries of Paris: A Romance of Rich and Poor*, trans. Henry Champion Deming (New York: J. Winchester, New World Press, 1844), and Eugène Sue, *The Mysteries of Paris, A Novel*, trans. Charles H. Town (New York: Harper & Bros., 1843). See Armbruster, "Translating the *Mysteries*." Before the books appeared the translations came out serially in "numbers." For references to these see a review in the *Subterranean*, October 28, 1843.

65   *"all the excitement"*: "Mysteries of Paris," *Weekly Ohio State Journal* (Columbus), November 22, 1843; "The Mysteries of Paris," *New York Herald*, November 24, 1843. The *Macon Georgia Telegraph*, November 14, 1843, reported, "It is said 15,000 copies of this work were sold in New York in a single day."

65   *It was immediately dramatized*: Performance at the Chatham Theater: "The Mysteries of Paris," *New York Herald*, November 24, 1843. "Infamous book": *Advocate of Moral Reform*, " 'Mysteries of Paris' and Other Trash," January 15, 1844. LMC, LNY111, January 1, 1844; Marx and Engels, *Holy Family*; [Edgar Allan Poe], "The Mysteries of Paris."

65   *George Wilkes was only one*: Zboray and Zboray count fourteen books with "mystery" in the title published just in 1844. These included "Mysteries" of Boston, Nashua, Haverhill, Fitchburg, and more. Zboray and Zboray, "Mysteries of New England," 457, and "works cited" list, 483–492.

66   *"It is the book of the people"*: "The Mysteries of Paris," *Boston Daily Atlas*, November 17, 1843.

66   *"the descriptions of the author"*: Wilkes, *Mysteries*, 33.

66   *"since the Mysteries of Paris"*: "Correspondence of the Boston Post," *Boston Post*, January 29, 1844.

67   *Mrs. Lechner*: On the Lechners and Norman's protection of Mrs. Lechner see "Correspondence of the North American," *North American* (Philadelphia), December 14, 1843; "Another Great Robbery!," *Pittsfield (MA) Sun*, December 21, 1843; "Another

Attempted Suicide," *New York Post*, January 15, 1844; "The Lost Trunk. . . ," *Boston Transcript*, January 15, 1844; "Suicide of Lachnar [*sic*], the Robber of Pomeroy & Co.," *New York Evening Post*, January 15, 1844; "Finale of the Express Robbery," *Boston Evening Transcript*, January 16, 1844; "The Suicide, Attempted Suicide, Strange Monomania," *New York Sun*, January 16, 1844; "End of the Pom[e]roy Robbery," *Maine Cultivator and Hallowell Gazette*, January 20, 1844.

67   *Norman also helped eighteen-year-old Jane MacDonald*: Lydia Maria Child's letters on Jane MacDonald are LMC, LNY8, *Boston Courier*, April 22, 1844, which is the same as 19/548 in Lydia Maria Child, *Collected Correspondence*, ed. Patricia G. Holland, Milton Meltzer, and Francine Krasno (New York: Kraus Microform, 1980), and LMC, LNY29, December 8, 1844, in Lydia Maria Child, *Letters from New-York*, 2nd Series (New York: C. S. Francis; Boston: J. H. Francis, 1845), 264. See also "A Hard Case," *New York Tribune*, April 11, 1844; "A Painful Case," *Boston Daily Atlas*, April 15, 1844. For MacDonald's pardon by New York's governor see *Newark Daily Advertiser*, April 23, 1844. Her name is given variously as McDonald and McDonnell.

68   *"everything indicated comfort"*: Wilkes, *Mysteries*, 42. On Melinda Hoag see Wilkes, *Mysteries*, 16–18. Wilkes already knew Hoag from his earlier role as editor of the *Sunday Flash*: see "Big Levy," *Sunday Flash*, October 17, 1841, in Cohen, Gilfoyle, and Horowitz, *Flash Press*, 200.

68   *"greatly wronged"*: "B," "The Last [Late] Attempt to Kill," *New York Tribune*, November 4, 1843; testimony of Joel Behrend, *New York Tribune*, January 19, 1844.

68   *But he showed his concern*: Testimony of William Callender, *New York Herald*, January 19, 1844.

68   *"in her situation"*: Testimony of Dr. Benjamin McCready, *New York Tribune*, January 19, 1844.

68   *"despondency"*: Testimony of Dr. Benjamin McCready, *New York Herald*, January 19, 1844.

69   *"repulsed her with disdain"*: Wilkes, *Mysteries*, 42.

5. A Great Heart

72   *"Over the River and through the Woods"*: "The New-England Boy's Song about Thanksgiving Day," in Lydia Maria Child, *Flowers for Children*, pt. 2 (New York: C. S. Francis, 1854), 25–26. For Lydia Maria Child's life see Carolyn L. Karcher, *The First Woman in the Republic: A Cultural Biography of Lydia Maria Child* (Durham, NC: Duke University Press, 1994). Older works on Child include Helene G. Baer, *The Heart Is Like Heaven: The Life of Lydia Maria Child* (Philadelphia: University of Pennsylvania Press, 1964), and Seth Curtis Beach, *Daughters of the Puritans: A Group of Brief Biographies* (Boston: American Unitarian Association, 1905). Contemporary observers include Thomas Wentworth Higginson, *Contemporaries* (Boston: Houghton, Mifflin, 1899), 108–141; James Russell Lowell, *A Fable for Critics* (London: Gay and Bird, 1890), 84; and Edgar Allan Poe, "The Literati of New York City," in *Essays and Reviews* (New York: Library of America, 1984), 1198–1199. There is also a voluminous scholarly journal literature on Child and her writing. Her letters are collected in *Collected Correspondence*, ed. Patricia G. Holland, Milton Meltzer, and Francine Krasno (New York: Kraus Microform, 1980) (hereafter *CC*), and *Selected Letters, 1817–1880*, ed. Milton Meltzer and Patricia G. Holland (Amherst: University of Massachusetts Press, 1982) (hereafter *SL*). A bibliography of her writings is included in Karcher, *First Woman*, 757–772. Modern, published editions of her writings are *A Lydia Maria Child Reader*, ed. Carolyn L. Karcher (Durham, NC: Duke University

Press, 1997), and *Letters from New-York*, ed. Bruce Mills (Athens: University of Georgia Press, 1998).

72   *"was by no means"*: John Greenleaf Whittier, introduction to *Letters of Lydia Maria Child* (Boston: Houghton Mifflin, 1883), xi.

72   *moved in intersecting abolitionist and Transcendentalist circles*: For Child's association with Transcendentalists in Boston see John Matteson, *The Lives of Margaret Fuller* (New York: W. W. Norton, 2012), 159. For her arrival in New York see Karcher, *First Woman*, xxii. For the editorship of the National Anti-Slavery Standard, Louis Hewitt Fox, *New York City Newspapers, 1820–1851: A Bibliography* (Chicago: University of Chicago Press, 1928), 71.

72   *"got hold of the strings"*: LMC to Anne Whitney, May 25, 1879, in *SL*, 558.

72   *Even those who worked*: The three-fifths clause of the federal Constitution is one example of this position. Another is the American Colonization Society, founded in 1817, which proposed sending enslaved African Americans "back" to Africa, establishing the colony of Liberia to do so. Still another is the gradual emancipation acts that freed slaves in the era of the American Revolution. For New York's gradual emancipation act see Arthur Zilversmit, *The First Emancipation: The Abolition of Slavery in the North* (Chicago: University of Chicago Press, 1967). For the bigger picture see Graham Hodges, *Root and Branch: African-Americans in New York and New Jersey, 1613–1863* (Chapel Hill: University of North Carolina Press, 1999), and Peter Kolchin, *American Slavery, 1619–1877* (New York: Hill & Wang, 2003).

72   *Garrison's ideas*: Robert A. Abzug, *Cosmos Crumbling: American Reform and the Religious Imagination* (New York: Oxford University Press, 1994), 129–162.

73   *Anti-abolitionist mobs*: For anti-abolitionist mobs in New York at the time see Tyler Anbinder, *Five Points: The 19th-Century New York City Neighborhood That Invented Tap Dance, Stole Elections, and Became the World's Most Notorious Slum* (New York: Penguin, 2002), 7–13. In 1838 a mob attacked a meeting of the Anti-Slavery Convention of American Women in Philadelphia: *SL*, 79. For Garrison's experience: Wendell Phillips Garrison and Francis Jackson Garrison, *William Lloyd Garrison, 1805–1879: The Story of His Life, Told by His Children*, vol. 2 (New York: Century, 1885), 1–24. For Child's own brush with anti-abolitionist mob violence see her letters to Louisa Loring, August 15, [1835] and Ellis Gray Loring, August 22, 1835, in *SL*, 31, 33–34.

73   *An Appeal*: (Boston: Allen and Ticknor, 1833). On the *Appeal* and its reception see Abzug, *Cosmos Crumbling*, 200–201; Karcher, *First Woman*, 191–192.

73   *"almost every door"*: Wendell Phillips, "Remarks of Wendell Phillips at the Funeral of Lydia Maria Child, October 23, 1880," in *Letters of Lydia Maria Child* (Whittier edition), 264–265; Harriet Martineau quoted in Higginson, *Contemporaries*, 122.

73   *Despite all this the* Appeal *sold*: For sales see Carolyn L. Karcher, "Censorship, American Style: The Case of Lydia Maria Child," *Studies in the American Renaissance*, 1986: 287. Higginson, *Contemporaries*, 123. Child's three subsequent anti-slavery works were *Authentic Anecdotes of American Slavery* (Newburyport, MA: Charles Whipple, 1835); *Anti-Slavery Catechism* (Newburyport, MA: Charles Whipple, 1836); *The Evils of Slavery, and the Cure of Slavery* (Newburyport, MA: Charles Whipple, 1836).

73   *The Society split*: For a contemporary description of the split in the American Anti-Slavery Society see Oliver Johnson, *W. L. Garrison and His Times* (1881; Miami: Mnemosyne, 1969), 292–297. For the roots of the American women's rights movement in the movement for the abolition of slavery see Eleanor Flexner, *Century of Struggle: The Woman's Rights Movement in the United States* (New York: Athenaeum, 1974).

74   *"say and do"*: LMC to William Lloyd Garrison, September 2, 1839, in *SL*, 123.

74   *"I never have entered"*: LMC to Lucretia Mott, March 5, 1839, in *SL*, 106.

74   *"rights-of-woman"*: LMC to Ellis Gray and Louisa Loring, July 10, 1838, in *SL*, 78; LNY34, February 23, 1843, in Karcher, *Reader*, 362. For the conservative values that some women reformers brought to their work see Lori Ginzberg, *Women and the Work of Benevolence: Morality, Politics, and Class in the Nineteenth-Century United States* (New Haven, CT: Yale University Press, 1990), and Carroll Smith-Rosenberg, who writes about the origins of the New York Female Moral Reform Society in *Religion and the Rise of the American City: The New York City Mission Movement, 1812–1870* (Ithaca, NY: Cornell University Press, 1971).

74   *Her abolitionist comrade*: Higginson wrote that Child "evidently looked with distrust, however, on that rising movement for the equality of the sexes, of which Frances Wright was then the rather formidable leader": Higginson, *Contemporaries*, 121. On Fuller: John Matteson, *The Lives of Margaret Fuller* (New York: W. W. Norton, 2012); on Wright: Celia Morris, *Fanny Wright: Rebel in America* (Urbana: University of Illinois Press, 1992). In 1843 Child wrote that the style of women's rights advocates "has often been offensive to taste, and unacceptable to reason," although "assuredly that of its opponents have been still more so," LNY34, in Karcher, *Reader*, 359.

74   *"Domestic love"*: Quotations: Lydia Maria Child, *Celebrated Women, or, Biographies of Good Wives* (Boston: Higgins, Bradley, and Dayton, 1858), 64, and LMC, LNY34, in Karcher, *Reader*, 363. Books: *The Frugal Housewife* (Boston: Marsh & Capen, 1829); *The Mother's Book* (Boston: Carter, Hendee & Babcock, 1831).

74   *"Reform always seemed"*: LMC to Eliza Scudder, February 6, 1870, in *SL*, 489.

74   *"vanity and ambition"*: LMC to Theodore Tilton, May 27, 1866, in *SL*, 461.

75   *"moral and intellectual development"*: LMC, LNY34, February 16 and 23, 1843, in Karcher *Reader*, 361.

76   *"more rational companions"*: LMC, LNY34, February 16 and 23, 1843, in Karcher, *Reader*, 363.

76   *"Would it not be an improvement"*: LMC, LNY34, February 16 and 23, 1843, in Karcher, *Reader*, 359.

76   *"ennobled and refined"*: LMC, LNY34, February 16 and 23, 1843, in Karcher, *Reader*, 363.

76   *"false structure of society"*: Child refers to the "false structure" or "false foundation" of society in relation to women in LNY5, February 6 and 22, 1844, in Karcher, *Reader*, 366, and in LNY34, in Karcher, *Reader*, February 16 and 23, 1843, 362, 264. In 1866 she was still writing about the "false customs, which men perpetuate for their own conveniences and then quarrel with the consequences": LMC to Theodore Tilton, May 27, 1866, in *SL*, 461. "Let her reflect why she is afraid to go out in the evening" is in LNY34, Karcher, *Reader*, 359.

76   *She was in agreement with "nonresistance"*: Merle E. Curti, "Non-resistance in New England," *New England Quarterly* 2 (January 1929): 34–57; John Demos, "The Anti-Slavery Movement and the Problem of Violent 'Means,'" *New England Quarterly* 37 (December 1963): 501–526; Lori D. Ginzberg, "Virtue and Violence: Female Ultraists and the Politics of Non-resistance," *Quaker History* 84 (Spring 1995): 17–25.

77   *"The non-resistance society"*: LMC to Francis Shaw, January 15, 1843, *SL*, 186. Child expressed comparable views in another letter to Shaw, February 15, 1842 (*SL*, 160–162), and in one to James Miller McKim, January 26, 1842 (*SL*, 158).

77   *Child was also opposed to violence in the form of capital punishment*: LMC, "Letter XXXI," November 19, 1842, 137–143, and "Letter XXXII," November 26, 1842, 143–147, in *Letters from New-York*, ed. Mills. These letters were devoted to the attempted execution of the murderer John Colt. Colt died of a stab wound under

mysterious circumstances before he could be executed. See Harold Schechter, *Killer Colt: Murder, Disgrace, and the Making of an American Legend* (New York: Ballantine Books, 2010).

77 *"Society had kindled all around me"*: LMC, "Letter XXXI," 138–139, in *Letters from New-York*, ed Mills.

77 chivalry: [Mike Walsh], "Trial of Amelia Norman," *Subterranean*, January 2, 1844. Here Walsh wrote of Norman, "Has she no male relative to avenge the wrongs which she has suffered[?]"; "Warm-blooded": [Mike Walsh], "Acquittal of Amelia Norman," *Subterranean*, January 27, 1844.

77 *"gallantry"*: LMC, LNY34, February 16 and 23, 1844, in Karcher, *Reader*, 360, 361.

77 *"Ah! How many of my sex"*: Sarah Grimké, Letter III, The Pastoral Letter of the General Association of Congregational Ministers of Massachusetts, July 1837, in *The Public Years of Sarah and Angelina Grimké*, ed. Larry Ceplair (New York: Columbia University Press, 1989), 216.

78 *"complete knight of chivalry"*: Karcher, *First Woman*, 48. "David Lee Child," *Dictionary of American Biography* (New York: Scribner's, 1936); "Death of David Lee Child," *New York Times*, September 28, 1874.

78 *"terrible year of toil and discord"*: LMC to Louisa Loring, June 22, 1845, in *SL*, 223. "My husband's deficiencies": LMC to Francis Shaw, August 2, 1846, in *SL*, 228–229. For the beet sugar experiment, Karcher, *First Woman*, 248–250.

78 *Isaac T. Hopper and his family*: Child's residence with the Hoppers can be traced in *Doggett's New York City Directory* (New York: John Doggett Jr., 1843–1847) at Isaac Hopper's addresses at 174 Grand Street (1843–1844) and 20 Third Street (1844–1847). Her husband's name is listed, even though he remained in Northampton. In 1846–1847 both Childs are listed at the Hoppers' address, with LMC listed as L. Maria Child, authoress. For the Hoppers: Margaret Hope Bacon, *Lamb's Warrior: The Life of Isaac T. Hopper* (New York: Thomas Y. Crowell, 1970); Lydia Maria Child, *Isaac T. Hopper: A True Life* (Boston: J. P. Jewett, 1853); Sarah Hopper Emerson, *The Life of Abby Hopper Gibbons, Told Chiefly through Her Correspondence* (New York: G. P. Putnam's, 1896–1897). For the involvement of Isaac Hopper and his son-in-law James Gibbons with the American Anti-Slavery Society and the founding and running of the *National Anti-Slavery Standard* see Johnson, *W. L. Garrison*, 296–297. On the *Standard*'s founding and editorship see Karcher, *First Woman*, 267–294.

79 *John Hopper was twice attacked*: Child recounts these stories in *Isaac Hopper*, 316–317, 319–334, without naming John Hopper. Margaret Hope Bacon confirms that it was John Hopper in *Lamb's Warrior*, 108, 112.

79 *Isaac and Hannah Hopper*: Child wrote an admiring biography of Isaac Hopper (*Isaac T. Hopper: A True Life*) and dedicated it to his widow, describing herself as Hannah Hopper's "grateful and attached friend." On varieties of male/female friendship in the early United States see Cassandra Good, *Founding Friendships: Friendships between Men and Women in the Early American Republic* (New York: Oxford University Press, 2015).

79 *"a miracle of fun"*: Joseph Hodges Choate, *The Life of Joseph Hodges Choate as Gathered Chiefly from His Letters*, ed. Edward Sandford Martin (New York: C. Scribner's Sons, 1920), 1:96, 98. "Earnest and ardent": Octavius Brooks Frothingham, *Words Spoken at the Funeral of John Hopper, July 31, 1864* (New York: Thitchener and Glastaeter, 1864), 4. A jokester: DeWolf Hopper, *Once a Clown, Always a Clown: Reminiscences of DeWolf Hopper* (Boston: Little Brown, 1927), 8. On seeing Fanny Kemble: Bacon, *Lamb's Warrior*, 144. John Hopper's son DeWolf Hopper recalled that his father saw the actress Laura Kean ninety-four times: *Once a Clown*, 5.

79   *When Lydia Maria Child arrived*: Karcher, *First Woman*, 296–299. "Little Zippy Damn": LMC to Ellis Gray Loring, June 17, 1841, in *SL*, 145. "Zippy Damn" might have had some relation to the song "Ole Zip Coon," which was written by George Washington Dixon, George Wilkes's partner in the *Sunday Flash*, and performed by him in blackface. See Patricia Cline Cohen, Timothy J. Gilfoyle, and Helen Lefkowitz Horowitz, *The Flash Press: Sporting Male Weeklies in 1840s New York* (Chicago: University of Chicago Press, 2008), 28. However, Child's gentility and abolitionist views make this unlikely.

79   *"My charms"*: LMC to Ellis Loring, July 27, 1841, quoted in Karcher, *First Woman*, 297. "Anything but fashionable": Edgar Allan Poe, "The Literati of New York City," in *Essays and Reviews* (New York: Library of America, 1984), 1198–1199.

80   *"natural love for sinners"*: Maria Lowell, quoted in Abigail Hopper Gibbons to her daughter Sally, April 3, 1874, in *The Life of Abby Hopper Gibbons: Told Chiefly through Her Correspondence*, ed. Sarah Hopper Emerson (New York: G. P. Putnam's Sons, 1897), 2:182.

80   *In Philadelphia*: Bacon, *Lamb's Warrior*; Child, *Isaac T. Hopper*. An advertisement for Hopper's store at 143 Nassau Street shows him selling works by and about Quakers and Quakerism. The ad is for H. Jackson, *Civilization of the Indians*; *Life of Thomas Cooper, Who Was a Fugitive Slave, and Became an Eminent Methodist Minister, an Authentic Narrative*; and other works, *National Anti-Slavery Standard*, October 7, 1841.

80   *the Prison Association of New York*: For the prison reform movement, the Prison Association of New York, and the Women's Prison Association of New York see LMC, LNY29, December 8, 1844, in *Letters from New York*, 2nd series (New York: C. S. Francis; Boston, J. H. Francis, 1845), 258–272; Dorothea Dix, *Remarks on Prisons and Prison Discipline in the United States* (1845; Montclair, NJ: Patterson Smith, 1984), 11, 57; [Margaret Fuller], "Asylum for Discharged Female Convicts," *New York Tribune*, June 19, 1845; see Estelle B. Freedman, *Their Sisters' Keepers: Women's Prison Reform in America* (Ann Arbor: University of Michigan Press, 1981), 30, for Fuller's authorship of this article. Abigail Hopper Gibbons, "Sketch of Miss Sedgwick's Connection with the Women's Prison Association of New York," in *Life and Letters of Catharine M. Sedgwick*, ed. Mary E. Dewey (New York: Harper and Bros., 1872), 419–425; Prison Association of New York, *First Annual Report*, December 1844 (New York: Prison Association of New York, [1844]).

80   *"'Murder!'"*: George Wilkes, *Mysteries of the Tombs: A Journal of Thirty Days Imprisonment in the New York City Prison for Libel* (New York, 1844), 30.

80   *The Hoppers' long-established practice*: In his testimony at Norman's trial, the Tombs' doctor, Benjamin McCready, said John Hopper visited Norman in jail and found her a lawyer: *New York Herald*, January 19, 1844. Child suggests that Isaac Hopper discovered Norman in jail. In two stories that blend fact with fiction, "The Umbrella Girl" and "An Affecting Tale of Truth," Child describes Isaac Hopper discovering the protagonist—a young woman for whom Child borrowed some elements from Norman's life—"lying on the floor of her cell, with her face buried in her hands, sobbing as if her heart would break," just as Child found Norman in the Tombs. "The Umbrella Girl," in Child, *Isaac T. Hopper*, 87, and "An Affecting Tale of Truth," in *The Mother's Assistant and Young Lady's Friend* 4–5 (April 1844): 85–90.

80   *"In prison"*: LMC, LNY5, in Karcher, *Reader*, 365.

80   *The bail*: LMC, LNY5, in Karcher, *Reader*, 365–367. Child obscures who these supporters were with the passive voice, writing "efforts were made to reduce this sum"

(365), but Norman's supporters were herself, the Hoppers, the moral reformers, and the "good-hearted stranger, a Mr. Carney of Boston" (367), who offered fifty dollars to pay Norman's legal fees. If there were others, she doesn't name them.

81   *"legion of heartless"*: Wilkes, *Mysteries*, 13, 52. Supporting Wilkes's view is the fact that Warner is not listed in biographical guides to lawyers of this period, such as Alden Chester, *Courts and Lawyers of New York: A History, 1609–1925* (New York: American Historical Society, 1925; reprint, Clark, NJ: Lawbook Exchange, 2005); L. B. Proctor, *The Bench and Bar of New York, Containing Biographical Sketches of Eminent Judges and Lawyers of the New-York Bar* (New York: Diossy, 1870); David McAdam, *History of the Bench and Bar of New York* (New York: New York History Co., 1897).

81   *"wise for him to settle"*: Charles Edwards, *Pleasantries about Courts and Lawyers of the State of New York* (New York: Richardson, 1867), 209.

81   *"noble-souled"*: LMC, LNY5, in Karcher, *Reader*, 367. Thomas Warner, lawyer, lived and worked at 18 City Hall Place: *Doggett's New York City Directory for 1845 & 1846* (New York: John Doggett, 1845). For the date Warner left Norman's case, LMC, LNY5, in Karcher, *Reader*, 366, and *New York Herald*, January 16, 1844. On Hopper and McCready's role in finding a new lawyer: *New York Herald*, January 19, 1844, and *New York Tribune*, January 19, 1844. Carney is never mentioned again in any of the records of or writings about the case. He does not seem to be a member of any of New York's reform organizations, and his Irish name, common in both New York and Boston, makes him hard to locate in the city directories. In the version of LNY5 that appeared in the *Boston Courier* on February 6, 1844, Child spells the name Kearny.

81   *Henry Leitga*: "The Murder of Mrs. Leitga," *New York Herald*, October 31, 1843; " 'Wo to the Bloody City,' " *Advocate of Moral Reform*, November 15, 1843, 173; *New York Herald* (all 1843): October 30, 31, November 1, 2, 4, 11, and December 19; and (in 1844), January 17, 18 (with a portrait of Leitga). His acquittal is reported in the *Whig Standard* (Washington, DC), January 20, 1844. This is just a sampling of the many articles about the Leitga case.

81   *"pallid faced"*: Wilkes, *Mysteries*, 15, 52.

82   *"sick at heart"*: LMC to Ellis Gray Loring, April 30, 1839, *SL*, 114.

82   *"fighting and controversy"*: LMC to Ellis Gray Loring, March 6, 1843, 193. Child expresses her reasons for leaving the *Standard* in this letter, 192–197 in *SL*.

82   the *Standard's* circulation: Karcher, *Reader*, 297.

82   *"individual freedom"* . . . *"I will work in my own way"*: LMC to Ellis Gray Loring, March 6, 1843, in *SL*, 194.

82   *"the freedom of my own spirit"*: LMC, "Farewell," *Standard*, May 4, 1843.

82   *Child's sympathy*: For the idea (with which I agree) that Child empathized with Norman's status as a fallen woman, even though she didn't inhabit that status herself, see Karcher, *Reader*, 339.

82   *to liberate herself from David*: In Anglo-American law women lost their separate civic identities when they married, as a result of which husbands controlled their wives' property and earnings. See Linda Kerber, *Women of the Republic: Intellect and Ideology in Revolutionary America* (Chapel Hill: University of North Carolina Press, 1980), 120, and Marylynn Salmon, *Women and the Law of Property in Early America* (Chapel Hill: University of North Carolina Press, 1986). The concept of "coverture," as it was called, was challenged by the married women's property laws passed by states starting in the middle of the nineteenth century. Before that, equity law provided a way for women and their families to retain or regain control of property, and Child did this,

making her friend Ellis Gray Loring her legal surrogate. The details of this transaction are vague—it may have been an informal arrangement—but see Karcher, *First Woman*, xxii, 293, 364–365, and LMC to Ellis Gray Loring, April 13, 1851, in *SL*, 258–259 and 259n2.

82   *"I have come to be* afraid": LMC to Ellis Gray Loring, March 6, 1843, in *SL*, 195.

83   *"supplies to me the place"*: LMC to Ellis Gray Loring, March 6, 1843, in *SL*, 195.

83   *"The fallen woman"*: Whittier, introduction to *Letters of Lydia Maria Child*, 267.

83   *ten-year-old orphan boy*: LMC to Anna Loring, December 26, [1843], in *SL*, 206.

83   *In later years*: Harriet Jacobs, *Incidents in the Life of a Slave Girl*, ed. Nellie Y. McKay (1861; New York: W. W. Norton, 2001).

83   *More spectacularly*: Karcher, *Reader*, 143–145.

83   *"When God"*: LMC to Ellis Loring, December 14, 1849, quoted in Karcher, *First Woman*, 367.

83   *In August 1843 she published*: Lydia Maria Child, *Letters from New York*, 1st series (New York: C. S. Francis; Boston: James Munroe, 1843; London: Bentley, 1843); Child, *Letters from New York*, 2nd series. For the publication history of the collected editions of *Letters from New-York* see Mills, ed., *Letters from New-York*, xxvi–xxxi. Mills discusses Child's decision to leave some letters out on xxx–xxxi. The column devoted to Norman was LNY5, which appeared in the *Boston Courier*, February 6, 1844, and the *National Anti-Slavery Standard*, February 22, 1844. The version that appeared in the *Standard* is published by Carolyn Karcher as the "Uncollected Letter": Karcher, *Reader*, 365–373. For more on the two versions of LNY5 see the appendix.

84   *"mostly based upon the sins"*: Higginson, *Contemporaries*, 130.

84   *The leadership of the American Female Moral Reform Society*: For the American Female Moral Reform Society, which began as the New York Female Moral Reform Society and later became the American Female Guardian Society, see American Female Guardian Society and Home for the Friendless, *Our Golden Jubilee: A Retrospect of the American Female Guardian Society and Home for the Friendless from 1834 to 1884* (New York: American Female Guardian Society, 1884), and *Wrecks and Rescues* (New York: American Female Guardian Society, 1859); Mrs. S. R. I. Bennett, *Woman's Work among the Lowly: Memorial Volume of the First Forty Years of the American Female Guardian Society and Home for the Friendless* (New York: American Female Guardian Society, 1877); Flora Northrup, *The Record of a Century, 1834–1934* (New York: American Female Guardian Society and Home for the Friendless, 1934); Smith-Rosenberg, *Religion and the Rise of the American City*. Smith-Rosenberg describes the social background of the moral reformers, and Northrup lists the names of the Society's leaders, but because the members did not sign their writings in the *Advocate* and did not speak publicly, it is impossible to know which members of the Society wrote in favor of Amelia Norman and attended her trial.

84   *"Mothers," they warned*: *Advocate of Moral Reform*, April 15, 1840.

84   *"Seduction is going on by wholesale"*: LMC, LNY5, Karcher, *Reader*, 371.

85   *Less open to joy*: From the *Advocate of Moral Reform*: " 'Mysteries of Paris' and Other Trash," January 15, 1844; Mrs. Turner, "Thoughts and Considerations on the Subject of Moral Purity" (novel reading), April 1, 1844, 52; "Immorality of Theatres," November 15, 1838, 171; "Balls, Houses of Infamy and Death," April 19, 1838, 53; "Tendency of the Waltz," November 15, 1838, 169; "Dangers of the Circus," April 15, 1838, 58.

85   *"cause of moral purity"*: *Advocate of Moral Reform*, November 15, 1840. In this issue the *Advocate* declared that "all the profits of this paper . . . will be faithfully expended in Missionary and other labors to promote the cause of Moral Purity."

85   *"the injustice"*: *Advocate of Moral Reform*, February 15, 1844. Under the heading "Female Labor" they reprinted from the *Portland (ME) Tribune*: "Females must be paid better for their labor, and they shall be if our influence can be felt": January 1, 1844, 7. On March 1, 1844, they published a poem, "Song of the Shirt," about the hard fate of a seamstress.

85   *visited Norman in jail*: In a letter to the editor of the *Tribune* signed "Several Moral Reformers," members of the American Female Guardian Society mentioned "visiting the prisoner in her cell": "Amelia Norman and the F.M.R.S. [Female Moral Reform Society]," *New York Tribune*, January 23, 1844.

86   *"The girl who gave the wound"*: "Police Office—the Stabbing Case near the Astor House," *Advocate of Moral Reform*, November 15, 1843. On the moral reformers' visiting Norman in jail see "Amelia Norman and the F.M.R.S," *New York Tribune*, January 23, 1844.

86   *At the same time*: For the Society's anti-seduction campaign see its fourteenth annual report, published in the *Advocate of Moral Reform*, June 1, 1848, describing the Society's ten-year effort to get a bill passed. The history of the campaign, which also targeted adultery, abduction, and the banning of "disorderly houses," can be traced in the pages of the *Advocate* from 1838 until 1848, when bills criminalizing seduction and abduction were passed. See, for example, "Who Will Circulate Petitions?," November 1, 1838; mention of "thousands of petitions" delivered to legislators "for the last five years" in "Trial and Acquittal of Amelia Norman," February 1, 1844; "Why Do You Ask a Law?," February 1, 1844; "Six Years Delay," July 15, 1844. See also Marilynn Wood Hill, *Their Sisters' Keepers: Prostitution in New York City, 1830–1870* (Berkeley: University of California Press, 1993), 142, and Larry Whiteaker, *Seduction, Prostitution, and Moral Reform in New York, 1830–1860* (New York: Garland, 1997), 141–145.

86   *"bent on revenge"*: "Police Office—the Stabbing Case near the Astor House," *Advocate of Moral Reform*, November 15, 1843.

86   *George W. Matsell*: On Matsell (1811–1877) see "Death of George W. Matsell," *New York Times*, July 26, 1877; Bob Drahozal, "George Washington Matsell, Remembering the Big Chief," *Linn County Time Lines* (Linn County Historical Society, Cedar Rapids, IA) 4 (June 1998): 1, 6–8; William Hunt, *American Biographical Panorama* (Albany: J. Munsell, 1849), 443–340; Christine Stansell, *City of Women: Sex and Class in New York, 1789–1860* (Urbana: University of Illinois Press, 1987), 194–197. For an example of his Dickensian style of writing see his *Semi-Annual Report of the Chief of Police from May 1, to October 31, 1849* (New York, 1849).

86   *Matsell interviewed*: Matsell worked at the lower police office at the Tombs: see David T. Valentine, *Manual of the Corporation of the City of New-York for the Years 1842 & 3* (New York: David T. Valentine, 1842), 118. His interview with Norman is in "The People vs. Amelia Norman, November 23, 1843" (indictment), District Attorney Indictment Records, New York County, MN 5221, Roll 221, Municipal Archives, Department of Records and Information Services, New York, NY.

87   *"the rogue fraternity"*: George Washington Matsell, *Vocabulum; or, The Rogue's Lexicon* (New York: George W. Matsell, 1859), [iii]; "I was naturally led," iv.

6. The Trial Begins

88   *Amelia Norman's trial was set to start*: "Another Attempted Suicide," *New York Post*, January 15, 1844; "Suicide of Lachnar, the Robber of Pomeroy & Co.," *New York Post*, January 15, 1844; "Attempted Suicide in the City Prison," *New York Herald*, January 16, 1844; "City News," *New York Morning Express*, January 16, 1844; "The Suicide—Attempted Suicide—Strange Monomania," *New York Sun*, January 16, 1844; "Attempted

Suicide," *New York Evangelist*, January 18, 1844; "Case of Amelia Norman" (testimony by Benjamin McCready about Amelia's suicide attempt), *New York Tribune*, January 19, 1844. There are some minor disagreements in these articles as to date and method (the *Post* says she used a handkerchief, the *Herald* a petticoat; the *Evangelist* says the attempt was Sunday night, the others Monday morning), but all agree that both suicides took place the weekend before Norman's trial and that Norman was aware of Lechner's suicide.

88   *"proved the drop too much"*: LMC, LNY5, in Carolyn L. Karcher, ed., *A Lydia Maria Child Reader* (Durham, NC: Duke University Press, 1997), 366.

88   *"extremely pallid"*: *New York Herald*, January 16, 1844.

89   *"almost to suffocation"*: *New York Tribune*, January 17, 1844.

89   *Child found the Egyptian style*: LMC, LNY5, in Karcher, *Reader*, 372–373. "Letters from New-York," which Child originated as a column in the *National Anti-Slavery Standard* while she was editor there, was by this time being published in the *Boston Courier*. "Letter from New-York No. V," which was published in the *Courier* on February 6, 1844, soon after the trial ended, is Child's fullest comment on Amelia Norman. When the *Standard* reprinted it on February 22, 1844, its angrier passages had been cut, probably by Child herself. For a comparison between the two texts of "Letter from New-York No. V" see the appendix.

89   *The courtroom was equally grand*: For the appearance of the Court of Sessions courtroom in the Tombs complex see American Female Guardian Society and Home for the Friendless, *Wrecks and Rescues* (New York: American Female Guardian Society, 1859), 206, 208; Richard G. Carrott, *The Egyptian Revival: Its Sources, Monuments, and Meaning, 1808–1858* (Berkeley: University of California Press, 1978), 166–167; John Doggett Jr., *The Great Metropolis: or New York in 1845* (New York: John Doggett Jr., [1845]), 62; James D. McCabe, Jr., *Lights and Shadows of New York Life; or, The Sights and Sensations of the Great City* (Philadelphia: National, 1872; reprint, New York: Farrar, Straus and Giroux, 1970), 239, 240; George Wilkes, *Mysteries of the Tombs: A Journal of Thirty Days Imprisonment in the New York City Prison for Libel* (New York, 1844), 11.

89   *a kind of theater*: Mary Henderson, *The City and the Theatre* (New York: Back Stage Books, 2004), map 2, "Theatres in New York from 1798 to 1850," 37, and 49–79. For crowds at the Court of Sessions—specifically the 1839 trial of Ezra White for the murder of Peter Fitzpatrick, where "the Court Room was thronged as soon almost as the doors were opened"—see letter, E. H. Faulkner to Thomas Mudgley, December 4, 1839, Thomas Mudgley, Miscellaneous Manuscripts, New-York Historical Society. Or the 1842 trial of John Colt for the murder of Samuel Adams, where "the large space allotted to the public was completely filled, and there was scarce standing room inside the railing": *New York Herald*, November 2, 1841.

90   *"thick-and-thin Democrat"*: "Old Bourbon," *Harper's Weekly*, March 12, 1887, 178. For Purdy's career on the Board of Aldermen from 1838 to 1843 see David Valentine, *Manual of the Corporation of the City of New-York for the Years 1842 & 3* (New York: Thomas Snowden, 1842), 233–237. According to William C. Gover, Purdy was "a veteran of Democratic warfare": *The Tammany Hall Democracy of the City of New York* (New York, 1875), 47. His funeral was an elaborate and well-attended Tammany Hall event, held at the height of the corrupt ring's power: "Funeral of Elijah F. Purdy," *New York Times*, January 13, 1866. Death notice, *Harper's Weekly*, January 20, 1866, 35.

90   *David Vandervoort*: As an alderman, 1844–1845, see Valentine, *Manual* (1842), 158–160, and in results of the New York charter election, *Hudson River Chronicle*,

April 20, 1841, where Vandervoort appears with Elijah Purdy on a list of elected aldermen, with party affiliations noted.

90   *As recorder*: For the history, function, and personnel of the Court of Sessions in New York see Oliver L. Barbour, *The Magistrate's Criminal Law: A Practical Treatise on the Jurisdiction, Duty, and Authority of Justices of the Peace in the State of New York, in Criminal Cases* (Albany: Gould, 1841; New York: Gould, Banks, 1841), 312–313; *Documents of the Board of Aldermen of the City of New York*, vol. 10, pt. 1, May 29, 1843, to January 3, 1844 (New York, 1844), 697; "New York's Old Bailey: A Sketch of the Great Criminal Court," *New York Times*, October 28, 1888.

90   *the Culper Ring*: For the spying and military career of Benjamin Tallmadge see his correspondence with George Washington in *Papers of George Washington, Colonial Series*, ed. W. W. Abbott (Charlottesville: University of Virginia Press, 1983–1995), and Morton Pennypacker, *George Washington's Spies on Long Island and in New York* (New York: Long Island Historical Society, 1938). For Benjamin Tallmadge's career in Congress see "Benjamin Tallmadge (1754–1835)," Biographical Directory of the United States Congress, http://bioguide.congress.gov.

90   *Frederick Tallmadge*: For Frederick Tallmadge's career see "Frederick Augustus Tallmadge (1792–1869)," Biographical Directory of the United States Congress, http://bioguide.congress.gov; L. B. Proctor, *The Bench and Bar of New-York* (New York: Diossy, 1870), 495; "Obituary, Hon. Frederick A. Tallmadge," *New York Times*, September 18, 1869. Tallmadge was an alderman from the Eighth Ward in 1836–1837: Valentine, *Manual*, 1843–1844, 155. By 1860 Tallmadge was one of the "former leaders" of the Native American Party: "Analysis of Our Local Contest," *New York Times*, November 9, 1860.

92   *The prosecutor in the case*: On the life, career, and family of Jonas B. Phillips: Charles P. Daly, *The Settlement of the Jews in North America*, ed. Max J. Kohler (New York: P. Cowen, 1893), 145–146; Helen Lefkowitz Horowitz, *Rereading Sex: Battles over Sexual Knowledge and Suppression in Nineteenth-Century America* (New York: Knopf, 2002), 182; Samuel Rezneck, *The Saga of an American Jewish Family since the Revolution: A History of the Family of Jonas Phillips* (Washington, DC: University Press of America, 1980), 185, 188, 192–193, 195; Jonathan Sarna, *Jacksonian Jew: The Two Worlds of Mordecai Noah* (New York: Holmes & Meier, 1981). "Obituary, Jonas B. Phillips," *New York Times*, May 16, 1867. This obituary estimates that Phillips wrote "over seventy plays." Despite his productivity he was, according to theater historian George Odell, "a very minor light in the history of the American drama": Odell, *Annals of the New York Stage*, vol. 3 (New York: AMS, 1970), 680. Phillips's career as a playwright can be traced in Odell: 3:523, 568, 680, 684–685; also 4:99, 136, 158, 182, 635.

92   *Prosecutors that were privately hired*: Robert M. Ireland, "Privately Funded Prosecution of Crime in the Nineteenth-Century United States," *American Journal of Legal History* 39 (January 1995): 43–58.

93   *Sandford was not only Ballard's lawyer*: For the friendship of Sandford and Ballard: LMC, LNY5, in Karcher, *Reader*, 367; for Sandford's role in persuading Norman to go to Mrs. Bird's, *New York Sun*, January 17, 1844; for his role in the seduction suit (identified as "his [Ballard's] counsel"), *Sun*, January 17, 1844; his presence in Ballard's store, statement of lawyer J. S. Carpentier, in *New York Post*, January 17, 1844. Biographical: Proctor, *Bench and Bar*, 469. For "indomitable industry" see "Loss of the Arctic," *New York Times*, October 12, 1854.

93   *"great energy"*: *New York Tribune*, January 20, 1844; LMC, LNY5, in Karcher, *Reader*, 367.

94   *Graham was born*: A. Oakey Hall, "The Legal Graham Family," *Green Bag: An Entertaining Magazine for Lawyers* (Boston), August 1894, 353–360; David McAdam, ed., *History of the Bench and Bar of New York* (New York: New York History Co., 1897), 1:335–336. Obituaries for David Graham Jr. are in *New York Evening Mirror*, *New York Tribune*, and *New York Daily Times*, June 19, 1852. J. Doggett Jr.'s *New York Business Directory* (1841) lists him at 136 Nassau Street. The obituary for his brother, lawyer John Graham, describes their mother's death in a fire: *New York Times*, April 10, 1894. David Graham Sr. evidently left Ireland for political reasons. In New York the Grahams were welcomed by Thomas Addis Emmet, a leader in the Irish republican movement who had emigrated to New York in 1804 after he was released from jail. David Graham Sr. studied law in Emmet's office in New York. Emmet was a brother of Robert Emmet, who was executed by the British and became a much revered martyr in Irish American memory. See McAdam, *History of the Bench and Bar*, 1:335n1; Hall, "Legal Graham Family," 354; and the obituary for John Graham, *New York Times*, April 10, 1894. For the Irish radicals who left Ireland after 1798 and found a home in the United States see Michael Durey, *Transatlantic Radicals and the Early American Republic* (Lawrence: University Press of Kansas, 1997), and David A. Wilson, *United Irishmen, United States: Immigrant Radicals in the Early Republic* (Ithaca, NY: Cornell University Press, 1998).

94   *At twenty-four he published*: David Graham Jr., *A Treatise on the Practice of the Supreme Court of the State of New York* (Albany: W. and A. Gould, 1832). According to A. Oakey Hall, it became "the *vade mecum* of the New York practitioner": Hall, "Legal Graham Family," 354. George Templeton Strong, a New York lawyer and author of a witty, chatty, and acutely observant diary of antebellum and Civil War–era New York, wrote of Graham that he wished "that man no worse punishment than to be condemned to read his own book": *Diary of George Templeton Strong*, ed. Allan Nevins and Milton Halsey Thomas, vol. 2 (New York: Macmillan, 1952), 92. Graham's later books were *An Essay on New Trials* (New York: Halsted and Voorhies, 1834), and *A Treatise on the Organization and Jurisdiction of the Courts of Law and Equity of the State of New York* (New York: Halsted and Voorhies, 1839). For his role at the law school see *Inaugural Addresses Delivered by the Professors of Law in the University of the City of New-York at the Opening of the Law School of that Institution* (New York, 1838).

94   *one of Graham's clients*: "Trial of Michael Walsh for Libel," *New York Atlas*, October 15, 1843.

94   *that of Ezra White*: A. Oakey Hall described the White case as the one that began Graham's "great rise": "Legal Graham Family," 355. See also Philip Hone, *The Diary of Philip Hone, 1828–1851*, vol. 1, ed. Alan Nevins (New York: Dodd, Mead, 1927), 434; "The Willett Street Murder," *New York Spectator*, February 28, 1839.

94   *"if ever [a] community"*: "Crime," *Public Ledger*, August 23, 1841. "Black as white" is cited in Hall, "Legal Graham Family," 355. The case is documented in *Ezra White vs. The People of the State of New York: Case on the Part of the Plaintiff in Error: D. Graham, Jr. for Plaintiff in Error, J. R. White for Defendants in Error* (New York: Bryant and Boggs, 1840).

95   *Graham achieved such results*: Hall, "Legal Graham Family," 354–355, 356, 358. Hall quotes Aaron Vanderpoel, who had been his law partner. Hall was New York district attorney, 1853–1869, and mayor, 1869–1872. He was also a playwright and actor. See, for example, his *A Coroner's Inquisition: A Farce in One Act, as Performed at Burton's Theatre* (New York: S. French, [1857?]), in which he also performed. As mayor

Hall was a central figure in the corrupt Tweed Ring. Its collapse in 1871 while he was mayor ended his legal career. McCabe, *Lights and Shadows*, 100–103.

95   *"individual whose ignorance"*: "Young Men's National Convention," *Commercial Advertiser*, November 19, 1831.

96   *At the national level*: For Graham's leadership positions in local National Republican and Whig organizations see, for example, "Second Ward," *Commercial Advertiser*, December 24, 1830 (secretary of the National Republican Electors of the Second Ward); "Young Men's National Convention," *Commercial Advertiser*, November 19, 1831 (delegate to the convention of the National Republican Young Men of the United States, Washington DC, May 1832); "Gathering of the Whigs Last Night at National Hall," *Commercial Advertiser*, March 20, 1834 (Graham speaks as an "organ" of the Democratic Whig Young Men); "Charter Election," "General Meeting of the Independent Republican Young Men of the Whig Party," *New York American*, April 5, 1834 (Graham offers a resolution "amid loud and continuous cheering"). For Graham as chair of the General Committee of Democratic Whig Young Men see *New York Tribune*, March 5, April 5, and October 11, 1844.

96   *"might have had any nomination"*: Obituary, *New York Evening Mirror*, June 19, 1852.

96   *his political activity was limited*: Assembly race: *Commercial Advertiser*, November 7, 1831. Graham is identified as an alderman or assistant alderman in Hall, "Legal Graham Family," 357; obituary, *New York Evening Mirror*, June 19, 1852; and "Whig Nomination of Mayor," *Commercial Advertiser*, March 25, 1840. A racy journal, *New York Polyanthos* (January 17, 1841, 16), includes him in a list of aldermen. As corporation counsel: Valentine, *Manual*, 1842–1843, 117. For the charter revision committee see Hall, "Legal Graham Family," 354. Hall claims that Graham was on a committee of lawyers that drafted a revised city charter when he was twenty-four (1832). The city's charter was revised in 1830, but newspaper reports don't show Graham taking part. They do show him participating in 1846, when the aldermen formed a committee to revise the charter again; see "Convention to Revise the Charter," *New York Post*, July 7, 1846, and "City News, City Convention," *New York Spectator*, July 8, 1846. In 1847 New York's legislature appointed Graham a member of its Commissioners on Practice and Pleadings: Arphaxad Loomis, David Graham, David Dudley Field, "Law Reform in New York—Report," *Western Law Journal* 2 (April 1850): 331.

96   *nominated Graham for mayor*: "Whig Nomination of Mayor," *Commercial Advertiser*, March 25, 1840; "City Convention," *Commercial Advertiser*, March 27, 1840; untitled notice, "Mr. David Graham declines. . . ," *North American* (Philadelphia), March 28, 1840. His obituary in the *New York Evening Mirror* (June 19, 1852) gets the story of his mayoral nomination wrong, claiming it took place in 1844, and that he ran but was defeated, but states that his "defeat" was the result of the "aberration of so many Whigs into the camp of Nativism." Graham opposed anti-Irish nativism. In 1844, at a Whig meeting, he declared that the Whigs would never exclude capable men from office because they were born elsewhere: "Meeting of the Whig Young Men at National Hall," *Commercial Advertiser*, March 29, 1844.

96   *"famished and suffering Irish"*: "Relief to Ireland," *Albion, a Journal of News, Politics and Literature*, January 2, 1847. For Graham as a supporter of Henry Clay: "The Clay Meeting," *Commercial Advertiser*, June 3, 1848; "Welcome to a Returning Friend," *Commercial Advertiser*, September 19, 1848; "Letter of Willis Hall," *New York Evening Post*, October 3, 1848. Henry Clay Graham: obituary, *New York Times*, July 30, 1870.

96   *"paramount duty"*: Graham's letter of March 26, 1840, printed in "City Convention," *Commercial Advertiser*, March 27, 1840.

96   *"numerous and expensive family"*: Strong, *Diary*, 2:87; Hall, "Legal Graham Family," 356.

97   *"I know I am unable"*: "The Great Whig Meeting at National Hall Last Night," *New York Herald*, November 1, 1843.

97   *"ruddy and youthful"*: "Whig Nomination of Mayor," *Commercial Advertiser*, March 25, 1840.

97   *"noble letter"*: LMC, LNY5, in Karcher, *Reader*, 367; Graham's refusal to take a fee is also lauded in "Liberality," *New York Post*, January 23, 1844. For the location of Graham's office, Valentine, *Manual*, 1842–1843, 117.

97   *John A. Morrill and James S. Carpenter*: *New York Post*, January 19, 1844; *New York Herald*, January 16, 1844. John A. Morrill's name is sometimes spelled Morrell, but since it most often appears as Morrill, including in the trial record, I am using Morrill.

97   *The abortionist Madame Restell*: *The Trial of Madame Restell, Alias Ann Lohman for Abortion and Causing the Death of Mrs. Purdy* (New York, 1841); Clifford Browder, *The Wickedest Woman in New York: Madame Restell, the Abortionist* (Hamden, CT: Archon Books, 1988), 23–46; A. Cheree Carlson, *The Crimes of Womanhood: Defining Femininity in a Court of Law* (Urbana: University of Illinois Press, 2009), 118–120; Eric Homberger, *Scenes from the Life of a City* (New Haven, CT: Yale University Press, 1994), 97–101.

97   *other infamous client was John Colt*: Harold Schechter, *Killer Colt: Murder, Disgrace, and the Making of an American Legend* (New York: Ballantine Books, 2010).

97   *"unrelenting public appetite for blood!"*: *Collected Writings of Walt Whitman: The Journalism*, vol. 2, ed. Herbert Bergman et al. (New York: P. Lang, 1998–2018), 205; "such an intense excitement," quoted in Schechter, *Killer Colt*, 164.

98   *Graham felt*: Schechter, *Killer Colt*, 268, 279.

98   *"corroding excitement"*: LMC, LNY31, November 19 and 24, 1842, in *Letters from New-York*, ed. Mills, 139. Child devoted this letter to the preparations for Colt's execution, and used it to protest capital punishment. "That the murder committed": *Letters from New-York*, ed. Mills, 241n4.

98   *Colt's brother*: Mills states that Samuel Colt approached Child after her LNY31 was published: see *Letters from New-York*, ed. Mills, 241n2.

98   *"Oh here is a rare chance"*: LMC to John Sullivan Dwight, December 1, 1842, in *SL*, 184. There was more to the story than Child knew. Henshaw was not John Colt's mistress but Samuel Colt's wife, and the child was Samuel's. See Schechter, *Killer Colt*, 300, and *Letters from New-York*, ed. Mills, 241n2. For Brook Farm see Henry W. Sams, ed., *Autobiography of Brook Farm* (Englewood Cliffs, NJ: Prentice-Hall, 1958). According to Schechter, Henshaw did not go to Brook Farm: *Killer Colt*, 302.

98   *James S. Carpentier*: For the rest of Carpentier's unremarkable but evidently honorable career he practiced both on his own and in a series of partnerships, including, after Norman's trial, with David Graham. Carpentier is listed at 85 Nassau Street in *New York Business Directory for 1841 and 1842* (New York: J. Doggett Jr., 1841) and at 15 Nassau Street, in partnership with Elias J. Beach, in *Trow's City Directory, 1864–1865* (New York: John F. Trow). As an associate of Warner's: "General Sessions," *New York Herald*, January 16, 1844. As a partner of Graham: "After a Lawyer with a 'Sharp Stick,'" *New York Times*, January 23, 1863. He died in 1885; see Jay Henry Mowbray, ed., *Representative Men of New York: A Record of Their Achievements*, vol. 3 (New York: New York Press, 1898), 87.

99   *"was very neatly dressed"*: *New York Herald*, January 17, 1844. The papers that followed Norman's trial most regularly and fully were the *Herald*, *Post*, *Sun*, and *Tribune*. The *Herald* was the most attentive, never missing a day, reporting often at greater length than the others, and with editor James Gordon Bennett interjecting occasionally with editorial comments. The *Herald* and *Tribune* both published their articles the following day; the *Post* on the same day. The *Post*'s reporters were the briefest and hastiest, often rushing out before the day's session was over, probably to meet their deadlines. Other New York papers, such as the *Express* and Mike Walsh's *Subterranean*, also reported or commented on the trial, and reports of Norman's trial from New York papers were reprinted in other papers around the country. Sometimes these papers added their own commentary. Because the titles of these articles were all largely the same (for example, this one from the *Herald* on January 17, 1844, was "General Sessions, before Recorder Tallmadge and Aldermen Purdy and Rawson. Jan. 16th—Trial of Amelia Norman for Assault and Battery with Intent to Kill"), I am just citing them with the paper's name and the date, as I do throughout this book. (This is the only place where Alderman Rawson is mentioned. Either this is a mistake, or else he was substituting for Vandervoort that day. He said nothing at the trial.) Out-of-town papers in which I found reports of Norman's trial included the *Albany (NY) Evening Journal*, *Boston Daily Atlas*, *Cleveland Herald*, *Daily National Intelligencer* (Washington, DC), *Farmer's Cabinet* (Amherst, NH), *Madisonian* (Washington, DC), *Massachusetts Ploughman and New England Journal of Agriculture* (Boston), *Newport (RI) Mercury*, *Pittsfield (MA) Sun*, *Charleston (SC) Southern Patriot*, and *Baltimore Sun*. I was only able to find these because of the searchable newspaper databases made available to me at the Library of Congress, the New-York Historical Society, and the New York Public Library.

99   *"a rush among the ladies"*: "The Newark Murder," *New York Herald*, January 19, 1844. The portrait was in the *Herald*, January 18, 1844. According to the *Sun*, witness Samuel Floyd reported that Norman wore both the veil and the muff on the night of the crime, as she did in the courtroom: *New York Sun*, January 17, 1844.

99   *"flush of red"*: *New York Herald*, January 19, 1844. References to Ballard's "genteel" appearance appear in the *Herald* on January 17 and 19, 1844.

99   *"long heavy face"*: [James Gordon Bennett], "The Case of Amelia Norman and Ballard—the Crime of Seduction," *New York Herald*, January 19, 1844. This is an unsigned editorial that appeared along with the day's reporting on the trial in the paper. Reporting and editorials were typically unsigned in nineteenth-century newspapers, but the editorials in the *Herald* were the work of Bennett, its editor. He wrote: "Every editorial article which appears in the *Herald*, is written in this office—by whom it matters not; but all written there under the control and superintendence of one mind": "The Case of Amelia Norman—the Jury and the Lawyers—Popular Opinion," *New York Herald*, January 22, 1844.

99   *"nowise distinguishable"*: [Bennett], "Case of Amelia Norman and Ballard," *New York Herald*, January 19, 1844.

99   With Norman in the courtroom: For the presence in the courtroom of Child and the Hoppers see "Trial of Amelia Norman for Assault and Battery with Intent to Kill," *New York Herald*, January 17 and 18, 1844; "The Trial of Amelia Norman," *Boston Post*, January 23, 1844; "The Trial of Amelia Norman for an Attempt to Kill," *Charleston (SC) Southern Patriot*, January 24, 1844.

99   *he had been subpoenaed*: In his closing statement Ballard's lawyer Charles Sandford revealed that Ballard was in the courtroom "on a subpoena as a witness for the defense": *New York Tribune*, January 20, 1844.

99   *"as there were witnesses in abundance"*: Graham's closing statement: *New York Tribune*, January 20, 1844.

100   *"perhaps, a prudent measure"*: LMC, LNY5, in Karcher, *Reader*, 371.

101   *"the outbreaking of deep sympathy"*: "New York Correspondence," *Madisonian* (Washington DC), January 17, 1844.

101   *"Don't come too near us!"*: LMC, LNY5, in Karcher, *Reader*, 371; [Mike Walsh], "Trial of Amelia Norman," *Subterranean*, January 20, 1844.

101   *In an editorial*: [Bennett], "The Case of Amelia Norman and Ballard," *New York Herald*, January 19, 1844. For an analysis of this view of society, Karen Halttunen, *Confidence Men and Painted Women: A Study of Middle-Class Culture in America, 1830–1870* (New Haven, CT: Yale University Press, 1982.)

101   *behind the stove*: *New York Herald*, January 18, 1844; "In the rear of the step leading to the bench of the court," *Herald*, January 19, 1844. Other references to Ballard hiding himself in the courtroom: *Herald*, January 18, 1844; [Bennett], "The Case of Amelia Norman and Ballard," January 19, 1844.

101   *"coward seducer"*: Lawyer John A. Morrill in *New York Herald*, January 20, 1844.

101   *"all eyes"*: *New York Herald*, January 17, 1844.

101   *The jurors were sworn*: Of the twelve jurors, the occupations of seven can be found in contemporary records. These records are "People vs. Amelia Norman" (trial record), Minutes, Court of General Sessions, vol. 70, January–September 1844, MN 10019, Roll 19, Manhattan, Municipal Archives, Department of Records and Information Services, New York, NY; New York City jury lists for First, Second, and Third Wards, 1843 and 1844, New-York Historical Society; John Doggett Jr., *New York City Directory for 1843–1844* (New York: John Doggett Jr., 1843) and 1844–1845 (1844), which includes addresses and occupations. The jurors were Charles Rose (grocer), David Bignall (broker), Zepheniah Frost (grocer), Joseph H. Horton, Samuel Wiswell (marketman), Gilbert Hatfield, John Conroy (fish tackle), John W. Howe (baker), Russell Dowd, James C. Coleman (there are three James Colemans in Doggett's: sawyer, foundryman, and cooper), Mark B. Markwald, Abner Lawton (merchant). For women and jury service see Linda Kerber, "A Constitutional Right to Be Treated Like American Ladies: Women and the Obligations of Citizenship," in *U.S. History as Women's History: New Feminist Essays*, ed. Linda Kerber, Alice Kessler-Harris, and Kathryn Kish Sklar (Chapel Hill: University of North Carolina Press, 1995), 29–32. According to Kerber (30) no woman served on a jury in New York State until 1937, almost a century after Norman's trial.

102   *"parlying with him"*: *New York Herald*, January 17, 1844; *New York Post*, January 16, 1844.

102   *"two thirds of the community"*: LMC, LNY5, *Boston Courier*, February 6, 1844, and *National Anti-Slavery Standard*, February 22, 1844.

102   *The crowd was primed*: Joanne B. Freeman, *The Field of Blood: Violence in Congress and the Road to Civil War* (New York: Farrar, Straus, and Giroux, 2018). Mike Walsh was in jail with Norman in part because of a charge of assault. In 1836 James Gordon Bennett, editor of the *Herald*, was attacked by another newspaper editor, James Watson Webb of the *Courier and Enquirer*; see [James Gordon Bennett], "To the Public," *New York Herald*, January 22, 1836.

102   *Crummie and Floyd each described*: Testimony of William Crummie, Samuel Floyd, and Alexander T. Watson are in *Herald*, *Express*, *Sun*, and *Tribune*, all January 17, 1844.

103   *The jury next heard from James S. Carpentier*: There is some confusion about the identity of the lawyer who gave the opening statement for the defense. The *Sun* (January 17, 1844) and the *Brooklyn Eagle* (January 17, 1844), copying from the *Plebeian*, say that it was David Graham. However, the "People vs. Amelia Norman" (trial record), the *Post* (January 17, 1844), and the *Herald* (January 17, 1844), all state that it was Carpentier. Because the trial record and the *Herald* are the two best sources, I am concluding that the opening speaker was Carpentier.

104   *"perpetual fighting"*: LMC, LNY5, in Karcher, *Reader*, 368.

105   *The insanity defense*: "The Legal Doctrine of Insanity," *American Law Magazine*, October and January 1843–1844, 346–357. Just at this time the insanity defense was being transformed from a concept in common law to a codified practice in England and, eventually, the United States. The 1843 case at the center of the law was that of Daniel McNaughton. See D. Cheryn Picquet and Reba A. Best, *The Insanity Defense: A Bibliographic Research Guide*, 3rd ed. (Suwanee, GA: Harrison, 2002).

105   *The "unwritten law"*: Hendrik Hartog, *Man and Wife in America: A History* (Cambridge, MA: Harvard University Press, 2000), 218–241; Hartog, "Lawyering, Husbands' Rights, and 'the Unwritten Law' in Nineteenth-Century America," *Journal of American History* 84 (June 1997): 67–96; Robert M. Ireland, "The Libertine Must Die: Sexual Dishonor and the Unwritten Law in the Nineteenth-Century United States," *Journal of Social History* 23 (Fall 1989): 27–44; Lewis H. Machen, "Should the Unwritten Law Be Written?," *Virginia Law Register* 13 (June 1907): 107–113.

105   *they too were usually acquitted*: Catharine A. MacKinnon, "Toward Feminist Jurisprudence," *Stanford Law Review* 34 (February 1982): 712.

105   *Lydia Maria Child struggled*: LNY5, *Boston Courier*, February 6, 1844. A portion of this was cut when the letter was reprinted in the *National Anti-Slavery Standard* on February 22, 1844. See the appendix.

106   *"fiction of romance"*: LMC, LNY5, in Karcher, *Reader*, 368. For the power of charismatic preachers over their audiences see, for example, Frances Trollope's description of a camp meeting, *Domestic Manners of the Americans* (New York: Vintage Books, 1949), first published in 1832. Henry Ward Beecher, brother of novelist Harriet Beecher Stowe, weekly attracted enormous audiences to his Brooklyn church with the charismatic power of his sermons. For Beecher's career, and the trouble his charisma eventually created, see Richard Wightman Fox, *Trials of Intimacy: Love and Loss in the Beecher Tilton Scandal* (Chicago: University of Chicago Press, 1999). For churchgoing as a form of entertainment for the young in New York see, for example, the diary of Henry A. Patterson, a young hardware merchant, vol. 4, March 1843–December 1845, New-York Historical Society, particularly entries for November 4, 1843, and January 21, 1844, when he describes hearing the sermons of Mr. Bellows at the First Unitarian Church.

106   *"the fame of a great lawyer"*: Hall, "Legal Graham Family," 354; "fairly compelled verdicts," 355.

106   *"we have plenty of such villains"*: Carpentier's opening statement: *New York Herald, New York Post, New York Sun*, January 17, 1844.

106   *"poor man"*: *New York Herald* and *New York Tribune*, January 17, 1844.

107   *"swarmed with an anxious and excited multitude"* . . . *"busy hum"*: *New York Herald*, January 18, 1844.

107   *"There stand our thirty witnesses"*: Child quoting David Graham, LMC, LNY5, in Karcher, *Reader*, 369.

107   *"most amusing daily performance"*: Wilkes, *Mysteries of the Tombs*, 10.

107   *"What was the conduct"*: *New York Herald*, January 18, 1844. The newspapers did not record which of Norman's lawyers asked the question.

108   *"delusion and lunacy"*: To make his point Sandford cited *American Law Magazine* for January 1844, probably "Art[icle]. III.—The Legal Doctrine of Insanity," 346–, and "Collinson's Law of Lunatics," probably George Dale Collinson, *A Treatise on the Law Concerning Idiots, Lunatics, and Other Persons Non Compotes Mentis. . . .* (London: W. Reed, 1812). Morrill also cited sources on lunacy, including "the trial of Stewart for the murder of Boswell in a duel, as contained in Scott's Law Report of 1731." Both sides cited the Singleton Mercer case, about which more below.

108   *John Morrill countered*: *New York Herald*, January 18, 1844.

108   *"great force and ability"*: *New York Tribune*, January 18, 1844. The *Post* reporter's early departure: *New York Post*, January 17, 1844.

108   *"It was an adroit game"*: LMC, LNY5, in Karcher, *Reader*, 367, 369.

108   *the trial of Singleton Mercer*: For the Singleton Mercer story see "Seduction in Philadelphia—Deliberate Murder of the Seducer by the Brother of the Seduced—Great Excitement," *New York Tribune*, February 13, 1843; "Horrible Tragedy," *Christian Observer*, February 17, 1843; "Seduction and Abduction, of a Young Lady at Philadelphia—Her Seducer's Fate," *Brother Jonathan*, February 18, 1843; "Mercer's Trial, Indictment," *New York Post*, March 28, 1843; "Trial of Singleton Mercer for the Murder of Hutchinson Heberton," *New York Herald*, March 29, 1843; "Trial of Singleton Mercer for Murder," *Herald*, March 30, 1843; *Herald*, March 31, 1843; "Trial of Singleton Mercer," *Herald*, April 1, 1843; "Trial of Singleton Mercer," *Herald*, April 4, 1843; "Trial of Singleton Mercer," *New York Spectator*, April 8, 1843; "Trial of Singleton Mercer," *Herald*, April 8, 1843; "Acquittal of Mercer," *Sunbury (PA) American and Shamokin Journal*, April 15, 1843; "The Trial of Young Mercer," *Christian Observer*, April 14, 1843. Also: Alvin V. Sellers, *Classics of the Bar: Stories of the World's Great Jury Trials and a Compilation of Forensic Masterpieces*, vol. 1 (Baxley, GA: Classic, 1909–1924), 302. Mercer's story inspired a novel by George Lippard published in 1845, *The Quaker City, or, The Monks of Monk Hall*, ed. David S. Reynolds (Amherst: University of Massachusetts Press, 1995), xii—xiii.

108   *copies of* Herald *extras*: For the display of extra *Heralds* in the courtroom with the Mercer-Heberton case, *New York Herald*, January 17, 1844. For explicit comparisons between Mercer's case and Norman's see "Another Mercer Case," "The Trial of Amelia Norman. . . ," *Baltimore Sun*, January 19, 1844; "The Case of Amelia Norman—the Jury and the Lawyers—Popular Opinion," *New York Herald*, January 22, 1844; "The Case of Amelia Norman," *New York Tribune*, January 22, 1844; "The Trial of Amelia Norman," *Boston Post*, January 23, 1844; "The Trial of Amelia Norman for an Attempt to Kill," *Charleston (SC) Southern Patriot*, January 24, 1844.

110   *"highly respectable"*: *New York Herald*, March 29, 1843.

110   *"an abandoned libertine"*: *New York Herald*, March 31, 1843.

110   *"social inequality"*: "Horrible Tragedy," *Christian Observer*, February 17, 1843; "Seduction and Abduction of a Young Lady at Philadelphia—Her Seducer's Fate," *Brother Jonathan*, February 18, 1843.

110   *"My dear son"*: The lawyer was Peter Browne: "Trial of Singleton Mercer," *New York Herald*, March 30, 1843.

111   *insanity at the time of the crime*: References to Mercer's insanity appear in articles in the *New York Herald* on March 29, 30, April 1, 4, 1843.

111   *"considerable importance"*: *New York Herald*, January 18, 1844.

111   *"A Hard Case"*: *New York Tribune*, January 18, 1844.

111   *"peculiar and racy"*: *New York Herald*, January 18, 1844.

7. Verdict

Epigraph: From *The Poetical Works of the Right Hon. George Granville, Lord Lansdowne: With the Life of the Author* (Edinburgh: Apollo, 1779), 91.

112   *"that deluded state of mind"*: New York Herald, January 19, 1844.

113   *"if the fact of the insanity"*: New York Tribune, January 19, 1844. The *Herald* and *Tribune* report this coda to Tallmadge's argument a little differently. The *Tribune* argues that Tallmadge added it after he was challenged by Graham, whom they identify only as "Counsel for accused." The *Herald* has Tallmadge making this statement unprodded, with Graham, whom they identify, agreeing to it.

113   *"What did you see"*: Testimony of John K. Liston: *New York Herald*, January 19, 1844; *New York Post*, January 18, 1844.

113   *The next witness was Madame Restell*: Testimony of Ann Lohman, aka Madame Restell, *New York Herald*, *New York Tribune*, and *New York Sun*, January 19, 1844. The papers don't specify which of the defense lawyers questioned her.

114   *"a monster in human shape"*: *The Trial of Madame Restell, Alias Ann Lohman for Abortion and Causing the Death of Mrs. Purdy* (New York, 1841), [3]. Eric Homberger locates the earliest anti-abortion denunciation that "specifically named Restell" in 1839: Homberger, *Scenes from the Life of a City: Corruption and Conscience in Old New York* (New Haven, CT: Yale University Press, 1994), 94.

114   *the case of Mary Rogers*: On Restell as "the phantom abortionist in the Rogers case" see Homberger, *Scenes from the Life*, 100. On Rogers: Karen Halttunen, *Murder Most Foul: The Killer and the American Gothic Imagination* (Cambridge, MA: Harvard University Press, 1998), 197–198; Daniel Stashower, *The Beautiful Cigar Girl: Mary Rogers, Edgar Allan Poe, and the Invention of Murder* (New York: Dutton, 2006); and Amy Gilman Srebnick, *The Mysterious Death of Mary Rogers: Sex and Culture in Nineteenth-Century New York* (New York: Oxford University Press, 1995).

114   *a scowling Restell*: In *National Police Gazette*, March 13, 1847.

114   *American midwives*: For the definition of "quickening" see James C. Mohr, *Abortion in America: The Origins and Evolution of a National Policy, 1800–1900* (New York: Oxford University Press, 1978), 3–6; on anti-abortion laws, Mohr, *Abortion in America*, 20–22; on attitudes, practices, and laws relating to abortion in the United States see, in addition to Mohr, Janet Farrell Brodie, *Contraception and Abortion in Nineteenth-Century America* (Ithaca, NY: Cornell University Press, 1994); James Reed, *From Private Vice to Public Virtue: The Birth Control Movement and American Society since 1830* (New York: Basic Books, 1978); Carroll Smith-Rosenberg, "The Abortion Movement and the AMA, 1850–1880," in *Disorderly Conduct: Visions of Gender in Victorian America* (New York: Oxford University Press, 1985). For a contemporary view of "irregular" medical practitioners see David Meredith Reese, *Humbugs of New York: Being a Remonstrance against Popular Delusion; Whether in Science, Philosophy, or Religion* (New York: John S. Taylor; Boston: Weeks, Jordan, 1838).

116   *"What was the conduct"*: Testimony of Isabella Hurley, *New York Herald* and *New York Tribune*, January 19, 1844. The *Herald* notes that after Hurley sat down, William Callender was called up to testify, but before he could say much Hurley was recalled for cross-examination. The *Tribune* doesn't record Callender's interrupted testimony. This is one of several discrepancies in the reporting of the various papers that covered Norman's trial.

117   *"a member of my family"*: Testimony of William Callender, *New York Herald*, January 18, 1844; *New York Tribune*, January 19, 1844.

117   *"dark brown hair"*: *New York Herald*, January 19, 1844.

117   *beamed "with silent tears"*: *New York Sun*, January 19, 1844.

117   *"crowd of painted harlots"*: [James Gordon Bennett], "The Case of Amelia Norman and Ballard—the Crime of Seduction," *New York Herald*, January 19, 1844.

117   *"Did you live with him?"*: Testimony of Sarah Ballard, *New York Herald* and *New York Tribune*, both January 19, 1844.

118   *Mary Moore*: Testimony of Mary Moore, *New York Herald* and *New York Tribune*, January 19, 1844. On breach-of-promise law in the nineteenth century see Michael Grossberg, *Governing the Hearth: Law and the Family in Nineteenth-Century America* (Chapel Hill: University of North Carolina Press, 1985) and Patricia Miller, *Bringing Down the Colonel: A Sex Scandal of the Gilded Age, and the "Powerless" Woman Who Took on Washington* (New York: Farrar, Straus and Giroux, 2018).

119   *"She has several times"*: Testimony of Dr. Benjamin McCready, *New York Herald* and *New York Tribune*, January 19, 1844.

119   *simply like "fits"*: In the 1830s and 1840s, well before Jean-Martin Charcot in France and Sigmund Freud in Vienna made hysteria their subject, American doctors could buy medical books about it. For example, on October 15, 1840, the *Charleston (SC) Courier* advertised "Laycock on Hysteria"—probably Thomas Laycock, *An Essay on Hysteria* (Philadelphia: Haswell, Barrington and Haswell, 1840)—and the *Commercial Advertiser*, April 20, 1840, included "Tate on Hysteria" in an advertisement for a Chatham Street bookseller. This was probably George Tate, *A Treatise on Hysteria* (London: Highley, 1830). On hysteria see Mark S. Micale, "A Short 'History' of Hysteria," in *Approaching Hysteria: Disease and Its Interpretations* (Princeton, NJ: Princeton University Press, 1995), 19–29; Micale, "On the 'Disappearance' of Hysteria: A Study in the Clinical Deconstruction of a Diagnosis," *Isis* 84 (September 1993): 496–526; Sigmund Freud and Josef Breuer, *Studies in Hysteria*, trans. Nicola Luckhurst (New York: Penguin Books, 2004). For hysteria and women see Carroll Smith-Rosenberg, "The Hysterical Woman: Sex Roles and Role Conflict in Nineteenth-Century America," in *Disorderly Conduct*, 197–216. Examples of patent medicines whose makers claimed they cured hysteria are Dr. Jayne's Carminative Balsam, advertised in *Auburn (NY) Journal and Advertiser*, January 15, 1840; Dr. Evans's medicine, advertised in the *New York Post*, April 17, 1839; and Saratoga Pavilion Fountain water, also in the *Post*, August 12, 1842.

120   *"constipation of the bowels"*: Testimony of Dr. Benjamin McCready, *New York Tribune* and *New York Herald*, January 19, 1844.

120   *"of a fragile frame"*: "Trial of Singleton Mercer for Murder," *New York Herald*, March 30, 1843.

120   *Sering Wade*: Wade, whose name was also spelled Siren or Saron, was married to Eliza Meriam's sister Rohamy. James P. Snell, *History of Sussex and Warren Counties, New Jersey* (Philadelphia: Evarts and Peck, 1881), 416. Eliza Meriam's testimony is in the *Herald* and *Tribune*, January 19, 1844.

121   *"'God alone can judge me'"*: LMC, LNY5, in Carolyn L. Karcher, ed., *A Lydia Maria Child Reader* (Durham, NC: Duke University Press, 1997), 365. Joel Behrend's testimony, and the very brief testimonies of Ann Pierson and Edward Stewart, are in the *Herald* and *Tribune*, January 19, 1844.

123   *"Woman to cards"*: Granville, "Women," from *Poetical Works*, 91.

123   *"'Let the galled jade wince'"*: *Hamlet*, 3.2.266–267. Morrill's closing statement (including the reference to "great applause') is in the *Herald*, January 20, 1844, and *Post*, January 19, 1844. For Shakespeare performances in New York in this period see George Clinton Densmore Odell, *Annals of the New York Stage* (New York: AMS, 1970), 4:569, 606–607 (for 1842); 5:20–21 (1843); 5:16, 26, 40 (1844). This is not

exhaustive. On Shakespeare in America: Lawrence Levine, *Highbrow/Lowbrow: The Emergence of Cultural Hierarchy in America* (Cambridge, MA: Harvard University Press, 1988), 11–81. James Shapiro, ed., *Shakespeare in America: An Anthology from the Revolution to Now* (New York: Library of America, 2014).

123 *"the mother of children"*: On the development of a movement for the welfare of children in the mid-nineteenth century see Julie Miller, *Abandoned: Foundlings in Nineteenth-Century New York* (New York: NYU Press), 9, and Steven Mintz, *Huck's Raft: A History of American Childhood* (Cambridge, MA: Harvard University Press), 154–184. The Children's Aid Society, for example, was founded in 1853: see Charles Loring Brace, *The Dangerous Classes of New York and Twenty Years Work among Them* (New York: Wynkoop & Hallenbeck, 1880).

124 *"calmness and argumentative ability"*: *New York Tribune*, January 20, 1844. Jonas Phillips's statement was also covered by the *Herald* and the *Post*, January 20, 1844. The *Post* usually reported the same day, but on the nineteenth the *Post*'s reporter left before Phillips began; see *New York Post*, January 19, 1844.

125 *"in the bud and beauty"*: *New York Tribune*, January 20, 1844. David Graham's statement on Friday was also in the *Herald*, January 20, 1844.

125 *Graham linked Norman's case*: There was confusion about the presence of members of the American Female Moral Reform Society in the courtroom. In his closing address, David Graham said that the American Moral Reform Society "had no connection whatever" with the "ladies who had so generously come forward to assist the prisoner in this her hour of trial" (*Post*, January 20, 1844). But the moral reformers protested that they *were* there: "Letter from Several Moral Reformers" (*Tribune*, January 23, 1844). The *Tribune* on January 19, 1844, also noted that they were there.

125 *"great ability"*: *New York Tribune*, January 20, 1844. "The blessing of God": LMC, LNY5, in Karcher, *Reader*, 367.

126 *"almost total want of sympathy"*: LMC, LNY5, in Karcher, *Reader*, 367.

126 *Sandford began*: Sandford's testimony, in *New York Herald*, *New York Post*, and *New York Tribune*, January 20, 1844.

126 *"12,000 public women"*: The American Female Moral Reform Society's claim that there were twelve thousand prostitutes in the city was one of several anxious estimates produced by reformers at midcentury at a time when the number of prostitutes was rising. Reformers failed to distinguish between career prostitutes, occasional practitioners, and women who lived with men as their mistresses—which inflated their numbers. See Estelle B. Freedman, *Their Sisters' Keepers: Women's Prison Reform in America* (Ann Arbor: University of Michigan Press, 1981); Timothy J. Gilfoyle, *City of Eros: New York City, Prostitution, and the Commercialization of Sex, 1790–1920* (New York: W. W. Norton, 1992); Marilynn Wood Hill, *Their Sisters' Keepers: Prostitution in New York City, 1830–1870* (Berkeley: University of California Press, 1993); William Sanger, *The History of Prostitution: Its Extent, Causes, and the Effects throughout the World* (New York: Harper and Bros., 1858).

127 *"deeply injured women"*: LMC, LNY5, in Karcher, *Reader*, 369–370; "Trial and Acquittal of Amelia Norman," *Advocate of Moral Reform*, February 1, 1844, 22.

127 *"I protest against"*: LMC, LNY5, *Boston Courier*, February 6, 1844. When LNY5 was reprinted in the *National Anti-Slavery Standard* on February 22, 1844, the paragraph that included this protest was left out.

127 *"Much had been said"*: *New York Herald*, January 20, 1844. The official charge was "Assault & Battery Nov 1 1843 with a knife with intent to kill," "People vs. Amelia Norman" (trial record), Minutes, Court of General Sessions, vol. 70,

January–September 1844, MN 10019, Roll 19, Manhattan, Municipal Archives, Department of Records and Information Services, New York, NY.

128   *"she wished she had killed him"*: *New York Tribune*, January 20, 1844.

128   *"I sincerely hope"*: [Mike Walsh], "Trial of Amelia Norman," *Subterranean*, January 20, 1844.

128   *"NOT GUILTY!"*: *New York Herald*, January 20, 1844. Had the jury simply disregarded the evidence of the prosecution, and the recorder's charge, and committed an act of jury nullification? Or did they believe that Norman had been unable to determine right from wrong when she stabbed Ballard? With no evidence surviving from any of the jurors, it is impossible to know, but the fact that they spent such a short time deliberating seems to argue for the former. For jury nullification see George C. Christie, "Lawful Departures from Legal Rules: 'Jury Nullification' and Legitimated Disobedience," *California Law Review* 62 (July–September 1974): 1289–1310.

128   *"the building shook"*: LMC, LNY5, in Karcher, *Reader*, 371.

128   *"in congratulation"*: *New York Herald*, January 20, 1844.

129   *"The jury were perfectly right"*: [Mike Walsh], "Acquittal of Amelia Norman," *Subterranean*, January 27, 1844.

129   *George Wilkes also had something to say*: Wilkes, *Mysteries of the Tombs*, 64.

129   *"a trial of handshaking"*: "Acquittal of Amelia Norman," *Farmer's Cabinet* (Amherst, NH), January 26, citing the *Commercial Advertiser*.

129   *John Morrill . . . was overcome*: Morrill's collapse is in "Trial and Acquittal of Amelia Norman," *Advocate of Moral Reform*, February 1, 1844. Norman's faint is in *New York Herald*, January 20, 1844. A small notice in the *Christian Register* ("Amelia Norman," February 3, 1843) reported that on the morning after the trial, Dr. McCready took Norman to Child's home to live "as an intimate of her family." Child was still a boarder at the Hopper family's home.

8. The Law of Seduction

Epigraph: *"The brand is on her cheek"*: The rest of the poem:

> For *him*, whose beastly lust has brought her shame,
> Whose guile has doomed her to eternal flame,
> Be every sail of prosperous life unfurled;
> On other charms he feeds, nor recks her moan.
> As looks the blinded world, so looks not God—
> So looked not ye, ye noble pair, whose throne
> Of high-raised thought obeyed not fashion's nod;
> Who dared to breast the vulgar shame, with one
> Whose name was evil, by the public trod

The poem's introductory heading reads: "The prisoner was attended in court by Mrs. Hopper, a Quaker lady, and Mrs. David L. Child." Lydia Maria Child and Hannah Hopper (the "Quaker lady") are probably the "noble pair" who appear in the last stanza. I was not able to learn the identity of C.C.B.

130   *"I do love you"*: [Lydia] Maria [Child] to Dear Husband [David Lee Child], [February 1844], CC.

130   *"From all we learn"*: "Amelia Norman," *Christian Register* (Boston), February 3, 1844.

131   *"as an intimate of her family"*: "Amelia Norman," *Christian Register* (Boston), February 3, 1844.

131   *"her constitution is naturally good"*: LMC, LNY5, in *Boston Courier*, February 6, 1844.

131   *"strong deep feelings"*: LMC to Maria White Lowell, December 22, 1845, CC 23/643. As far as "Indian implacability," Child knew Indians on the Maine frontier, where she lived with an older sister after her mother's death, and she wrote about Indians throughout her career, starting with her first novel, *Hobomok: A Tale of Early Times* (Boston: Cummings, Hilliard, 1824).

131   *"docile to the influence"*: LMC, LNY5, in *A Lydia Maria Child Reader*, ed. Carolyn L. Karcher (Durham, NC: Duke University Press, 1997), 372.

131   *"If treated with friendly interest"*: LMC to Maria White Lowell, December 22, 1845, CC 23/643.

131   *"A proper education"*: LMC, LNY5, in Karcher, *Reader*, 372.

132   *"May I be forgiven"*: Lydia Maria Child, "Letter from New-York No. 5," *Boston Courier*, February 6, 1844; *National Anti-Slavery Standard*, February 22, 1844. For ease in locating quotations I am citing the version of the letter published in *A Lydia Maria Child Reader*, ed. Karcher, 365–373. Karcher published the version that appeared in the *Standard*, and she calls it the "Uncollected Letter."

132   *"a kind of ability"*: LMC, LNY5, in Karcher, *Reader*, 367.

132   *Throughout she dwelled*: LMC, LNY5, in Karcher, *Reader*, 365, 367, 371, 372.

133   *"Let me not be understood"*: LMC, LNY5, *Boston Courier*, February 6, 1844.

133   *the stories she published in magazines*: For example: "An Affecting Tale of Truth," *The Mother's Assistant and Young Lady's Friend* 4–5 (April 1844), 85–90, reprinted as "The Umbrella Girl," in LMC, *Isaac T. Hopper: A True Life* (Boston: J. P. Jewett, 1853), 229–237; "Home and Politics," *National Era*, November 16, 1848; and, in LMC, *Fact and Fiction* (New York: C. S. Francis, 1846), "Elizabeth Wilson," "Hilda Silfverling," "The Quadroons," and "Rosenglory." Most of these were published and republished in magazines, many in the *Columbian Lady's and Gentleman's Magazine*. For the publication history of Child's stories and other writings see Carolyn Karcher, *First Woman in the Republic: A Cultural Biography of Lydia Maria Child* (Durham, NC: Duke University Press, 1994), 757–772.

133   *titled* Fact and Fiction: (New York: C. S. Francis, 1846). Child's magazine stories of the 1840s draw heavily on features from her own life, such as close brother-sister relationships, the early loss of a mother, and the arrival of a stepmother. Almost all contain irresponsible or cruel husbands and lovers. For a more detailed discussion of Child's stories see Karcher, *First Woman*, 330–333 and 344–346. For a discussion of the complicated relationship between fact and fiction in eighteenth-century writing see Jill Lepore, *Book of Ages: The Life and Opinions of Jane Franklin* (New York: Vintage Books, 2013), 237–242.

133   *A few of Child's stories*: "An Affecting Tale of Truth," *Mother's Assistant*, 85–90; reprinted as "The Umbrella Girl," in Child, *Isaac T. Hopper*, 229–237. Other stories borrow a few facts from Norman's life; for example, in "Elizabeth Wilson," *Fact and Fiction*, 129, the eponymous character, like Norman, has fits.

133   *"as ignorant of the dangers"*: "Affecting Tale," *Mother's Assistant*, 85.

133   *"stirred the deep fountains"*: "Affecting Tale," 86.

133   *"as the recollection"*: "Affecting Tale," 87.

134   *"sufficient presence of mind"*: "Affecting Tale," 89.

134   *"lying on the floor"*: "Affecting Tale," 87.

134   *"highly respectable man"*: "Affecting Tale," 89–90.

134   *"men should be magistrates"*: "Rosenglory," *Fact and Fiction*, 255.

134   *"Those who deem"*: "Rosenglory," 256.

134   *"keep out of his way"*: "Rosenglory," 259.

134   *"I was like a withered leaf"*: "Rosenglory," 259.

134   *"a haggard spectre"*: "Rosenglory," 257, 258, 259. For Gibbons and the Hopper Home see Julie Miller, *Abandoned: Foundlings in Nineteenth-Century New York City* (New York: NYU Press, 2008), 157, and [Margaret Fuller], "Asylum for Discharged Female Convicts," *New York Tribune*, June 19, 1845. The article is unsigned, but the attribution to Fuller is from Estelle B. Freedman, *Their Sisters' Keepers: Women's Prison Reform in America* (Ann Arbor: University of Michigan Press, 1981), 31.

135   *"looking well, and escorted"*: LMC, "To the Editor of the True Sun," reprinted in *New York Tribune*, January 25, 1844; *Spirit of the Times*, March 30, 1844; *Brooklyn Eagle*, March 6, 1844, copying the *Aurora*. A biographer of Child believed that while Norman was living with Child she "admitted being guilty of a number of minor crimes," but gives no source: Helene G. Baer, *The Heart Is Like Heaven: The Life of Lydia Maria Child* (Philadelphia: University of Pennsylvania Press, 1964).

135   *"little episodes"*: "The Grand, Fashionable, Fouriette, Metropolitan, Free-and-Easy, Joint Stock Fancy Ball at Miss Smuggins', a Fancy Sketch," *New York Herald*, February 11, 1844.

135   *"Amelia Norman came directly"*: LMC, "To the Editor of the True Sun," reprinted in *New York Tribune*, January 25, 1844. The comment from the *Post* is reprinted in the *Brooklyn Eagle*, March 6, 1844, along with the notice from the *Aurora*, to which it refers. The comment from the *New York American* is reprinted in the *Boston Daily Atlas*, February 15, 1844. In addition to these, the *Berkshire County Whig* (Pittsfield, MA), April 18, 1844, (also copying from other papers) commented: "In the name of all that is kind, benevolent and christian, let the poor girl rest in peace, encourage her efforts, and let her hear nothing from the world but the mild rebuke, 'go thou and sin no more.' "

136   *"three indictments"*: "The Normans," *Baltimore Sun*, February 8, 1844.

136   *That spring the phrenologist*: J.R.L., "The Parentage of Amelia Norman, with Other Hereditary Facts," *American Phrenological Journal* 6 (June 1844): 157.

136   *As Norman recovered*: LMC, LNY5, *Boston Courier*, February 6, 1844; LMC, "To the editors of the True Sun," reprinted in the *New York Tribune*, January 25, 1844.

136   *By the end of April*: Child's effort to find Norman a job is documented in LMC to unknown recipient, April 23, 1844, typescript copy, CC, 19/550, and LMC to Maria W. [White] Lowell, December 22, 1845, CC, 23/643. In October small notices appeared in the press stating that Norman was settled as a housekeeper in a country town in Massachusetts: *Boston Evening Transcript*, October 7, 1845; "Amelia Norman," *Boston Courier*, October 9, 1845; *National Police Gazette*, October 11, 1845; *Subterranean*, October 18, 1845.

137   *"Intelligent, worthy"*: LMC to Maria W. Lowell, December 22, 1845; "highly respectable": "Amelia Norman," *Boston Evening Transcript*, October 7, 1845.

137   *"for her own state of mind"*: LMC to Maria W. Lowell, December 22, 1845.

137   *"When I look at this poor misguided girl"*: LMC to unknown recipient, April 23, 1844, CC, 19/550.

137   *They had linked their support*: "Police Office—the Stabbing Case near the Astor House," *Advocate of Moral Reform*, November 15, 1843.

137   *"Let seduction be at once made a state prison offence"*: [James Gordon Bennett], "The Case of Amelia Norman and Ballard—the Crime of Seduction," *New York Herald*, January 19, 1844; *Christian Watchman*, February 2, 1844; "Amelia Norman," *Berkshire County Whig* (Pittsfield, MA), February 1, 1844. These are just samples.

The *Brooklyn Eagle* ("A Tale of Crime," January 17, 1844) argued that Norman's case "seems to demand that a law, for the adequate punishment of such monstrous and unblushing knaves, should be enacted by the Legislature." The *New York Herald* ("Legislation on Social Crimes," February 12, 1844) argued that "there cannot be any difference of opinion on this most important subject. The necessity of some legislative action is undeniable." The *Western Law Journal* (Cincinnati, March 1844) argued that "the seducer should at least share the infamy of his victim; and this can only be done by putting the brand of the law on him." The *Advocate of Moral Reform* ("The Cause and the Remedy," February 15, 1844) warned, "Let the murderer of virtue know and feel that unless truly penitent, he can have no more place in the esteem of the virtuous than the felon in his cell." More commentary appears in "Amelia Norman," *Christian Reflector*, February 1, 1844; "A Righteous Verdict—Amelia Norman," *Christian Secretary*, February 2, 1844; "The Seducer and the Seduced," *Liberator*, February 9, 1844; "Libertinism a Crime," *New York Tribune*, February 12, 1844.

137　*"We cannot but hope"*: "Trial and Acquittal of Amelia Norman," *Advocate*, February 1, 1844. Also from the *Advocate*: "Why Do You Ask a Law?," February 1, 1844, and "The Cause and the Remedy," February 15, 1844. On February 15, 1844, the *Advocate* reprinted a piece from the *New York Evangelist* that argued that the only way to halt seduction "is to brand the crime with the same degree of infamy and disgrace, in the *eye of law*, as are attached to the crime of theft, or robbery, or murder. Let seduction be at once made a *State Prison Offence*."

138　*"with joy"*: "Amelia Norman and the F.M.R.S.," letter to the editor signed "Several Moral Reformers," *New York Tribune*, January 23, 1844.

138　*"extraordinary moral impulse"*: "Legislation on Social Crimes," *New York Herald*, February 12, 1844. The *Herald* included "the recent extraordinary case of Amelia Norman" as one among several creating this excitement. For the Norman case as a "focal point" of the anti-seduction movement in 1844 see Marilynn Hill Wood, *Their Sisters' Keepers: Prostitution in New York City, 1830–1870* (Berkeley: University of California Press, 1993), 141. "Morals," *Magazine for the Million*, February 24, 1844, also explicitly linked Norman's trial with the anti-seduction effort in 1844.

138　*"Those who lie in wait"*: "Six Years Delay," *Advocate of Moral Reform*, July 15, 1844. For petitions from "224 ladies" in Madison County, New York, see *New York Tribune*, January 20, 1844 (this article appeared on the same page as one reporting Norman's trial). For petitions from 968 people in favor of a law to punish seduction and adultery see *New York Tribune*, January 26, 1844. For the introduction of the bill, more petitions, and equation of Norman's trial with the legislation see "Legislation on Social Crimes," *New York Herald*, February 12, 1844; "Morals," *Magazine for the Million*, February 24, 1844, 32. Notices on the bill in the legislature: *Advocate of Moral Reform*, March 1, 1844, 34 and 35. For the bill's failure: "Crimes against Women," *Philadelphia Public Ledger*, June 25, 1844. For the failure of previous bills see Wood, *Sisters' Keepers*, 142.

138　*"Act to Punish Seduction as a Crime"*: Chapter III, *Laws of the State of New-York Passed at the Seventy-First Session of the Legislature, January 4–April 12, 1848* (Albany, 1848), 148. The text is "Any man, who, shall under promise of marriage, seduce and have illicit connexion with any unmarried female of previous chaste character, shall be guilty of a misdemeanor, and upon conviction shall be punished by imprisonment in a state prison not exceeding five years, or by imprisonment in a county jail not exceeding one year; provided that no conviction shall be had under the provisions of this act, on the testimony of the female seduced, unsupported by other evidence, nor unless indictment shall be found within two years after the commission of the offence; and provided further, that the subsequent marriage of the parties may be plead in bar of a conviction."

138   *A few other states*: States that had movements to criminalize seduction in this period or that actually did so included Massachusetts ("Iniquity in High and in Low Places," *Christian Watchman*, February 2, 1844); New Jersey (*Advocate of Moral Reform*, May 15, 1844); and Pennsylvania ("Crimes against Women," *Philadelphia Public Ledger*, June 25, 1844). For the revision of the tort of seduction in the nineteenth century see Jane E. Larson, " 'Women Understand So Little, They Call My Good Nature "Deceit" ': A Feminist Rethinking of Seduction," *Columbia Law Review* 93 (March 1993): 374–472; M. B. W. Sinclair, "Seduction and the Myth of the Ideal Woman," *Law and Inequality* 5 (1987): 33–102; Lea VanderVelde, "The Legal Ways of Seduction," *Stanford Law Review* 48 (April 1996): 817–901. According to Sinclair, between 1846 and 1913 "some nineteen states or territories" abolished the "requirement of alleging or proving services" and granted women the right to sue for themselves: "Seduction and the Myth of the Ideal Woman," 61. The tort and the criminal law persisted side by side in the nineteenth century. According to Marilynn Hill Wood, the criminal law was rarely used: *Sisters' Keepers*, 143. The revised tort, on the other hand, was used heavily. According to Jane Larson, "In the late nineteenth century, the tort of seduction was among the most common civil actions": " 'Women Understand So Little,' " 383. My thanks to Nathan Dorn of the Law Library of Congress for helping me think this through.

138   *New York was among the states*: New York took steps, but while Section 604 of New York's revised code of laws, known as the Field Code, gave women the right to sue on their own behalf, it appears that it was not included in the portions of the Field Code passed by the New York legislature. Sinclair lists the states and territories that between 1846 and 1913 disconnected the seduction tort from the idea of compensation for loss of services and granted a woman the right to sue on her own behalf, and New York is not among them. Sinclair, "Seduction and the Myth of the Ideal Woman," 61n209.

139   *In 1847 New York's legislature appointed*: The three commissioners explain the scope of their work in the introduction to their final report: Arphaxad Loomis, David Graham, and David Dudley Field, "Law Reform in New York—Report," *Western Law Journal* 2 (April 1850): 331. For the connection between codification and Jacksonianism see Arthur Schlesinger Jr., *The Age of Jackson* (New York: Book Find Club, 1945), 329–332.

139   *"all this beastly Latin jargon"*: [Mike Walsh], "Deserved Compliment to the New-York Bar," *Subterranean*, January 31, 1846; "Mike Walsh in Albany," *Subterranean*, April 3, 1847.

139   *Graham really did make a sacrifice*: T.G.S., "Law Reforms and Law Reformers," *American Law Register* 12 (July 1864): 524. T.G.S. connects Graham's selflessness to his appointment on the commission, remarking that "it is highly honorable to his sense of good faith and of loyalty to his constituents" that Graham abandoned "his nature, his associations, his interests as a lawyer and an author, his pride of consistency, and his pride of opinion" to join the commission.

139   *The leader of the codification movement*: Preceding David Dudley Field as a promoter of codification were Jeremy Bentham in Britain, Napoleon in France, and Edward Livingston in Louisiana. For Field and the history of codification see Philip J. Bergan, "David Dudley Field: A Lawyer's Life," in Bergan, Owen M. Fiss, and Charles W. McCurdy, *The Fields and the Law* (New York: Federal Bar Council, 1986), 29–30; Mildred V. Coe and Lewis W. Morse, "Chronology of the Development of the David

Dudley Field Code," *Cornell Law Quarterly* 238 (1941–1942): 238–245; Lawrence Meir Friedman, *A History of American Law*, 3rd ed. (New York: Simon & Schuster, 2005), 341–343, 351; Alison Reppy, ed., *David Dudley Field: Centenary Essays* (New York: New York University School of Law, 1949); T.G.S., "Law Reforms and Law Reformers," *American Law Register* 12 (July 1864): 513–529; Daun Van Ee, *David Dudley Field and the Reconstruction of the Law* (New York: Garland, 1986).

139   *"Seduction"*: Section 604, "Seduction," *The Code of Civil Procedure of the State of New-York, Reported Complete by the Commissioners on Practice and Pleadings* (Albany: Weed, Parsons, 1850; reprint, Union, NJ: Lawbook Exchange, 1998), 245–247.

140   *"The woman and her seducer"*: Section 604, "Seduction," *Code of Civil Procedure of the State of New-York* (1850), 245–247. See also "Law Reform in New York—Report," *Western Law Journal* (April 1850): 331, which gives a slightly different version of the commissioners' explanation of Section 604, and omits the quotation from Paley.

141   *"revolution in women's standing to sue for seduction"*: VanderVelde, "Legal Ways of Seduction," 893. VanderVelde, uncertain why the commissioners were moved to compose Section 604, with "almost no public pressure and little public recognition of a need for reform of this writ," speculates that "notorious cases" may have moved the commissioners; she doesn't mention the Norman trial or David Graham's connection with it (891, 894). Andrea Hibbard and John Parry note VanderVelde's question, and make the connection between Graham and the composition of Section 604: "Law, Seduction, and the Sentimental Heroine: The Case of Amelia Norman," *American Literature* 78 (June 2006): 340–341.

141   *The family structure*: For this process see Carole Shammas, *A History of Household Government in America* (Charlottesville: University of Virginia Press, 2002).

141   *The unmarried daughters*: For women who worked as servants in cities in the antebellum United States see Faye Dudden, *Serving Women: Household Service in Nineteenth-Century America* (Middletown, CT: Wesleyan University Press, 1983), and Christine Stansell, *City of Women: Sex and Class in New York, 1789–1860* (Urbana: University of Illinois Press, 1987). On the reinterpretation of loss of services in seduction as a "legal fiction" see Michael Grossberg, *Governing the Hearth: Law and the Family in Nineteenth-Century America* (Chapel Hill: University of North Carolina Press, 1985), 45, and Larson, " 'Women Understand So Little,' " 385–386.

142   "What *is the redress"*: LMC, LNY5, in *Boston Courier*, February 6, 1844. Feminist author Caroline Dall (1822–1912), who knew Child's work, made a similar protest against the seduction tort in one of a series of lectures she delivered in the 1850s: "No single woman, having been seduced, has any remedy at common law; neither has her mother nor next friend. If her father can prove *service* rendered, he may sue for loss of service. In what 'bosom of divinitye' does this law rest? Here is a remedy for the loss of a few hours, but no penalty held up in *terrorem*, to warn man that he may not trifle with honor, womanly purity, and childish ignorance or innocence. In the eye of this law, female chastity is only valuable for the work it can do." Caroline Dall, *The College, the Market, and the Court: Or Woman's Relation to Education, Labor, and Law* (Boston: Lee and Shepard, 1867), 293. For Dall's awareness of Child see Karcher, *First Woman*, 58, 131, 170–171, 311. VanderVelde identifies Dall as the only nineteenth-century feminist thinker who protested the seduction tort ("Legal Ways of Seduction," 891n357), but it appears Child got there first as a result of her involvement with Amelia Norman.

142   *"life and property are protected"*: LMC, LNY5, in Karcher, *Reader*, 371. "Lamentable want of law": *New York Tribune*, January 20, 1844. The *Herald*, January 20, 1844,

wrote that Graham "argued in favor of the passage of enactments making the offence punishable by imprisonment and fine."

142   *"involved considerations higher"*: LMC, LNY5, in Karcher, *Reader*, 367.

142   *One was an 1847 bill*: The 1847 bill to punish "licentiousness" included seduction along with adultery and several other offenses; see "Bill on Licentiousness," *National Police Gazette*, April 17, 1847; "Report of the Committee of the New-York Senate . . . Seduction and Adultery," *National Police Gazette*, April 24, 1847; "Legal Punishment of Licentiousness," *New York Evangelist*, August 12, 1847. "Legislative," *Rondout Freeman* (Kingston, NY), March 20, 1847, reports Graham's appointment to the Commission on Practice and Pleadings, along with two members who were afterward dropped, and the introduction of the 1847 bill. Hibbard and Parry note that Graham's term on the code commission coincided with the passage of the 1848 bill criminalizing seduction: "Law, Seduction," 340–341.

142   *The Field Code became a model*: For the wide influence of the Field Code: T.G.S., "Law Reforms," 527–528, and Philip J. Bergan, "David Dudley Field: A Lawyer's Life," in *The Fields and the Law*, ed. Philip J. Bergan et al. (New York: Federal Bar Council, 1986), 30.

142   *Between 1851 and 1930*: The thirteen states were Iowa (1851), Alabama (1852), Indiana (1852), Tennessee (1872), Montana (1877), Mississippi (1880), Washington (1881), Idaho (1887), Utah (1888), Alaska (1900), South Dakota (1903), Nevada (1912), and Oregon (1930): VanderVelde, "Legal Ways of Seduction," 893 and 893n369.

143   *"wounded"*: Friedman, *History of American Law*, 341; "fragmentary": T.G.S., "Law Reforms and Law Reformers," *American Law Register* 12 (July 1864): 527.

143   *Among the sections of the Field Code*: On New York's failure to adopt Section 604: neither Sinclair ("Seduction," 61n209, and see 48–71 for a longer discussion of the seduction tort) nor VanderVelde ("Legal Ways of Seduction," 893 and 893n369) includes New York among the states they list that granted a woman the right to sue for seduction on her own behalf. My review of New York's nineteenth-century laws corroborates this. The final report of New York's code commission, passed in 1865, does not include the text of Section 604: *The Civil Code of the State of New York* (Albany: Weed, Parsons, 1865), S1866, Damages for Seduction, p. 578. As late as 1897 New York still recognized loss of services as a cause of action for seduction and did not recognize a woman's right to sue on her own behalf. See *Digest of the Reports and Statutes of the State of New York from January 1, 1890 to January 1, 1897* (Albany: James B. Lyon, 1898), Seduction, 2613–2614.

143   *Exhausted by their work*: By the 1850s the moral reformers were opening industrial schools for poor and vagrant children and campaigning for a truancy act. See American Female Guardian Society and Home for the Friendless, *Our Golden Jubilee: A Retrospect of the American Female Guardian Society and Home for the Friendless from 1834 to 1884* (New York: American Female Guardian Society, 1884); Mrs. S. R. I. Bennett, *Woman's Work among the Lowly: Memorial Volume of the First Forty Years of the American Female Guardian Society and Home for the Friendless* (New York: American Female Guardian Society, 1877); Carroll Smith-Rosenberg, *Religion and the Rise of the American City: The New York Mission Movement, 1812–1870* (Ithaca, NY: Cornell University Press, 1971), 97–124 and 203–224.

143   *the criminal law languished*: Larry Whiteaker, *Seduction, Prostitution, and Moral Reform in New York, 1830–1860* (New York: Garland, 1997), 144, and Ellen Carol DuBois, introduction to *The Elizabeth Cady Stanton—Susan B. Anthony Reader*, ed. DuBois (Boston: Northeastern University Press, 1992), 7.

143   *Meanwhile, even in places*: For the popularity of the seduction tort by the late nine-
       teenth century in the United States and Canada see Larson, " 'Women Understand So
       Little,' " 383–384.
143   *"gold diggers"*: The seduction tort was one of four so-called heartbalm actions. The
       others were breach of promise to marry, criminal conversation, and alienation of affec-
       tions. For their fate in the 1930s see Larson, " 'Women Understand So Little,' " 394–
       401, and Sinclair, "Law and Inequality," 65–71. For New York, Sinclair, "Law and
       Inequality," 66 and 66n248.
143   *On April 7, 1848*: New York's legislature passed the law to criminalize seduction on
       March 22, 1848, and the Married Women's Property Act on April 7, 1848. It accepted
       the first report of the Commissioners on Practice and Pleadings during the same term.
       That report was Arphaxad Loomis, David Graham, and David Dudley Field, *First Re-
       port of the Commissioners on Practice and Pleadings: Code of Procedure* (Albany:
       Charles Van Benthuysen, 1848). Section 604, on seduction, did not appear in this pre-
       liminary report. The text of "An Act for the effectual protection of the property of
       married women, Passed April 7, 1848" is in "Married Women's Property Laws," in
       "American Women: Resources from the Law Library," Library of Congress, https://
       guides.loc.gov/american-women-law/state-laws, accessed August 11, 2019.
143   *New York's married women's property act*: On the history of the Married Women's
       Property Act in the New York legislature see Judith Wellman, *The Road to Seneca
       Falls: Elizabeth Cady Stanton and the First Woman's Rights Convention* (Urbana: Uni-
       versity of Illinois Press, 2004), 147.
143   *to dismantle coverture*: For coverture see Linda Kerber, *Women of the Republic: Intel-
       lect and Ideology in Revolutionary America* (Chapel Hill: University of North Caro-
       lina Press, 1980), 137–155. For the context in which the end of coverture took place
       see Shammas, *History of Household Government*.
143   *In the middle of the nineteenth century*: Joan Hoff, *Law, Gender, and Injustice:
       A Legal History of Women* (New York: NYU Press, 1991), 127; Carole Shammas,
       "Re-assessing the Married Women's Property Acts," *Journal of Women's History* 6
       (Spring 1994): 9; Richard Chused finds that the first married women's property laws
       were passed in the 1830s but that they came in a "deluge" in the 1840s: Chused,
       "Married Women's Property Law, 1800–1850," *Georgetown Law Journal* 71 (1983):
       1398, 1400. See also Marylynn Salmon, *Women and the Law of Property in Early
       America* (Chapel Hill: University of North Carolina Press, 1986).
144   *Among those who lobbied*: For Stanton's lobbying efforts for the married women's
       property bill see Elizabeth Cady Stanton, *Eighty Years and More: Reminiscences,
       1815–1897* (New York: European Publishing Co., 1898), 135, 150, and Ellen Carol
       DuBois, " 'The Pivot of the Marriage Relation': Stanton's Analysis of Women's Sub-
       ordination in Marriage," in *Elizabeth Cady Stanton, Feminist as Thinker: A Reader
       in Documents and Essays*, ed. DuBois and Richard Cándida Smith (New York: NYU
       Press, 2007), 83, 91n3. On the Married Women's Property Act and the Panic of 1837:
       Hoff, *Law, Gender, and Injustice*, 122; Chused, "Married Women's Property Law,"
       1361. For the state earnings acts that succeeded the married women's property acts see
       Amy Dru Stanley, "Conjugal Bonds and Wage Labor: Rights of Contract in the Age of
       Emancipation," *Journal of American History* 75 (September 1988): 471–500. For New
       York's Earnings Act of 1860 see Shammas, "Re-assessing," 15, and Nancy Cott, *Pub-
       lic Vows: A History of Marriage and the Nation* (Cambridge, MA: Harvard Univer-
       sity Press, 2000), 53. The degree to which the married women's property acts passed
       by American states in the nineteenth century helped to liberate women from the "civil

death" of coverture has been debated by historians, starting with Mary Beard, *Woman as a Force in History* (New York: Macmillan, 1946). For an outline of this debate see Shammas, "Re-assessing." Shammas concludes that by the end of the nineteenth century women controlled significantly more property than they had at the start, and that these laws did play a role (20–23).

144   *a weekday gathering*: For Seneca Falls see DuBois, introduction to *Stanton–Susan B. Anthony Reader*, 2–26; Wellman, *Road to Seneca Falls*; and Stanton's memoir, *Eighty Years and More*. There is no record that David Graham knew about the Seneca Falls Convention or read the Declaration of Sentiments, but he could have. In New York the *Herald* published the Declaration on July 30, and a scoffing editorial a few days later ("The most amusing part is the preamble, where they assert their equality"): "Woman's Rights Convention," *Herald*, July 30, 1848; editorial with the same title, August 3, 1848.

144   *ever ambivalent*: Stanton described meeting Child in Boston after Stanton moved there in 1843, including her among the "noble men and women among reformers, whom I had long worshiped at a distance": *Eighty Years and More*, 127. For Stanton's invitation to Child: Wellman, *Road to Seneca Falls*, 191.

144   *she plundered Child's*: Stanton's reference to the "Arabian Kerek, whose wife is obliged to steal from her husband to supply the necessities of life" (Stanton, "Address Delivered at Seneca Falls," in DuBois, *Stanton–Susan B. Anthony Reader*, 29) comes from Child, *History of the Condition of Women, in Various Ages and Nations*, vol. 1 (Boston: John Allen, 1835), 41. Her statement about the "Mohametan who forbids, pigs, dogs, and women and other impure animals, to enter a mosque" (Stanton, "Address," in DuBois, *Stanton–Susan B. Anthony Reader*, 29) is in 1:68 of Child's *History of the Condition of Women*.

145   *"nourishing her vanity"*: "Address Delivered at Seneca Falls," in DuBois, *Stanton–Susan B. Anthony Reader*, 32–33.

145   *"abuses and usurpations"*: The Declaration of Sentiments, published in "Woman's Rights Convention," *New York Herald*, July 30, 1848.

146   *"Would to God"*: Elizabeth Cady Stanton, "Address to the Legislature of New York, Albany, February 14, 1854," in DuBois, *Elizabeth Cady Stanton, Feminist as Thinker*, 167.

Epilogue

147   *Mike Walsh*: For the later life and death of Mike Walsh see Robert Ernst, "The One and Only Mike Walsh," *New-York Historical Society Quarterly* 36 (January 1952): 43–65, and the many obituaries and tributes to him in the press, including "Death of Mike Walsh," *New York Post*, March 17, 1859; "The Hon. Mike Walsh Killed," *New York Tribune*, March 18, 1859; "A Life Wasted," *New York Ledger*, April 9, 1859; "The Murder of Mike Walsh," *New York Tribune*, March 19, 1859; "Funeral of Mike Walsh," *New York Tribune*, March 21, 1859; "Frightful Death of the Hon. Mike Walsh, Ex-Congressman," *Frank Leslie's Illustrated Weekly*, March 21, 1859; "Arrest of Mulholland on Suspicion of the Murder of Mike Walsh," *New York Post*, September 1, 1859.

148   *"Were the proceedings of the trial irksome to you?"*: George Wilkes, *Mysteries of the Tombs: A Journal of Thirty Days Imprisonment in the New York City Prison for Libel* (New York: 1844), 62. Wilkes's *Life of Babe, the Pirate* is advertised on the back cover of *Mysteries of the Tombs* with the information that "the Work Will Be Prepared for

the Press by George Wilkes and Published on the Morning of the Execution." I could not find a copy.

148   *In later years Wilkes*: Clarence B. Bagley, "George Wilkes," *Washington Historical Quarterly* 5 (January 1914): 3–11 (Bagley reprints the obituary for Wilkes published in *Spirit of the Times*, September 26, 1885); "Burial of George Wilkes," *New York Herald*, September 27, 1885; "Dropped Out, the Mutability of Life as Illustrated by the Career of Mr. George Wilkes," *New Hampshire Sentinel*, October 21, 1885; "George Wilkes," (obituary) *New York Herald*, September 25, 1885; Alexander Saxton, "George Wilkes: The Transformation of a Radical Ideology," *American Quarterly* 33 (Autumn 1981): 437–458. Wilkes's books from this period include *History of Oregon* (New York: W. H. Colyer, 1845); *Proposal for a National Railroad to the Pacific Ocean, for the Purpose of Obtaining a Short Route to Oregon and the Indies* (New York: the author, 1845); *The Lives of Helen Jewett and Richard P. Robinson* (New York, 1849); *Europe in a Hurry* (New York: H. Long, 1853); *The Great Battle, Fought at Manassas . . . from Notes Taken on the Spot* (New York: Ryan and Brown, 1861); *McClellan: Who He Is and What He Has Done* (New York: S. Tousey, 1863); *Shakespeare, from an American Point of View . . . with the Baconian Theory Considered* (New York: D. Appleton, 1882).

148   *He escorted an American prizefighter*: John C. Heenan, who fought Englishman Tom Sayers at Farnborough, England, on April 17, 1860: "Heenan v. Sayers: The Fight That Changed Boxing Forever," *Guardian*, April 14, 2010.

148   *"manly, high toned"*: "George Wilkes" (obituary), *New York Herald*, September 25, 1885.

149   *"His death caused no more sensation"*: "Dropped Out, the Mutability of Life as Illustrated by the Career of Mr. George Wilkes," *New Hampshire Sentinel*, October 21, 1885. Similarly, "Burial of George Wilkes," *New York Herald*, September 27, 1885.

149   *"prosperity and business interests"*: "Hon. Frederick A. Tallmadge," *New York Times*, September 18, 1869.

149   *besieged the Astor Place Opera House*: Tallmadge "made a memorable record in dealing with the Astor Place riots": L. B. Proctor, *The Bench and Bar of New-York* (New York: Diossy, 1870), 495. On the Astor Place riots: Peter Buckley, "To the Opera House: Culture and Society in New York City, 1820–1860" (PhD diss., State University of New York at Stony Brook, 1984); Edwin G. Burrows and Mike Wallace, *Gotham: A History of New York City to 1898* (New York: Oxford University Press, 1999), 761–766; Edward K. Spann, *The New Metropolis, New York City, 1840–1857* (New York: Columbia University Press, 1981), 235–239. Also, "Account of the New York Mob," *Newark (NJ) Daily Advertiser*, May 11, 1849; "The Awful Events of Thursday," *New York Herald*, May 12, 1849; "Additional Particulars of the Terrible Riot at the Astor Place Opera House," *New York Herald*, May 12, 1849.

149   *"the minds of many," "Three groans," "Hang them up"*: "Additional Particulars," *New York Herald*, May 12, 1849.

150   *the two departments . . . operated simultaneously*: The "police war" of 1857 is described in Burrows and Wallace, *Gotham*, 835–839; Spann, *New Metropolis*, 386–393; and "Death of George W. Matsell," *New York Times*, July 26, 1877. For Matsell as chief of police see James F. Richardson, *The New York Police: Colonial Times to 1901* (New York: Oxford University Press, 1970), 69–72.

150   *"Bloodshed!"*: Advertisement for the *Police Gazette*, in *New York Tribune*, June 18, 1857. Wilkes edited the *National Police Gazette* between 1845 and 1852; Matsell took over in 1858, with others in between. See the paper's catalog record at the Library of

Congress: http://lccn.loc.gov/ca08002606, accessed January 24, 2020. George W. Matsell, *Vocabulum; or, The Rogue's Lexicon* (New York: George W. Matsell, 1859).

150   *The abortionist Madame Restell*: On Restell's bribery of Matsell and others see Eric Homberger, *Scenes from the Life of a City: Corruption and Conscience in Old New York* (New Haven, CT: Yale University Press, 1994), 99, 101, 107, 115, 116, 119, 319n59.

150   *performing an abortion on Maria Bodine*: "Arrest of the Wretch Restell," *National Police Gazette*, September 11, 1847; Cheree Carlson, *Trials of Womanhood: Defining Femininity in a Court of Law* (Urbana: University of Illinois Press, 2009), 123–125; Homberger, *Scenes from the Life*, 108–116; *Wonderful Trial of Caroline Lohman, Alias Restell, with Speeches of Counsel, Charge of Court and Verdict of Jury, Reported in Full for the National Police Gazette* (New York: Burgess, Stringer, 1847).

151   *"seemed to feel"*: Homberger, *Scenes from the Life*, 115, 116.

151   *captured by Anthony Comstock*: Ellen Chesler, *Woman of Valor: Margaret Sanger and the Birth Control Movement in America* (New York: Doubleday, 1973), 66–70, 72–73; Homberger, *Scenes from the Life*, 129–133. The "Comstock Law" is Chap. 258, "An Act for the Suppression of Trade in, and Circulation of, Obscene Literature and Articles of Immoral Use," passed March 3, 1873, *United States Statutes at Large*, 42nd Congress, vol. 17, ed. George P. Sanger (Boston: Little, Brown), 598–600.

151   *brownstone mansion*: Restell's mansion is described in "Her Last Appeal," *New York Herald*, April 2, 1878.

152   *"a bloody ending"*: New York Society for the Suppression of Vice, Records, vol. 1, pp. 111–112, Manuscript Division, Library of Congress. The story of Comstock's entrapment of Restell and her suicide is in Homberger, *Scenes from the Life*, 129–140; "Her Last Appeal," *New York Herald*, April 2, 1878; "End of a Criminal Life, Mme Restell Commits Suicide," *New York Times*, April 2, 1878; "End of an Infamous Life," *New York Tribune*, April 2, 1878; "Did Restell Commit Suicide?," *North American* (Philadelphia), April 4, 1878.

152   *"He is very ill"*: Charles Edwards, *Pleasantries about Courts and Lawyers in the State of New York* (New York: Richardson, 1867), 65. Henry Field, brother of David Dudley Field, remarked that "the labor involved [on the code commission] was almost incredible." Daun Van Ee, *David Dudley Field and the Reconstruction of the Law* (New York: Garland, 1986), 38.

152   *"some very painful, harassing disease"*: The Diary of George Templeton Strong, ed. Allan Nevins and Milton Halsey Thomas (New York: Macmillan, 1952), 2:87. Also on Graham's death: A. Oakey Hall, "The Legal Graham Family," *Green Bag: An Entertaining Magazine for Lawyers*, August 1894, 357; "Death of David Graham, Esq," *New York Daily Times*, June 19, 1852; "Death of David Graham," *New York Tribune*, June 19, 1852.

152   *Years later John Graham*: Hendrik Hartog, "Lawyering, Husbands' Rights, and 'the Unwritten Law' in Nineteenth-Century America," *Journal of American History* 84 (June 1887): 67–96.

153   *"obedience to the instincts of our natures"*: John Graham, *Opening Speech of John Graham, Esq., to the Jury on the Part of the Defence, on the Trial of Daniel E. Sickles in the Criminal Court of the District of Columbia, Judge Thomas H. Crawford, Presiding, April 9th and 11th, 1859* (New York: T. R. Dawley, [1859]), 71.

153   *"whether a man could be other than frenzied"*: The Richardson-McFarland Tragedy, Containing All the Letters and Other Interesting Facts and Documents Not Before Published, Being a Full and Impartial History of This Most Extraordinary Case (Philadelphia: Barclay, 1870), 85.

153   *"with indescribable interest"*: Graham, *Opening Speech*, 71; *Richardson-McFarland Tragedy*, 85.

153   *"the City was filled with mourning"*: "Loss of the Arctic," *New York Times*, October 12, 1854.

153   *"from one failure to another"*: Susan Lyman Leslie, quoted in Carolyn L. Karcher, *The First Woman in the Republic: A Cultural Biography of Lydia Maria Child* (Durham, NC: Duke University Press, 1994), 361.

154   *"Child, L. Maria, Authoress"*: Doggett's *New-York City Directory, for 1846 and 1847* (New York: John Doggett Jr., 1846).

154   *"could never see my way clear"*: LMC to Louisa Loring, April 29, 1847, in *SL*, 237.

154   *"like a thunder clap"*: LMC to Susan Lyman, March 28, 1847, quoted in Karcher, *First Woman*, 355.

154   *"in great glee"*: Joseph Choate to his mother, April 8, 1861, in Edward Sandford Martin, *The Life of Joseph Hodges Choate as Gathered Chiefly from His Letters* (New York, C. Scribner's Sons, 1920), 1:219. Choate was a lawyer and reformer and a friend of Hopper's.

154   *When his poor eyesight*: Sarah Hopper Emerson, ed., *Life of Abby Hopper Gibbons, Told Chiefly through Her Correspondence* (New York: G. P. Putnam's Sons, 1896), 2:106–107; Julie Miller, *Abandoned: Foundlings in Nineteenth-Century New York* (New York: NYU Press, 2008), 156. "John is at work": Joseph Choate to his wife, August 6, 1862, in Martin, *Life of Joseph Hodges Choate*, 1:240. John Hopper may have been the "young lawyer" who, according to Thomas Wentworth Higginson, was persuaded to abandon his legal career after learning from Child to hate the "injustices" of the courts. Thomas Wentworth Higginson, *Contemporaries* (Boston: Houghton Mifflin, 1899), 128.

155   *"What power of love"*: Octavius B. Frothingham, *Words Spoken at the Funeral of John Hopper, July 31, 1864* (New York: Thitchener and Glastaeter, 1864), 9. The *New York Times* printed a death notice for him on July 21, 1864.

155   *A single headstone*: John Hopper's tombstone reads, "In the grave with him sleeps Robert F. Denyer, the orphaned cripple from Randall's I., his adopted son." A photograph of the tombstone is on www.findagrave.com. A death notice in the *New York Times*, October 16, 1861, identifies the boy as Robert F. Denyer Hopper. The story of Hopper's adoption of Denyer is in Frothingham, *Words Spoken*, 8.

155   *The Hoppers' son*: Early in his career DeWolf Hopper performed with Georgie Drew Barrymore, mother of Ethel, Lionel, and John Barrymore. He made a splash reading "Casey at the Bat," which became associated with his name, and he became a well-known interpreter of Gilbert and Sullivan. DeWolf Hopper, *Once a Clown, Always a Clown: Reminiscences of DeWolf Hopper* (Boston: Little, Brown, 1927); George Eells, "Hedda Hopper," in *Notable American Women, the Modern Period*, ed. Barbara Sicherman and Carol Hurd Green (Cambridge, MA: Radcliffe College, 1980), 350–351.

155   *"And it may also surprise you"*: "DeWolf Hopper 75 and Spry as Ever," *New York Times*, March 31, 1933. "A rabid abolitionist" in Hopper, *Once a Clown*, 5.

155   *Child continued to help young women*: The "adopted daughters" included a family-less young Spanish woman, Dolores, about whom Child wrote, "When God lays a forlorn fellow creature in my arms, and says, 'There! take her and warm her!' I cannot otherwise than do it": quoted in Karcher, *First Woman*, 367. Another was author Mattie Griffith (ca. 1825–1906), who, like Child's friends Sarah and Angelina Grimké, rejected her heritage as a Southern slave owner to become an abolitionist: see Karcher, *First Woman*, 413, 585, and Joe Lockard, "Griffith Browne, Mattie," http://www.anb.org/articles/16/16-03522.html, American National Biography Online, October 2007,

accessed May 11, 2016. A third was African American / Chippewa sculptor Edmonia Lewis (1844–1907): see Karcher, *First Woman*, 474–475, and "Edmonia Lewis," Smithsonian American Art Museum, http://americanart.si.edu/collections/search/artist/?id=2914, accessed May 22, 2016.

156   *"under the circumstances"*: LMC to Harriet Jacobs, September 27, 1860, in Harriet Jacobs, *Incidents in the Life of a Slave Girl*, ed. Nellie Y. McKay and Frances Smith Foster (New York: W. W. Norton, 2001), 194.

156   *"soon found the way"*: Harriet Jacobs to Amy Post, October 8, [1860], quoted in Jean Fagin Yellin, "Written by Herself: Harriet Jacobs' Slave Narrative," in Jacobs, *Incidents in the Life*, 206–207.

156   *Child continued to support*: For the history of Child, Jacobs, and Jacobs's book see Yellin, "Written by Herself," in Jacobs, *Incidents in the Life*, 203–209; LMC to Harriet Jacobs, August 13, 1860, and September 27, 1860, and LMC to John Greenleaf Whittier, April 4, 1861, in Jacobs, *Incidents in the Life*, 193–195, 163–164; and Karcher, *First Woman*, 435–437.

157   *"resolute rebuke"*: "Remarks of Wendell Phillips at the Funeral of Lydia Maria Child, October 23, 1880," in *Letters of Lydia Maria Child, with a Biographical Introduction by John G. Whittier and an Appendix by Wendell Phillips* (Boston: Houghton, Mifflin, 1883; reprint, New York, AMS, 1971), 267. For the Childs' activities before and during the Civil War see Karcher, *First Woman*, xxiv, 446, 447.

157   *"the names of the colored authors"*: Lydia Maria Child, *The Freedmen's Book* (Boston: Ticknor and Fields, 1865). Child's antislavery writings of the 1860s include *Duty of Disobedience to the Fugitive Slave Act: An Appeal to the Legislators of Massachusetts* (Boston: American Anti-Slavery Society, 1860); *The Right Way, the Safe Way: Proved by Emancipation in the British West Indies, and Elsewhere* (New York, 1860); *The Patriarchal Institution, as Described by Members of Its Own Family* (New York: American Anti-Slavery Society, 1860).

157   *"Believing in peace principles"*: LMC to John Brown, in *SL*, 324; LMC to the editor *New York Tribune*, November 10, 1859, in *Letters of Lydia Maria Child*, 117; Karcher, *First Woman*, 416–442; *Correspondence between Lydia Maria Child and Gov. Wise and Mrs. Mason, of Virginia* (Boston: American Anti-Slavery Society, 1860); John G. Whittier, introduction, in *Letters of Lydia Maria Child*, xviii–xix.

158   *"sex in souls"*: LMC wrote, "I am not of those who maintain there is 'no sex in souls' ": LNY34, in *A Lydia Maria Child Reader*, ed. Carolyn L. Karcher (Durham, NC: Duke University Press, 1997), 363 (February 16 and 23, 1843), and in LMC to Theodore Tilton, May 27, 1866, in *SL*, 461.

158   *"It is in vain to speculate"*: LMC to Theodore Tilton, May 27, 1866, in *SL*, 461.

158   *"I sympathize entirely"*: LMC to Elizabeth Cady Stanton, [before December 6, 1866] in *SL*, 467. The friend was Henrietta Sargent: October 13, 1860, in *SL*, 361.

158   *"they seem to have no discretion"*: LMC to Sarah Shaw, [September? 1869] in *SL*, 486.

158   *"I am old"*: LMC to Elizabeth Cady Stanton, [before December 6, 1866] in *SL*, 467.

158   *"Yours for the unshackled exercise"*: LMC to Iowa woman's suffrage group, May 30, 1870, *SL*, 491–492.

158   *"entirely dependent"*: "Lydia Maria Child Memorial Book for David Lee Child, 1824–1875," 13, Cornell University, Division of Rare and Manuscript Collections, Ithaca, NY. LMC's writings after the Norman trial include *Isaac T. Hopper: A True Life* (Boston: J. P. Jewett, 1853); *Progress of Religious Ideas, through Successive Ages* (New York: C. S. Francis, 1855); *Looking toward Sunset: From Sources Old and New*,

Original and Selected (Boston: Ticknor and Fields, 1865); *A Romance of the Republic* (Boston: Ticknor and Fields, 1867); *An Appeal for the Indians* (New York: William P. Tomlinson, 1868).

159   *"pecuniary necessities"*: LMC, "Memorial Book for David Lee Child," 13.

159   *"My good, darling David"*: LMC to Lydia Bigelow Child, February 11, 1875, in *SL*, 530–531.

159   *a eulogy*: LMC, "William Lloyd Garrison," *Atlantic Monthly*, August 1879, 237–238. Child's death: Karcher, *First Woman*, 604–605.

159   *"ready to die"*: Wendell Phillips, "Remarks of Wendell Phillips at the Funeral of Lydia Maria Child," in *Letters of Lydia Maria Child*, 268.

159   *He left New York*: Ballard's movements are traceable in notices in the *Philadelphia Public Ledger*, January 25, 1844 ("An Unenviable Notoriety"); *Boston Courier*, January 29, 1844; and the *Farmer's Cabinet* (Amherst, NH), February 1, 1844. The *Boston Courier* reports that "New York journals mentioned on Saturday the propriety of his arrest, as being accessory to the death of his children, and doubtless he took himself off immediately in the Bridgeport boat." One of these reports was in the *Advocate of Moral Reform*, February 1, 1844, reprinting a notice that appeared earlier in the *Tribune*: "Is not inducing a friendless, dependent girl to destroy her own unborn offspring, on the part of its father, an indictable offense, especially where threats and even violence are resorted to?"

160   *The importing business*: In 1845 and 1846 H. S. Ballard and Co. Importers was at 28 Pine Street, as it had been since 1844, but while Francis had a home address in Brooklyn, only the office address is listed for Henry. In 1847 Henry and Francis are both gone. See *New-York City Directory for 1845 and 1846* (New York: John Doggett Jr., 1845); *New-York City Directory for 1846 and 1847* (New York: John Doggett Jr., 1846); *New-York City Directory for 1847 and 1848* (New York: John Doggett Jr., 1847). Francis Ballard appears in a Boston city directory in 1847, selling house furnishings on Bromfield Street near other Ballard family businesses: *Adams's Boston Directory, 1847–1848* (Boston: James French, Charles Stimpson, 1847), and subsequent volumes through 1860–1861. Henry does not appear in the Adams Boston directory. His death record identifies him as a merchant with an address at 266 Washington Street in Boston: *Massachusetts Town and Vital Records, 1620–1988* (Provo, UT; Ancestry.com, 2011), accessed May 31, 2016.

160   *he died of erysipelas*: Death notices for Henry Ballard appeared in the *Boston Daily Evening Transcript*, December 6, 1849, and the *Boston Daily Atlas*, December 7, 1849. His birth and death but nothing else are noted in Charles Frederick Farlow, *Ballard Genealogy* (Boston: Charles H. Pope, 1911).

160   *"every sail of prosperous life"*: C.C.B., "Amelia Norman," *Liberator*, March 8, 1844.

160   *"now in a country town"*: "Amelia Norman," *Boston Evening Transcript*, October 7, 1845; "Amelia Norman," *Boston Courier*, October 9, 1845; *National Police Gazette*, October 11, 1845; *Subterranean*, October 18, 1845.

160   *"certain difficulties"*: LMC to Maria White Lowell, December 22, 1845, CC, 23/643. Blanche Lowell was born on December 25, 1845: *Letters of James Russell Lowell*, ed. Charles Eliot Norton (New York: Harper and Bros., 1894), 1:102. Neither these letters, nor Martin Duberman's biography of James Russell Lowell (*James Russell Lowell* [Boston: Houghton Mifflin, 1966]) mention Amelia Norman. Lowell's reply is not preserved in Child's letters.

161   *In 1851 Peter Norman made his will*: Peter Norman, Will, March 31, 1853, filed April 15, 1863, Surrogate Court, Sussex County, NJ, 3248S, New Jersey State

Archives, Trenton. The mortgage and bond were owed by James L. Munson, who lived to the east of Peter Norman, and is visible on the map of Sparta in Griffith Morgan Hopkins Jr. and Carlos Allen, *Map of Sussex Co., New Jersey: From Actual Surveys & Records* (Philadelphia: Carlos Allen, 1860), Library of Congress, Geography and Map Division, https://www.loc.gov/item/2012593681/. The value of Norman's farm is listed in the 1860 census, when he was eighty-two: www.ancestrylibrary.com, p. 13. Oliver Norman was convicted of assault and battery and sentenced to five years starting on August 6, 1847: Oliver Norman, Sussex County, Court of Common Pleas, box 19, folder 6, New Jersey State Archives, Trenton. The 1850 census shows him in the New Jersey State Penitentiary, Nottingham Township, Mercer County: US Census, 1850, Roll M432–454, p.335A, www.ancestry.com.

161   *"straight-forward nobleness"*: Margaret Fuller, *Woman in the Nineteenth Century*, ed. Madeleine B. Stern and Joel Myerson (1845; Columbia: University of South Carolina Press, 1980), 134–135.

161   *"fiendish daring"*: "Woman, Her Character, Sphere, Influence, and Consequent Duties, and Education," *American Phrenological Journal*, October 1846: 304.

162   *the novelist George Thompson*: The Author [George Thompson], *The Countess; or Memoirs of Women of Leisure: Being a Series of Intrigues with the Bloods, and a Faithful Delineation of the Private Frailties of Our First Men* (Boston: Berry and Wright, 1849), 9, 36–41. One more recollection of Norman's violence appeared in 1859 in the *Herald* ("The Centre of Fashion and Fights—Crime and Crinoline on Broadway," September 29, 1859) in an article bemoaning the decline of Broadway from "the most orderly, peaceful street in the city" to a place where "crime and disorder, emboldened by impunity, rear their hideous heads almost in the broad light of day." The article listed recent cases of "homicide in Broadway in recent years," including "Young Ballard," who was "nearly killed on the Astor House steps by Amelia Norman." David S. Reynolds discusses Thompson in *Beneath the American Renaissance: The Subversive Imagination in the Age of Emerson and Melville* (New York: Knopf, 1988), 212–220.

162   *Singleton Mercer*: David S. Reynolds, introduction to George Lippard, *The Quaker City; or, The Monks of Monk Hall* (Amherst: University of Massachusetts Press, 1995), xii–xiii. The story of Mercer and the threatened theater riot is in Francis Courtney Wemyss, *Theatrical Biography, or, The Life of an Actor and Manager* (Glasgow: R. Griffin, 1848), 317–320.

163   *Norman's story*: The most sustained treatment of Amelia Norman's story before this book is Andrea L. Hibbard and John T. Parry, "Law, Seduction, and the Sentimental Heroine: The Case of Amelia Norman," *American Literature* 78 (June 2006): 325–355. Hibbard and Parry uncovered the connection between Norman's trial and the possible role of David Graham, as a member of New York's Commission on Practice and Pleadings, in the creation of the law granting women the right to sue for seduction. Cynthia L. Karcher, Child's most recent biographer, briefly mentions Norman, in *First Woman*, 328–329; she mentions Norman in her *Lydia Maria Child Reader*, 40, and publishes LNY5, which she calls the "Uncollected Letter," 365–373. An older biography of Child, Helene G. Baer, *The Heart Is Like Heaven: The Life of Lydia Maria Child* (Philadelphia: University of Pennsylvania Press, 1964), mentions Norman. Other authors who touch on Norman include Phyllis Chesler, "A Woman's Right to Self-Defense: The Case of Aileen Carol Wuornos," *St. John's Law Review* 66 (Fall–Winter 1993): 936n6; Timothy Gilfoyle, *City of Eros: New York City, Prostitution, and the Commercialization of Sex, 1790–1920* (New York: W. W. Norton, 1992), 82, 143–144; Gilfoyle, "Strumpets and Misogynists: Brothel 'Riots' and the Transformation of

Prostitution in Antebellum New York City," *New York History* 68 (January 1987): 54; Jennifer Rae Greeson, "The 'Mysteries and Miseries' of North Carolina: New York City, Urban Gothic Fiction, and *Incidents in the Life of a Slave Girl*," *American Literature* 73 (June 2001): 283n17; Marilynn Wood Hill, *Their Sisters' Keepers: Prostitution in New York City, 1830–1870* (Berkeley: University of California Press, 1993), 141–144; Julie Husband, "Anticipating Progressive Era Reformers: Lydia Maria Child and the Mothering State," *ESQ: A Journal of the American Renaissance* 50 (2004): 289; Robert M. Ireland, "Frenzied and Fallen Females: Women and Sexual Dishonor in the Nineteenth-Century United States," *Journal of Women's History* 3 (Winter 1992): 98, 103, 104, 106, 107, 110; Ireland, "Privately Funded Prosecution of Crime in the Nineteenth-Century United States," *American Journal of Legal History* 39 (January 1995): 54; Rebecca E. Ivey, "Destabilizing Discourses: Blocking and Exploiting a New Discourse at Work in Gonzales v. Carhart," *Virginia Law Review* 94 (October 2008): 1502n219; Ann Jones, *Women Who Kill* (New York: Feminist Press, 2009), 177–183; Catharine A. MacKinnon, "Toward Feminist Jurisprudence," review of *Women Who Kill*, by Ann Jones, *Stanford Law Review* 34 (February 1982): 706; Melissa Murray, "Marriage as Punishment," *Columbia Law Review* 112 (January 2012): 8–9; Karen Renner, "Seduction, Prostitution, and the Control of Female Desire in Popular Antebellum Fiction," *Nineteenth-Century Literature* 65 (September 2010): 168n5.

163   *Child wrote her friend Sarah Shaw*: LMC to Sarah Shaw, July 9, 1878, *SL*, 552–553.

164   *one shaky genealogical source*: "Amena" Norman (1818–1855), Ancestry.com. The only source Ancestry gives is one family tree submitted by an Ancestry member. The spelling "Amena" also appears in Peter Norman's will at the New Jersey State Archives in Trenton.

Appendix

167   *Lydia Maria Child's most sustained*: Carolyn Karcher published the *Standard*'s version of the letter in *A Lydia Maria Child Reader* (Durham, NC: Duke University Press, 1997), 365–373. Because it didn't appear in any of the collected editions of Child's "Letters from New-York," she calls it the "Uncollected Letter." Some newspapers that reprinted "Letter from New-York No. V" included passages that were cut from the version that appeared in the *Standard*. See, for example, "The Case of Amelia Norman Described by Mrs. Child," *Evansville (IN) Journal*, March 7, 1844, and "Amelia Norman's Case," *Newark (NJ) Daily Advertiser*, February 8, 1844.

167   *Other newspapers*: in addition to the two cited above were the *Boston Daily Times*, February 7, 1844; *Newburyport (MA) Morning Herald*, February 8, 1844; *New York Tribune*, February 8, 1844; *Baltimore Sun*, February 15, 1844; *Universalist Watchman and Christian Repository* (Montpelier, VT), March 2, 1844; and others.

167   *Child became the editor*: Louis Hewitt Fox, *New York City Newspapers, 1820–1850: A Bibliography* (Chicago: University of Chicago Press, 1928), 71; Lydia Maria Child, *Letters from New-York*, ed. Bruce Mills (Athens: University of Georgia Press, 1998); Carolyn L. Karcher, *The First Woman in the Republic: A Cultural Biography of Lydia Maria Child* (Durham, NC: Duke University Press, 1994), 267–319; Heather Leland Roberts, "'The Public Heart': Urban Life and the Politics of Sympathy in Lydia Maria Child's Letters from New York," *American Literature* 76 (December 2004): 749–775.

167   *She resigned*: For LMC's resignation from the *Standard* see Karcher, *First Woman*, xxii. Her parting editorial was "Farewell," May 4, 1843. For Buckingham's invitation see Karcher, *First Woman*, 311.

168   *When Child left the* Standard: Lydia Maria Child was editor, with David Lee Child as assistant editor, from May 20, 1841, until July 27, 1843. David Lee Child appears as editor for the first time on August 3, 1843. He lasted less than a year, until May 23, 1844. Fox, *New York City Newspapers*, 71. The editors of Child's letters note that David Child did not leave Northampton, Massachusetts, where the couple had a farm, until mid-July 1843, and "whether Maria continued to manage the paper in his absence is unclear" during this gap. Lydia Maria Child, *Selected Letters, 1817–1880*, ed. Milton Meltzer and Patricia G. Holland, Francine Krasno, associate ed. (Amherst: University of Massachusetts Press, 1982), 201. A letter from LMC to Lucretia Mott, September 3, [1843], suggests she continued to have a hand in editing the *Standard*, even after David arrived in New York: *SL*, 201–202. The evidence for David Child's whereabouts in February 1844 is shaky. Karcher states that David was in New York with his wife "approximately from August 1843 to January 1844," when he left for Washington: *First Woman*, 299. The letter from Child to her husband in which she writes that Amelia Norman "has returned, and is *very* sick. I hope she will die" is undated, but an editorial hand has dated it "Feb 1844" (*CC*, 19/540).

168   *"If God spares my life"*: LMC to Francis Shaw, January 15, 1843, in *SL*, 186.

168   *"I am exceedingly anxious"*: LMC to Ellis Loring, April 11, 1843, quoted in Karcher, *First Woman*, 309.

168   *As part of this effort*: As she selected columns to include in the first edition of *Letters from New-York*, Child solicited advice from her friend Ellis Gray Loring, in the process describing her decisions, against his advice, to exclude letters about women's rights and capital punishment: LMC to Ellis Loring, February 21, 1843, 188, and March 6, 1843, 195, in *SL*. She also excluded letters on slavery: see Karcher, *First Woman*, 687n27. For Child's decision to exclude these letters in the first edition, and her wish to appeal to a wide audience, see *Letters from New-York*, ed. Mills, xxi–xxii, and Karcher, *First Woman*, 301–302, 308–309. None of this addresses Child's decision to exclude "Letter from New-York No. V" in the second edition of *Letters from New York*, but the success of the first edition must have convinced her that moderation was the right path.

168   *By December 1843*: For the publication history of *Letters from New-York* see: Karcher, *First Woman*, 308–309 and 689n42, and *Letters from New-York*, ed. Mills [xxix]–xxxi. For references to the completion of the second edition by February 1844 see Karcher, *First Woman*, 689n42, and *Letters from New-York*, ed. Mills, xxix. The first two editions were Lydia Maria Child, *Letters from New-York* (New York: C. S. Francis; Boston, J. Munroe, 1843) and *Letters from New York*, 2nd ed. (New York: C. S. Francis; Boston: Joseph H. Francis, 1844). By 1850 there was an eleventh edition (*Letters from New-York*, ed. Mills, [xxix]), and the book was still being reissued at the end of the nineteenth century.

169   *[For the* Courier*]*: The heading in the *Standard* reads

From the Boston Courier
Letter from New-York
By L. Maria Child

171   *William Thom*: Thom was a Scottish poet and weaver known for his poems about the hardships of the poor. Stephen Roberts, "William Thom (1798?–1848)," *Oxford Dictionary of National Biography* (Oxford: Oxford University Press, 2019), https://doi.org/10.1093/ref:odnb/27194.

171   *The young friend*: John Hopper, to whom Child dedicated the first (1843) edition of *Letters from New-York*.

173   *The counsel for the prisoner*: A footnote was added to LNY5 when it was republished in the *Standard*. It reads: "He stated that a deliberate plad [plan] of seduction had been laid, that Ballard had lived with the prisoner at various respectable boarding-houses, calling her his wife, assuming the name of Mr. and Mrs. Brown, Mr. and Mrs. Williams, &c. That he had afterward left her at a house of prostitution, pretending it was a respectable boarding-house, and had gone to Europe without her knowledge, leaving her without money. That she left the house as soon as she discovered its character, and strove to earn her living by honest industry. That when he returned from Europe, she remonstrated with him for deserting her, and he answered, 'Damn you, go and get your living, as other prostitutes do.'"

175   *"I beseech you"*: Merchant of Venice, 4.1.222–225.

177   *"She had no brother to avenge her wrongs"*: Child may have meant Mike Walsh, who wrote, "Has she no male relative to avenge the wrongs which she has suffered at his hands[?]": [Mike Walsh], "Trial of Amelia Norman," *Subterranean*, January 20, 1844.

179   *L.M.C.*: Child's initials are absent from the bottom of the letter in the *Standard*; instead, her name appears at the top.

Selected Bibliography

Unpublished Sources

Cornell University, Division of Rare and Manuscript
Collections, Ithaca, NY

   Lydia Maria Child, "Memorial Book for David Lee Child, 1824–1875"

*Harvard University Business School, Special Collections, Baker Library,
Cambridge, MA*

   J. and J. Amory Collection
   R. G. Dun and Co. Collection

Library of Congress, Manuscript Division, Washington DC

   New York Society for the Suppression of Vice, Records

Municipal Archives, Department of Records and Information Services, New York, NY

   "The People vs. Amelia Norman, November 23, 1843" (indictment and witness
   interviews). District Attorney Indictment Records, New York County, MN 5221,
   Roll 221.

"The People vs. Amelia Norman" (trial record). Minutes, Court of General Sessions, vol. 70, January–September 1844, MN 10019, Roll 19, Manhattan.
Police Office Watch Returns Docket Book, vol. 5, June 26, 1843–June 7, 1844

New Jersey State Archives, Trenton

Sussex County Court of Common Pleas, Indictments, 1754–1936
Sussex County Marriages, Book A, 1795–1853
Sussex County Marriages, Book B, 1834–1878
Sussex County Surrogate Court (Peter Norman's will, March 31, 1853, filed April 15, 1863, 3248S)

New-York Historical Society, New York, NY

Diaries: James Burtin, 1843–1844; John George Cayley, January–April 1844; Andrew Lester, vol. 3, July 1843–December 1844; Henry A. Patterson, vol. 4, March 1843–December 1845; James Riker, January 1843–February 1852
New York City jury lists, First, Second, and Third Wards, 1843 and 1844

Sussex County Historical Society, Newton, NJ

Norman Family Genealogical File

Published Sources

American Female Guardian Society and Home for the Friendless. *Our Golden Jubilee: A Retrospect of the American Female Guardian Society and Home for the Friendless from 1834 to 1884.* New York: American Female Guardian Society, 1884.
——. *Wrecks and Rescues.* New York: American Female Guardian Society, 1859.
Anbinder, Tyler. *Five Points: The Nineteenth-Century New York City Neighborhood That Invented Tap Dance, Stole Elections, and Became the World's Most Notorious Slum.* New York: Penguin, 2001.
Armbruster, Carol. "Translating the *Mysteries of Paris* for the American Market: The Harpers vs the New World." *Revue Française d'Études Américaines* 1, no. 138 (2014): 25–39.
Bacon, Margaret Hope. *Lamb's Warrior: The Life of Isaac T. Hopper.* New York: Thomas Y. Crowell, 1970.
Baer, Helene G. *The Heart Is Like Heaven: The Life of Lydia Maria Child.* Philadelphia: University of Pennsylvania Press, 1964.
Bailyn, Bernard. *Voyagers to the West: A Passage in the Peopling of America on the Eve of the Revolution.* New York: Knopf, 1986.
Barbour, Oliver L. *The Magistrate's Criminal Law: A Practical Treatise on the Jurisdiction, Duty, and Authority of Justices of the Peace in the State of New York, in Criminal Cases.* Albany: Gould, 1841.

Beach, Seth Curtis. "Lydia Maria Child, 1802–1880." In *Daughters of the Puritans: A Group of Brief Biographies.* Boston: American Unitarian Association, 1905.

Bennett, Mrs. S. R. I. *Woman's Work among the Lowly: Memorial Volume of the First Forty Years of the American Female Guardian Society and Home for the Friendless.* New York: American Female Guardian Society, 1877.

Bergan, Philip J., Owen M. Fiss, and Charles W. McCurdy. *The Fields and the Law.* San Francisco: United States District Court for the Northern District of California Historical Society; New York: Federal Bar Council, 1986.

Bezís-Selfa, John. "Slavery and the Disciplining of Free Labor in the Colonial Mid-Atlantic Iron Industry." *Pennsylvania History* 64 (Summer 1997): 270–286

——. "A Tale of Two Ironworks: Slavery, Free Labor, Work, and Resistance in the Early Republic." *William and Mary Quarterly* 56 (October 1999): 677–700.

Blumin, Stuart M. *The Emergence of the Middle Class: Social Experience in the American City, 1760–1900.* Cambridge: Cambridge University Press, 1989.

Boyer, Charles. *Early Forges and Furnaces in New Jersey.* Philadelphia: University of Pennsylvania Press, 1931.

Brodie, Janet Farrell. *Contraception and Abortion in Nineteenth-Century America.* Ithaca, NY: Cornell University Press, 1994.

Browder, Clifford. *The Wickedest Woman in New York: Madame Restell, the Abortionist.* Hamden, CT: Archon Books, 1988.

Buckley, Peter. "To the Opera House: Culture and Society in New York City, 1820–1860." PhD diss., State University of New York at Stony Brook, 1984.

Buntline, Ned. [E. Z. C. Judson]. *The Mysteries and Miseries of New York: A Story of Real Life.* New York: Bedford, 1847.

Burrows, Edwin G., and Mike Wallace. *Gotham: A History of New York City to 1898.* New York: Oxford University Press, 1999.

Campbell, Helen. *Darkness and Daylight; or, Lights and Shadows of New York Life.* Hartford, CT: Hartford Publishing Co., 1895.

Carlson, A. Cheree. *The Crimes of Womanhood: Defining Femininity in a Court of Law.* Urbana: University of Illinois Press, 2009.

Carlson, Oliver. *The Man Who Made News: James Gordon Bennett.* New York: Duell, Sloane, and Pearce, 1942.

Carrott, Richard G. *The Egyptian Revival: Its Sources, Monuments, and Meaning, 1808–1858.* Berkeley: University of California Press, 1978.

Case, Howard E. *Sussex County, New Jersey, Marriages.* Bowie, MD: Heritage Books, 1992.

Ceplair, Larry, ed. *The Public Years of Sarah and Angelina Grimké: Selected Writings, 1835–1839.* New York: Columbia University Press, 1989.

Chambers, Theodore F. *Proceedings of the Centennial Anniversary of the Presbyterian Church at Sparta, New Jersey, November 23, 1886, Together with a History of the Village.* New York: Williams Printing Co., 1887.

Child, Lydia Maria. *The Collected Correspondence of Lydia Maria Child, 1817–1880.* Edited by Patricia G. Holland, Milton Meltzer, and Francine Krasno, associate editor. Millwood, NY: Kraus Microform, 1980.

——. *Fact and Fiction*. New York: C. S. Francis, 1846.

——. *Isaac T. Hopper: A True Life*. Boston: J. P. Jewett, 1853.

——. *Letters from New-York*. Edited by Bruce Mills. Athens: University of Georgia Press, 1998.

——. *Letters of Lydia Maria Child, with a Biographical Introduction by John G. Whittier and an Appendix by Wendell Phillips*. Boston: Houghton, Mifflin, 1883.

——. *A Lydia Maria Child Reader*. Edited by Carolyn L. Karcher. Durham, NC: Duke University Press, 1997.

——. *Lydia Maria Child, Selected Letters, 1817–1880*. Edited by Milton Meltzer and Patricia G. Holland. Amherst: University of Massachusetts Press, 1982.

Christie, George C. "Lawful Departures from Legal Rules: 'Jury Nullification' and Legitimated Disobedience." *California Law Review* 62 (July–September 1974): 1289–1310.

The Code of Civil Procedure of the State of New-York, Reported Complete by the Commissioners on Practice and Pleadings. Albany: Weed, Parsons, 1850. Reprint, Union, NJ: Lawbook Exchange, 1998.

Cohen, Daniel A. *Pillars of Salt, Monuments of Grace: New England Crime Literature and the Origins of Popular Culture, 1674–1860*. New York: Oxford University Press, 1993.

Cohen, Patricia Cline. *The Murder of Helen Jewett*. New York: Vintage Books, 1998.

Cohen, Patricia Cline, Timothy J. Gilfoyle, and Helen Lefkowitz Horowitz. *The Flash Press: Sporting Male Weeklies in 1840s New York*. Chicago: University of Chicago Press, 2008.

Cooke, Henry. "Notes of a Loiterer in New York." *Bentley's Miscellany* 16 (1844): 596–602.

Cory, Harry Harmon. *The Cory Family, a Genealogy*. Minneapolis: Argus, 1941.

Cott, Nancy. *The Grounding of Modern Feminism*. New Haven, CT: Yale University Press, 1987.

——. *Public Vows: A History of Marriage and the Nation*. Cambridge, MA: Harvard University Press, 2000.

Crouthamel, James L. *Bennett's New York Herald and the Rise of the Popular Press*. Syracuse, NY: Syracuse University Press, 1989.

——. "James Gordon Bennett, the *New York Herald*, and the Development of Newspaper Sensationalism." *New York History* 54 (July 1973): 294–316.

——. "The Newspaper Revolution in New York, 1830–1860." *New York History* 45 (April 1964): 91–113.

Dall, Caroline. *The College, the Market, and the Court: Or Woman's Relation to Education, Labor, and Law*. Boston: Lee and Shepard, 1867.

Davidson, Cathy N. *Revolution and the Word: The Rise of the Novel in America*. New York: Oxford University Press, 1986.

Deák, Gloria. *Picturing New York: The City from Its Beginnings to the Present*. New York: Columbia University Press, 2000.

Denning, Michael. *Mechanic Accents: Dime Novels and Working-Class Culture in America*. London: Verso, 1987.

Dennis, Donna. *Licentious Gotham: Erotic Publishing and Its Prosecution in Nineteenth-Century New York*. Cambridge, MA: Harvard University Press, 2009.

Dickens, Charles. *American Notes for General Circulation*. London: Chapman and Hall, 1842. Reprint, edited by John S. Whitley and Arnold Goldman. London: Penguin Books, 1985.

[Disturnell, John]. *Guide to the City of New York; Containing an Alphabetical Listing of Streets &c*. New York: J. Disturnell, 1836.

Dix, Dorothea. *Remarks on Prisons and Prison Discipline in the United States*. 1845. Reprint, Montclair, NJ: Patterson Smith, 1984.

Doerflinger, Thomas. "Rural Capitalism in Iron Country: Staffing a Forest Factory, 1808–1815." *William and Mary Quarterly* 59 (January 2002): 3–38.

Doggett, John, Jr. *The Great Metropolis: Or New York in 1845*. New York: John Doggett Jr., [1845].

DuBois, Ellen Carol, ed. *Elizabeth Cady Stanton, Feminist as Thinker: A Reader in Documents and Essays*. New York: NYU Press, 2007.

———. ed. *The Elizabeth Cady Stanton–Susan B. Anthony Reader*. Boston: Northeastern University Press, 1981.

Dudden, Faye. *Serving Women: Household Service in Nineteenth-Century America*. Middletown, CT: Wesleyan University Press, 1983.

Durey, Michael. *Transatlantic Radicals and the Early American Republic*. Lawrence: University Press of Kansas, 1997.

Edwards, Charles. *Pleasantries about Courts and Lawyers in the State of New York*. New York: Richardson, 1867.

Eppler, Mary Elinor. *Behold and See, as You Pass By: Epitaphs in the Old Cemetery, 1787–1924, of the First Presbyterian Church of Sparta*. Sparta, NJ: Mary Elinor Eppler, 1976.

Ernst, Robert. "The One and Only Mike Walsh." *New-York Historical Society Quarterly* 36 (January 1952): 43–65.

Farlow, Charles Frederick. *Ballard Genealogy*. Boston: Charles H. Pope, 1911.

Foster, George G. *New York by Gas-Light and Other Urban Sketches by George G. Foster*. Edited by Stuart M. Blumin. Berkeley: University of California Press, 1990.

Fox, Louis Hewitt. *New York City Newspapers, 1820–1850: A Bibliography*. Chicago: University of Chicago Press, 1928.

Free Loveyer. *A Directory to the Seraglios in New York, Philadelphia, Boston, and All the Principal Cities in the Union*. New York: Printed and published for the trade, 1859.

Freedman, Estelle B. *Their Sisters' Keepers: Women's Prison Reform in America*. Ann Arbor: University of Michigan Press, 1981.

Freeman, Joanne. *The Field of Blood: Violence in Congress and the Road to the Civil War*. New York: Farrar, Straus and Giroux, 2018.

Freud, Sigmund, and Josef Breuer. *Studies in Hysteria*. Translated by Nicola Luckhurst. New York: Penguin Books, 2004.

Friedman, Lawrence Meir. *A History of American Law*. 3rd ed. New York: Simon & Schuster, 2005.

Frothingham, Octavius B. *Words Spoken at the Funeral of John Hopper, July 31, 1864.* New York: Thitchener and Glastaeter, 1864.

Fuller, Margaret. *Woman in the Nineteenth Century.* Edited by Madeleine B. Stern and Joel Myerson. Columbia: University of South Carolina Press, 1980.

Garrison, Wendell Phillips, and Francis Jackson Garrison. *William Lloyd Garrison, 1805–1879: The Story of His Life, Told by His Children.* New York: Century, 1885.

Gilfoyle, Timothy J. *City of Eros: New York City, Prostitution, and the Commercialization of Sex, 1790–1920.* New York: W. W. Norton, 1992.

Ginzberg, Lori. *Elizabeth Cady Stanton: An American Life.* New York: Hill & Wang, 2009.

———. *Women and the Work of Benevolence: Morality, Politics, and Class in the Nineteenth-Century United States.* New Haven, CT: Yale University Press, 1990.

Gordon, Thomas F. *Gazetteer of the State of New Jersey.* Trenton, NJ: Daniel Fenton, 1834.

Gorn, Elliot. "'Good-Bye Boys, I Die a True American': Homicide, Nativism, and Working-Class Culture in Antebellum New York City." *Journal of American History* 74 (September 1987): 388–410.

———. "'Gouge and Bite, Pull Hair and Scratch': The Social Significance of Fighting in the Southern Backcountry." *American Historical Review* 90 (supplement), (February 1985): 18–43.

Graham, John. *Opening Speech of John Graham, Esq., to the Jury on the Part of the Defence, on the Trial of Daniel E. Sickles in the Criminal Court of the District of Columbia, Judge Thomas H. Crawford, Presiding, April 9th and 11th, 1859.* New York: T. R. Dawley, [1859].

[Green, Asa]. *A Glance at New York.* New York: A. Green, 1837.

Grossberg, Michael. *Governing the Hearth: Law and the Family in Nineteenth-Century America.* Chapel Hill: University of North Carolina Press, 1985.

Hall, A. Oakey. "The Legal Graham Family." *Green Bag: An Entertaining Magazine for Lawyers* (Boston), August 1894, 353–360.

Halttunen, Karen. *Confidence Men and Painted Women: A Study of Middle-Class Culture in America, 1830–1870.* New Haven, CT: Yale University Press, 1982.

———. *Murder Most Foul: The Killer in the American Gothic Imagination.* Cambridge, MA: Harvard University Press, 1998.

Hardwick, Elizabeth. *Seduction and Betrayal: Women and Literature.* New York: Vintage Books, 1975.

Hartog, Hendrik. "Lawyering, Husbands' Rights, and 'the Unwritten Law' in Nineteenth-Century America." *Journal of American History* 84 (June 1887): 67–96.

Headley, Russel, ed. *The History of Orange County, New York.* Middletown, NY: Van Deusen and Elms, 1908.

Henderson, Mary. *The City and the Theatre: The History of New York Playhouses; A 250 Year Journey from Bowling Green to Times Square.* New York: Back Stage Books, 2004.

Hibbard, Andrea L., and John T. Parry. "Law, Seduction, and the Sentimental Heroine: The Case of Amelia Norman." *American Literature* 78 (June 2006): 325–355.

Higginson, Thomas Wentworth. "Lydia Maria Child." In *Contemporaries*. Boston: Houghton, Mifflin, 1899.

Hill, Marilynn Wood. *Their Sisters' Keepers: Prostitution in New York City, 1830–1870*. Berkeley: University of California Press, 1993.

Hodges, Graham Russell. *Root and Branch: African Americans in New York and East Jersey, 1613–1863*. Chapel Hill: University of North Carolina Press, 1999.

Hoff, Joan. *Law, Gender, and Injustice: A Legal History of Women*. New York: NYU Press, 1991.

Homberger, Eric. *Scenes from the Life of a City: Corruption and Conscience in Old New York*. New Haven, CT: Yale University Press, 1994.

Hone, Philip. *The Diary of Philip Hone, 1828–1851*. Edited by Alan Nevins. 2 vols. New York: Dodd, Mead, 1927.

Honeyman, Abraham Van Doren, ed. *Northwestern New Jersey: A History of Somerset, Morris, Hunterdon, Warren, and Sussex Counties*. New York: Lewis Historical, 1927.

Hopper, DeWolf, and Wesley Winans Stout. *Once a Clown, Always a Clown: Reminiscences of DeWolf Hopper*. Boston: Little, Brown, 1927.

Horowitz, Helen Lefkowitz. *Rereading Sex: Battles over Sexual Knowledge and Suppression in Nineteenth-Century America*. New York: Knopf, 2002.

Howe, Daniel Walker. *What Hath God Wrought: The Transformation of America, 1815–1848*. New York: Oxford University Press, 2007.

Ireland, Robert M. "The Libertine Must Die: Sexual Dishonor and the Unwritten Law in the Nineteenth-Century United States." *Journal of Social History* 23 (Fall 1989): 27–44.

——. "Privately Funded Prosecution of Crime in the Nineteenth-Century United States." *American Journal of Legal History* 39 (January 1995): 43–58.

Jacobs, Harriet. *Incidents in the Life of a Slave Girl*. Edited by Nellie Y. McKay and Frances Smith Foster. New York: W. W. Norton, 2001.

Jones, Ann. *Women Who Kill*. New York: Feminist Press, 2009.

Karcher, Carolyn L. *The First Woman in the Republic: A Cultural Biography of Lydia Maria Child*. Durham, NC: Duke University Press, 1994.

——. *A Lydia Maria Child Reader*. Durham, NC: Duke University Press, 1997.

Kerber, Linda. *Women of the Republic: Intellect and Ideology in Revolutionary America*. Chapel Hill: University of North Carolina Press, 1980.

Kerber, Linda, Alice Kessler-Harris, and Kathryn Kish Sklar, eds. *U.S. History as Women's History: New Feminist Essays*. Chapel Hill: University of North Carolina Press, 1995.

Kessner, Thomas. *Capital City: New York City and the Men behind America's Rise to Economic Dominance, 1860–1900*. New York: Simon & Schuster, 2003.

King, Moses. *King's Handbook of New York City*. Boston: Moses King, 1892.

Kury, Theodore W. "Labor and the Charcoal Iron Industry: The New Jersey–New York Experience." *Material Culture* 25 (Fall 1993): 19–33.

L., J. R. "The Parentage of Amelia Norman, with Other Hereditary Facts." *American Phrenological Journal* 6 (June 1844): 157.

Larson, Jane E. " 'Women Understand So Little, They Call My Good Nature "Deceit" ': A Feminist Rethinking of Seduction." *Columbia Law Review* 93 (March 1993): 374–472.

Levine, Lawrence. *Highbrow/Lowbrow: The Emergence of Cultural Hierarchy in America.* Cambridge: MA: Harvard University Press, 1988.

Lippard, George. *The Quaker City; or, The Monks of Monk Hall: A Romance of Philadelphia Life, Mystery, and Crime.* Edited by David S. Reynolds. Amherst: University of Massachusetts Press, 1970.

Loomis, Arphaxad, David Graham, and David Dudley Field. "Law Reform in New York—Report." *Western Law Journal* 2 (April 1850): 331.

Lowell, James Russell. *A Fable for Critics; with Vignette Portraits of the Authors.* London: Gay and Bird, 1890.

Matteson, John. *The Lives of Margaret Fuller.* New York: W. W. Norton, 2012.

McAdam, David, ed. *History of the Bench and Bar of New York.* New York: New York History Co., 1897.

McCabe, James D., Jr. *Lights and Shadows of New York Life; or, The Sights and Sensations of the Great City.* Philadelphia: National, 1872. Reprint, New York: Farrar, Straus and Giroux, 1970.

McCormick, Richard P. *New Jersey: From Colony to State, 1609–1789.* Newark: New Jersey Historical Commission, 1981.

Mecabe, William H. *A History of the Norman Family of Northern New Jersey.* Watertown, CT: W. H. Mecabe, 1958.

Micale, Mark S. *Approaching Hysteria: Disease and Its Interpretations.* Princeton, NJ: Princeton University Press, 1995.

Miller, Julie. *Abandoned: Foundlings in Nineteenth-Century New York City.* New York: NYU Press, 2008.

Mohr, James C. *Abortion in America: The Origins and Evolution of a National Policy, 1800–1900.* New York: Oxford University Press, 1978.

Northrup, Flora. *The Record of a Century, 1834–1934.* New York: American Female Guardian Society and Home for the Friendless, 1934.

Odell, George Clinton Densmore. *Annals of the New York Stage.* New York: AMS, 1970.

Poe, Edgar Allan. *Doings of Gotham.* Edited by Jacob Spannuth. Pottsville, PA: Jacob Spannuth, 1929.

——. "The Literati of New York City." In *Essays and Reviews,* 1198–1199. New York: Library of America, 1984.

Pomfret, John. *Colonial New Jersey: A History.* New York: Scribner's, 1973.

Pope, Charles Henry. *Merriam Genealogy in England and America.* Boston: Pope, 1906.

Proctor, L. B. *The Bench and Bar of New-York.* New York: Diossy, 1870.

Reynolds, David S. *Beneath the American Renaissance: The Subversive Imagination in the Age of Emerson and Melville.* New York: Knopf, 1988.

Reynolds, Donald Martin. *Architecture of New York City.* New York: Macmillan, 1984.

Richardson, James F. *The New York Police: Colonial Times to 1901.* New York: Oxford University Press, 1970.

The Richardson-McFarland Tragedy, Containing All the Letters and Other Interesting Facts and Documents Not Before Published, Being a Full and Impartial History of This Most Extraordinary Case. Philadelphia: Barclay, 1870.

Roberts, Alasdair. *America's First Great Depression: Economic Crisis and Political Disorder after the Panic of 1837.* Ithaca, NY: Cornell University Press, 2012.

Rothman, David. *The Discovery of the Asylum: Social Order and Disorder in the New Republic.* Boston: Little, Brown, 1971.

Royall, Anne. *Sketches of History, Life, and Manners in the United States, by a Traveller.* New Haven, CT: Printed for the author, 1826.

Salmon, Marylynn. *Women and the Law of Property in Early America.* Chapel Hill: University of North Carolina Press, 1986.

Saxton, Alexander. "George Wilkes and the Transformation of a Radical Ideology." *American Quarterly* 33 (Autumn 1981): 437–458.

———. *The Rise and Fall of the White Republic: Class Politics and Mass Culture in Nineteenth-Century America.* London: Verso, 1990.

Schaeffer, Casper. *Memoirs and Reminiscences, Together with Sketches of the Early History of Sussex County, New Jersey.* Hackensack, NJ: Privately printed, 1907.

Schechter, Harold. *Killer Colt: Murder, Disgrace, and the Making of an American Legend.* New York: Ballantine Books, 2010.

Sellers, Charles. *The Market Revolution: Jacksonian America, 1815–1846.* New York: Oxford University Press, 1991.

Shammas, Carole. *A History of Household Government in America.* Charlottesville: University of Virginia Press, 2002.

———. "Re-assessing the Married Women's Property Acts." *Journal of Women's History* 6 (Spring 1994): 9–30.

Shapiro, James, ed. *Shakespeare in America: An Anthology from the Revolution to Now.* New York: Library of America, 2014.

Sinclair, M. B. W. "Seduction and the Myth of the Ideal Woman." *Law and Inequality* 5 (1987): 33–102.

Smith-Rosenberg, Carroll. *Disorderly Conduct: Visions of Gender in Victorian America.* New York: Oxford University Press, 1985.

———. *Religion and the Rise of the American City: The New York Mission Movement, 1812–1870.* Ithaca, NY: Cornell University Press, 1971.

Snell, James P. *History of Sussex and Warren Counties, New Jersey.* Philadelphia: Everts and Peck, 1881.

Spann, Edward K. *The New Metropolis: New York City, 1840–1857.* New York: Columbia University Press, 1981.

Srebnick, Amy Gilman. *The Mysterious Death of Mary Rogers: Sex and Culture in Nineteenth-Century New York.* New York: Oxford University Press, 1995.

Stansell, Christine. *City of Women: Sex and Class in New York, 1789–1860.* Urbana: University of Illinois Press, 1987.

Stanton, Elizabeth Cady. *Eighty Years and More: Reminiscences, 1815–1897.* New York: European Publishing Co., 1898.

Stashower, Daniel. *The Beautiful Cigar Girl: Mary Rogers, Edgar Allan Poe, and the Invention of Murder.* New York: Dutton, 2006.

Still, Bayrd. *Mirror for Gotham: New York as Seen by Contemporaries from Dutch Days to the Present*. New York: Fordham University Press, 1994.

Strong, George Templeton. *The Diary of George Templeton Strong*. 4 vols. Edited by Allan Nevins and Milton Halsey Thomas. New York: Macmillan, 1952.

Sue, Eugène. *The Mysteries of Paris: A Novel*. Translated by Charles H. Town. New York: Harper & Brothers, 1843.

———. *The Mysteries of Paris: A Romance of Rich and Poor*. Translated by Henry Champion Deming. New York: J. Winchester, New World, 1844.

A Summary Historical, Geographical, and Statistical View of the City of New York. New York: J. H. Colton, 1836.

Sutton, Charles. *The New York Tombs: Its Secrets and Its Mysteries*. New York: United States Publishing Co., 1874.

[Thompson, George]. *The Countess; or Memoirs of Women of Leisure: Being a Series of Intrigues with the Bloods, and a Faithful Delineation of the Private Frailties of Our First Men*. Boston: Berry and Wright, 1849.

Thorp, Margaret Farrand. *Female Persuasion: Six Strong-Minded Women*. New Haven, CT: Yale University Press, 1949.

The Trial of Madame Restell, Alias Ann Lohman for Abortion and Causing the Death of Mrs. Purdy. New York, 1841.

Valentine, David T. *Manual of the Corporation of the City of New-York for the Years 1842 & 3*. New York: Thomas Snowden, 1842.

———. *Manual of the Corporation of the City of New-York for the Years 1844–5*. New York: J. F. Trow, 1844.

VanderVelde, Lea. "The Legal Ways of Seduction." *Stanford Law Review* 48 (1996): 818–901.

Van Ee, Daun. *David Dudley Field and the Reconstruction of the Law*. New York: Garland, 1986.

Walsh, Michael. *Sketches of the Speeches and Writings*. New York, 1843.

Wellman, Judith. *The Road to Seneca Falls: Elizabeth Cady Stanton and the First Woman's Rights Convention*. Urbana: University of Illinois Press, 2004.

Whiteaker, Larry. *Seduction, Prostitution, and Moral Reform in New York, 1830–1860*. New York: Garland, 1997.

Wilentz, Sean. *Chants Democratic: New York City and the Rise of the American Working Class, 1788–1850*. New York: Oxford University Press, 1984.

Wilkes, George. *Mysteries of the Tombs: A Journal of Thirty Days Imprisonment in the New York City Prison for Libel*. New York, 1844.

Wilson, David A. *United Irishmen, United States: Immigrant Radicals in the Early Republic*. Ithaca, NY: Cornell University Press, 1998.

Zboray, Ronald J., and Mary Saracino Zboray. "The Mysteries of New England: Eugène Sue's American 'Imitators,' 1844." *Nineteenth-Century Contexts* 22 (2000): 457–492.

INDEX

Page numbers in *italics* indicate illustrations. Authored works are under the name of the author.